Plone
Content Management Essentials

Julie Meloni

SAMS

800 East 96th Street, Indianapolis, Indiana 46240

Plone Content Management Essentials

Copyright © 2005 by Sams Publishing

All rights reserved. No part of this book shall be reproduced, stored in a retrieval system, or transmitted by any means, electronic, mechanical, photocopying, recording, or otherwise, without written permission from the publisher. No patent liability is assumed with respect to the use of the information contained herein. Although every precaution has been taken in the preparation of this book, the publisher and author assume no responsibility for errors or omissions. Nor is any liability assumed for damages resulting from the use of the information contained herein.

International Standard Book Number: 0-672-32687-6

Library of Congress Catalog Card Number: 2004091353

Printed in the United States of America

First Printing: October 2004

07   06   05   4   3   2

Trademarks

All terms mentioned in this book that are known to be trademarks or service marks have been appropriately capitalized. Sams Publishing cannot attest to the accuracy of this information. Use of a term in this book should not be regarded as affecting the validity of any trademark or service mark.

Warning and Disclaimer

Every effort has been made to make this book as complete and as accurate as possible, but no warranty or fitness is implied. The information provided is on an "as is" basis.

Bulk Sales

Sams Publishing offers excellent discounts on this book when ordered in quantity for bulk purchases or special sales. For more information, please contact

    U.S. Corporate and Government Sales

    1-800-382-3419

    corpsales@pearsontechgroup.com

For sales outside of the U.S., please contact

    International Sales

    international@pearsoned.com

Acquisitions Editor
Shelley Johnston

Development Editor
Mark Cierzniak

Managing Editor
Charlotte Clapp

Project Editor
George E. Nedeff

Copy Editor
Krista Hansing

Indexer
Chris Barrick

Proofreader
Tracy Donhardt

Technical Editor
Steve Heckler

Publishing Coordinator
Vanessa Evans

Multimedia Developer
Dan Scherf

Book Designer
Gary Adair

Page Layout
Michelle Mitchell

Contents at a Glance

	Introduction	1
1	Introduction to Plone and Content Management	5
2	Installing Plone	21
3	Using Your New Plone Site	39
4	Additional Plone Elements	73
5	Customizing Plone	103
6	Creating and Implementing a Custom Skin	127
7	Advanced Content-Related Techniques	149
8	Technical Administration	169

Appendixes

A	Using Python for Greater Customization	191
B	Introduction to Zope and the ZMI	209
	Index	225

Table of Contents

	Introduction	1
1	**Introduction to Plone and Content Management**	**5**
	Plone Basics	6
	Underlying Architecture of Plone	6
	When to Use Plone	7
	Examples of Plone in Use	8
	Why a Content-Management System?	13
	Features of a Content-Management System	13
	Anatomy of a Plone Site	16
	Plone Slots	16
	Troubleshooting	20
	Summary	20
2	**Installing Plone**	**21**
	Plone User Roles	21
	The Manager Role	21
	The Member Role	22
	Workflow Roles	22
	Installation and Access Requirements	23
	Obtaining Plone	24
	Installing Plone	25
	Installing on Windows	25
	Installing on Mac OS X	28
	Installing on Linux/Unix	30
	Upgrading Plone	33
	Where Do We Go from Here?	35
	Troubleshooting	37
	Summary	38
3	**Using Your New Plone Site**	**39**
	Joining a Plone Site	39
	Logging In	41
	The Member Home Page	43
	The Member Folder	44

	User Preferences	46
	Undo	48
	Working with Content in Plone	48
	Creating and Modifying Documents	49
	Adding and Modifying Events and News	61
	Adding and Editing Files	63
	Adding and Editing Other Content Types	64
	Publishing Content in Plone	66
	Utilizing the Content Discussion Feature	69
	Searching Content	70
	Using Advanced Search	70
	Troubleshooting	72
	Summary	72
4	**Additional Plone Elements**	**73**
	Using the CMF Collective	73
	Working with CMFBoard	74
	Installing CMFBoard	75
	Creating a CMFBoard Forum	77
	Setting Up ForumNBs	78
	Adding Topics and Posts	78
	Member Preferences for CMFBoard	82
	Additional CMFBoard Information	82
	Working with CMFMessage and CMFUserTrackTool	82
	Installing CMFMessage and CMFUserTrackTool	83
	Viewing the CMFMessage and CMFUserTrackTool Slots	83
	Sending an Instant Message	84
	Taking Action After Receiving an Instant Message	84
	Working with CMFPhoto and CMFPhotoAlbum	87
	Installing CMFPhoto and CMFPhotoAlbum	87
	Creating a Photo Album with CMFPhotoAlbum	87
	Adding Photos to a Photo Album	88
	The End-User View of a Photo Album	89
	Working with SimpleBlog	90
	Installing CMFWeblog	91
	Adding a Blog Folder	93
	Adding a Blog Entry	94
	Publishing Your Blog Entries	94
	Additional SimpleBlog Configuration	95

Working with Wikis ... 96
    Installing Zwiki ... 97
    Wiki Basics ... 99
    Working with Your Zwiki Wiki ... 99
Troubleshooting ... 102
Summary ... 102

5 Customizing Plone   103

Working with Standard Slots ... 103
    Changing the Location of Slots ... 103
    Modifying the Visibility of Standard Slots ... 107
    Making Slots Visible to Members Only ... 109
Creating and Maintaining Custom Slots ... 112
Customizing Tabs and Graphics ... 114
    Changing the Tabs ... 115
    Customizing Logos and Other Images ... 119
Internationalization and Localization of Your Plone Site ... 120
    Localizing Your Plone Site ... 121
    International Character Sets ... 124
Troubleshooting ... 125
Summary ... 125

6 Creating and Implementing a Custom Skin   127

What's a Skin? ... 127
Elements of a Plone Skin ... 128
    Preparing to Use a Custom Skin ... 129
Working with the Plone Base Properties File ... 132
Working with the Plone Style Sheet ... 138
    Quick Style Sheet Primer ... 138
    Structure of the Plone Style Sheet ... 139
Pulling It All Together ... 141
    Define Your Goals ... 142
    Developing the Overall Site Architecture ... 142
    Determine Your Navigational Elements ... 144
    Developing the Look and Feel ... 144
    Fitting the Pieces Together ... 145
    Plone Customization Example ... 145
Troubleshooting ... 148
Summary ... 148

Contents

7 Additional Content-Related Techniques — **149**

Working with Plone Page Templates — 149
- The Zope Template Language — 150
- Working with Existing Templates — 151
- Creating a New Plone Template — 153

Implementing Content Syndication — 156
- How RSS Works — 156
- Syndicating a Plone Folder — 157

Creating and Using New Content Types — 161
- Customizing the New Content Type — 162
- Other Methods for Adding Content Types — 167

Troubleshooting — 167
Summary — 168

8 Technical Administration — **169**

Basic Plone Administration — 169
- The Plone Setup Screen — 169

Backing Up Your Plone Site — 177
Caching Elements in Plone — 178
- ZODB Caching — 179
- Additional Cache Managers — 180

Using Plone with Other Applications — 182
- Zope Virtual Hosts — 182
- Running Plone with Apache — 183
- Running Plone with Microsoft IIS — 185

Troubleshooting — 186
Summary — 187

Appendixes — **189**

A Using Python for Greater Customization — **191**

Getting Started with Python — 192
- Working with the Interpreter — 192
- Working with Strings — 194
- Working with Lists — 196
- Operator Overview — 199
- Basic Flow Control in Python — 200
- File Access with Python — 203

	Defining Your Own Functions and Modules in Python	204
	What's in the Standard Library?	205
	More Information	207

B Introduction to Zope and the ZMI — 209

Fun with Application Servers — 209
The Zope Framework — 210
    The Components of the Zope Framework — 211
Zope and Objects — 211
    The Basics About Objects — 212
    Publishing and Managing Objects — 213
The Zope Management Interface (ZMI) — 213
    The ZMI Navigator Frame — 215
    The ZMI Workspace Frame — 216
    The Status Frame — 217
    Working with Objects in the ZMI — 218
    Undoing Actions — 220
    Object History — 222
Where to Find More Information — 223

Index 225

About the Author

Julie C. Meloni is the technical director for i2i Interactive (http://www.i2ii.com), a multimedia company located in Los Altos, California. She has been developing web-based applications since the web first saw the light of day and remembers the excitement surrounding the first GUI web browser. She has authored several books and articles on web-based programming languages and database topics, most notably PHP, MySQL, and Apache. You can find translations of her work in several languages, including Chinese, Danish, Italian, Portuguese, Polish, and even Serbian. Although Julie can't read these languages, she thinks that's very cool. Julie is also a course developer and instructor at Sessions.edu Online School of Design, where she teaches students the wonders of dynamic websites.

Dedication

For "the team."

Acknowledgments

A simple acknowledgment doesn't do justice to the hard work and dedication put forth by the developers working on all aspects of Plone. Specifically, thanks goes to Alexander Limi of Plone Solutions (http://www.plonesolutions.com/), Andy McKay at ZopeZen (http//www.zopezen.org), and Alan Runyan of Enfold Systems (http://www.enfoldtechnology.com/); definitely seek out their work after getting your feet wet with this introductory guidebook.

Great thanks to all the editors and layout folks at Sams who were involved with this book, for all their hard work in seeing this through! This book truly would not have come into existence without them.

We Want to Hear from You!

As the reader of this book, *you* are our most important critic and commentator. We value your opinion and want to know what we're doing right, what we could do better, what areas you'd like to see us publish in, and any other words of wisdom you're willing to pass our way.

You can email or write me directly to let me know what you did or didn't like about this book—as well as what we can do to make our books stronger.

Please note that I cannot help you with technical problems related to the topic of this book, and that due to the high volume of mail I receive, I might not be able to reply to every message.

When you write, please be sure to include this book's title and author as well as your name and phone or email address. I will carefully review your comments and share them with the author and editors who worked on the book.

Email: webdev@samspublishing.com

Mail: Mark Taber
            Associate Publisher
            Sams Publishing
            800 East 96th Street
            Indianapolis, IN 46240 USA

Reader Services

For more information about this book or another Sams Publishing title, visit our website at www.samspublishing.com. Type the ISBN (0672326876) or the title of a book in the Search field to find the page you're looking for.

Introduction

Welcome to *Plone Content Management Essentials* This book serves as a guide for working with Plone 2.0, from installation (or upgrading) to ongoing administration and customization. You'll learn about the underlying reasons for using a content-management system (CMS) through examples and practical application. You'll also learn how to work with the core feature set of Plone, and you'll see examples of third-party add-ons, including how to install and integrate them within your Plone site. Additionally, a basic Python primer is included at the end of the book, if you want to get your feet wet with the language used to extend Plone even further by writing modules and implementing custom code.

Who Should Read This Book?

Just as Plone is a fully administrable application geared toward "the masses," this book is aimed at users who do not possess an in-depth knowledge of Python programming and Zope/Plone administration. If you have any sort of working knowledge in these areas, all the more power to you, and you can probably skip the appendixes and skim certain portions of other chapters. However, before you begin, you must be familiar with installing software on your operating system of choice, either via the command line or by following wizard-based installers. You must already have, or have access to obtaining, the proper permissions on your operating system for installing server software. Finally, you must be familiar enough with installation processes to understand how to troubleshoot installation and configuration issues as they are explained in the book or as they come up on their own because of the esoteric nature of various operating systems.

By the end of this book, you will thoroughly understand how and when to utilize a content-management system—specifically, how to install, configure, and maintain a Plone-based web site. Although this is by no means a comprehensive, technically oriented book on the inner workings of Plone and the Zope application server, it serves its intended purpose: to introduce new users to the features of Plone and guide them through the creation and maintenance of their first Plone-based websites.

How This Book Is Organized

This book contains eight chapters and two appendixes. Although the chapters are meant to be read linearly—that is, you'll find installation instructions at the beginning of the book, not at the end—you can skip around when you get a feel for how to operate within Plone and Zope.

- Chapter 1, "Introduction to Plone and Content Management," discusses the underlying architecture of Plone and the basics of using a content-management system. Then it dissects the anatomy of a standard Plone site (for example, the elements found in the standard Plone template).

- Chapter 2, "Installing Plone," goes through the installation process for Windows, Mac OS X, and Linux/Unix users. It also covers the upgrade process, if you are coming to Plone 2.0 from Plone 1.0.

- Chapter 3, "Using Your New Plone Site," walks you through how to join a Plone site and what you gain by doing so—your own home page, folder, and presence in the content-publishing workflow. This chapter also shows you how to add and modify the various types of content within Plone, such as documents, new items, and events. Other content-related topics are explained, including the discussion feature and how to search through content stored in your Plone site.

- Chapter 4, "Additional Plone Elements," describes how to obtain, install, and configure the freely available third-party add-ons for Plone, such as wikis, photo album software, blogging tools, and so forth.

- Chapter 5, "Customizing Plone," details how to add, modify, or remove elements of the standard Plone template, including side slots, navigation tabs, and custom graphics. Internationalization and localization of your Plone template is also discussed, with examples.

- Chapter 6, "Creating and Implementing a Custom Skin," discusses the files used to create a Plone "look and feel," how to modify these files, and the process behind creating and implementing a skin—that is, a set of thematic display elements—for your Plone site.

- Chapter 7, "Additional Content-Related Techniques," discusses how to work with page templates and the Zope Template Language, how to syndicate your content (and the reasons for doing so), and how to create new content types beyond the standard set found in Plone.

- Chapter 8, "Technical Administration," discusses the process of ongoing maintenance for your Plone site, as well as how to accomplish other technical tasks, such as running Plone with web servers other than the built-in Zope web server.

- Appendix A, "Using Python for Greater Customization," introduces you to the Python language. Here you create scripts and work with the Python interpreter.

- Appendix B, "Introduction to Zope and the ZMI," provides a very basic overview of the Zope application server, as well as a quickstart guide (of sorts) to working with the Zope Management Interface.

At the end of each chapter, you will find general troubleshooting information for the items discussed, including pointers for where to look for more information or additional help.

Conventions Used in This Book

This book uses different typefaces to differentiate between code and plain English, and also to help you identify important concepts. Throughout the lessons, code, commands, and text that you type or see onscreen appear in a `computer typeface`. New terms appear in *italics* at the point in the text where they are defined. Additionally, icons accompany special blocks of information:

> **Note**
> A Note presents an interesting piece of information related to the current topic.

> **Tip**
> A Tip offers advice or teaches an easier method for performing a task.

> **Caution**
> A Caution warns you about potential pitfalls and explains how to avoid them.

Introduction to Plone and Content Management

IN THIS CHAPTER

- ▶ Plone Basics
- ▶ Why a Content-Management System?
- ▶ Anatomy of a Plone Site
- ▶ Troubleshooting

The software application known as Plone is an open-source, user-friendly, carefully structured content-management system. The sole purpose of Plone is to make your life easier—well, your life and the life of anyone else in your organization who needs to store, maintain, and share documents and other information with team members.

In general, a content-management system (CMS) manages content; accepting that definition requires no great leap of faith. But the types of CMS (web-based or offline), and the feature sets of the scores of CMS products available on the market, vary greatly. Just as CMS products differ, sometimes the needs of a company are so specific that internal developers create their own CMS to manage their own content, forgoing any out-of-the-box product that could take longer to customize than to build from scratch.

The Plone Team has created a web-based product that contains a vast yet customizable feature set, intended to meet the needs of most organizations looking for a way to manage and distribute their content. Plone is especially useful for intranets and educational institutions for which the primary goal is the dissemination of content—period.

In this chapter, you are introduced to the underlying architecture of Plone, the goals of a CMS in general, and the individual elements that make up a standard Plone site.

Plone Basics

First and foremost, Plone is open source. It is licensed under the GNU General Public License, enabling you to freely use and modify Plone however you see fit. Compare the cost of Plone (free) to other CMS software (tens of thousands of dollars), and you have an important item in the Pro column of your pros and cons list.

It's important to remember that *open source* does not necessarily mean "unsupported" or "looks cheap," just like *commercial* doesn't necessarily mean "bug free" and "beautifully designed." Often it's quite the opposite, but that's a topic left for another book. The Plone Team is made up of hundreds of developers worldwide, many of whom are usability experts, as evidenced by the fact that the Plone interface is highly usable and meets or exceeds the standards for accessibility. Standards compliance is often so difficult for web-design firms to achieve; having a compliant template set upon installation should be another item in your Pro column. After all, what good is content if your users can't find it?

Underlying Architecture of Plone

Plone itself is built on top of the Zope Application Server, an open-source product that is stable and rich in features, if not as widely publicized as the basic Apache Web Server. The Zope Application Server contains not only a web server, but also an object database and other elements such as the Content Management Framework (CMF). The CMF is a toolkit containing items that can be used individually or in a bundle, as Plone uses them. The Zope CMF contains all the logic and functionality that drives the workflow, personalization, and cataloging elements of Plone. In fact, you can think of Plone as a usable wrapper around the guts of the Zope CMF.

> **Tip**
>
> For a detailed look at the Zope architecture, see Chapter 3 of the Zope book, *Zope Concepts and Architecture*, by Amos Latteier and Michael Pellatier (Pearson Education, 2001), at http://zope.org/Documentation/Books/ZopeBook/2_6Edition/ZopeArchitecture.stx.

All things Zope are written in the Python programming language. Because Zope, the CMF, and Plone are all open source, if something about the inner workings of these parts is not to your liking, you can simply change it. But the beauty of Plone is this: Anyone with Python skills can modify the underlying elements, but knowledge of the Python language, technical architecture tricks, and even database design is absolutely *not required* to successfully build and maintain a Plone site. The end users of a typical Plone site—content maintainers and readers—tend not to have these skill sets.

> **Tip**
>
> You can find information on Zope at http://www.zope.org/; another outstanding resource is *The Zope Book,* by Amos Latteier and Michael Pellatier (Pearson Education, 2001). Python information can be found at http://www.python.org/ and in Appendix A, "Using Python for Greater Customization."

Previously, I mentioned that Zope has its own object database, and it contains its own web server. As you would imagine with a well-designed open-source product, using the built-in features is not required. Although Plone stores its content in the Zope Object Database (ZODB) by default, you can customize it to use LDAP or other relational databases, just as you can run Plone itself on any other web server, such as Apache. Some of these topics are covered in Chapter 8, "Technical Administration."

When to Use Plone

The short answer to the question "When should I use Plone?" is "Anytime you want to share a document or other content with anyone else." But more than that, Plone helps you institute security, workflow, categorization, and customization into content sharing.

For example, suppose that you are the human resources manager at a company and you need to provide everyone with employee-related forms for health insurance and stock purchase plans. Those aren't documents that you would want to put on the company's public website, for security reasons, nor would you email copies of the documents to all the employees in the company—although those are both ways in which users could possibly receive the documents.

With a Plone-driven intranet, you could create a section that only you, the HR manager, could maintain but that all employees could access. You could post the documents with accompanying notes and then update the files and add to the notes to your heart's content. You would be the content owner, and the security settings for your little slice of the Plone world would allow only you (and those above you in the hierarchy) to add, modify, and remove these documents. Those with basic end-user permissions could only retrieve the documents.

Extrapolate this simple example to all the various departments that you might find within the enterprise: Human Resources, Operations, Sales and Marketing, and so forth. Within these groups you could even have smaller groups; for example, the Sales and Marketing department might want to have a document set made available only to inside sales representatives.

Beyond the enterprise example, think of how Plone could be used in an educational setting, perhaps by the English Department of your favorite university (or the Math Department, Computer Science Department, and so forth). The websites of individual departments within a college or university tend to be designed and maintained by students or volunteer staff members, whose primary skill set is not website usability and content management. As such, these sites tend to be haphazardly organized and utilize an unpleasant or inconsistent display style. With Plone, you not only can utilize content-grouping rules, but the standard template styles are already designed to adhere to rules of usability and display.

This is not to say that you cannot customize the display templates, but changing a *skin*, or the overall template style, requires more knowledge than simply selecting the bright pink color swatch in a WYSIWYG HTML editor.

> **Note**
> You'll learn more about customizing the Plone display in Chapter 6, "Creating and Implementing a Custom Skin."

A negative comment often made about CMS-driven sites is that they all look the same, or that you can look at a site and immediately identify the CMS or template engine in use. In the next section, you'll see a few examples of completely different types of Plone-driven sites. These vastly different sites exemplify the fact that using a CMS does not lock you into a standard look and feel, nor are you stuck using flat colors and no graphics.

Examples of Plone in Use

As you've already learned, Plone can be used in any setting in which the dissemination of content is the primary goal. In this section, we take a brief look at two very different Plone-driven sites:

- The NASA/Jet Propulsion Labs Mars Rover Site, at http://mars.telascience.org/home/
- Southern Utah Online, at http://www.southernutah.com

First is the Mars Rover site from NASA/JPL. The Mars Rovers are a big deal right now, not only because it's incredibly cool that we're driving two golf carts on Mars, but also because information about this project has been made very accessible to the public. The Mars Rover site is quite simple and has only five main sections:

- **Home**—The main page of the site and a gateway for all other links, as shown in Figure 1.1
- **Download Maestro**—Instructions for obtaining Maestro, the software application necessary to view data from the Mars Rovers
- **Updates**—The data sets and images from the Mars Rovers, viewable via Maestro
- **Forums**—End-user discussion forums, as shown in Figure 1.2
- **Help**—Support documentation

The Mars Rover home page contains all the elements you would normally see on the main page of a website: introductory text, images, a standard navigation set, and supplementary items. Take a closer look at the navigation set and supplementary items, shown in Figure 1.1.

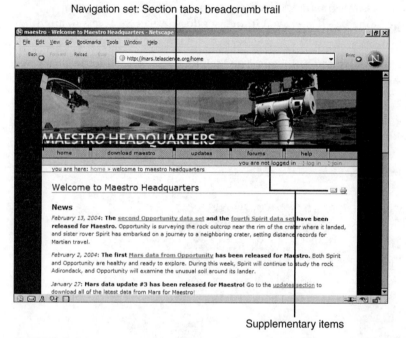

FIGURE 1.1 Close-up of the Mars Rover site's navigation set and supplementary items.

The Mars Rover site takes advantage of some core Plone components: the section tabs, breadcrumb trail, login status/links to login, and Print and Email icons. "Core" components are elements that are part of the standard Plone template but that you can modify or turn off as desired.

Use of navigation tabs reflects the custom categories of the Mars Rover site. Navigation tabs can say anything you want, but they should reflect the content that they contain. In this case, the tabs reflect the four main sections of the Mars Rover site, plus the home page itself.

A breadcrumb trail is a usability element that alerts the user to the title of the document being browsed, within the hierarchy of the site (if applicable). Think of it like a kiosk in a shopping mall, where the big red X shows where you are and the dashed line shows you how to get out. In the case of a website, a breadcrumb trail shows you the hierarchy in which the current document is situated, relative to the home page of the site. In this instance, actually viewing the home page of the site doesn't show you much of a trail, but imagine that it is a document three levels deep: The linked hierarchical elements would provide a quick exit.

The login status is another element in Plone sites. Plone sites are essentially user communities, potentially requiring accounts to access specific items, so the omnipresent login status reminds you to log in if you haven't already. The login status is usually found next to a Join link, which enables you to create an account if you don't have one already. Not all Plone sites require accounts to access information, but accounts can enable the end user to customize elements of the Plone-based site, even if the user doesn't receive access to anything special after creating an account.

Finally, Figure 1.1 shows the Mail and Print icons. The Mail icon can be used for feedback, either for an article, for a document, or in general. The Print icon is self-explanatory: It enables you to print the article or document.

Discussion forums are often an integral part of a community-oriented website. The Mars Rover site utilizes this Plone add-on, as shown in Figure 1.2.

FIGURE 1.2 The Mars Rover discussion forums.

After a user has created an account, he can start a topic, add or reply to a post, and so forth. Often users need not have accounts or be logged in to read posts, but only account holders can make contributions. You'll learn about Plone add-ons such as forums in Chapter 4, "Additional Plone Elements."

An entirely different kind of Plone-based site is the Southern Utah Online example, shown in Figure 1.3. The examples of the Mars Rover site and the Southern Utah Online site prove that just because two sites use the same underlying architecture (Plone), it does not mean that they will look the same.

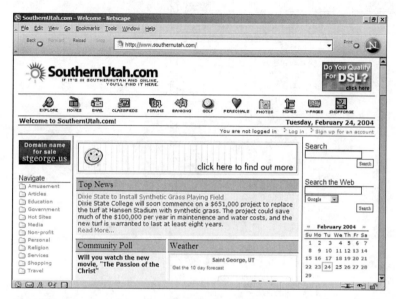

FIGURE 1.3 The Southern Utah Online home page.

The Southern Utah Online site is a prime example of a geography-based community site—in this case, one that provides information for residents and visitors to southern Utah. The number of core Plone elements on the Mars Rover site pales in comparison to those used here. Instead of tabs, you can see numerous icons across the top of the page, corresponding to content sections such as Movies, Golf, Homes, and Yellow Pages. Similarly, the Navigate section on the left side of the page shows entries such as Education, Government, and Religion.

Within the body of the main page, you can see such segments as Top News, a user poll, and an entry for weather information. On the sides of the site you can see a login form, search boxes, a calendar, and a listing of upcoming events—all of which are standard Plone elements that require no programming by the site administrator. Finally, although there's no breadcrumb trail on this main page, you do see the login status in the upper right of the page, directly under the current date.

The Southern Utah site might be a little on the busy side, but it exemplifies a lot of the possible elements that can be added to a standard Plone site without any knowledge of programming or application architecture. Figure 1.4 shows a subpage of the Southern Utah site, providing an example of content architecture.

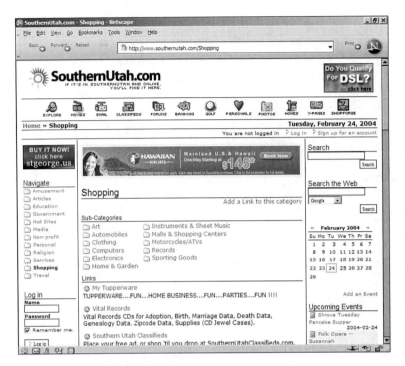

FIGURE 1.4 The Southern Utah Online Shopping main page.

When navigating to the Shopping page of the Southern Utah site, you can see the beginnings of content architecture. The breadcrumb trail is now used, in the upper left. The overall look and feel of the page has not changed; icon-based navigation elements are still present, as are the login status, the search boxes, the calendar, and so forth.

However, the body of the page now contains a list of subcategories within the shopping section, such as Automobiles, Electronics, and Sporting Goods. Links are also present and seem to follow a general structure: icon, hyperlinked link title, link description on the next line.

Additionally, an Add Link to This Category link takes you to a form that enables you to add your own information to the list of links. As the links are structured, so is the form. When it is stored, the information is displayed in the proper format because the elements entered in the form would match predetermined elements marked for display in the site.

The Mars Rover and Southern Utah sites show the wide range of possibilities for using Plone to share content and create a user-based community. In the next section, we take a look at some other motivating factors for using a CMS.

Why a Content-Management System?

Now that you've seen a few examples of content being managed in the Plone web-based management system, let's try to answer the question "Why use a CMS?" Although you could easily make a list a mile long with positive reasons for using a CMS—and we will in the next section—many companies and institutions simply do not use one or else use a poor implementation.

Organizations might think that although it is a wonderful idea to structure and maintain content in a secure and usable fashion, the fact remains that someone must still spend some time planning and implementing the overall hierarchy and business rules related to the content. Even if the actual technical creation of the structure comes via a stepwise set of web-based forms, some forethought by a human is still required. That little detail can be enough of an excuse to eschew the implementation.

Similarly, after a system is in place, all users must be trained in its usage. No matter how simple the system might be, there will be late adopters and laggards, as in the lifecycle of any new product. Unfortunately, the implementation of a CMS is only as successful as its weakest and most resistant user.

All of these negative situations are realities in an institutional environment, and they serve more to answer the question "Why should you *not* use a CMS?" If you are the champion for implementing a CMS—and Plone, in particular—come armed with all the positive benefits that it brings to the table, which you'll now see.

Features of a Content-Management System

Anyone who has created a website as part of a team of designers, usability experts, and content owners knows that the biggest problem is making everybody happy. Designers want it to be pretty, which sometimes means not so usable. Usability experts want it to be useful, which sometimes means not so pretty. Content owners tend not to be concerned about design or usability; they just want their document posted (yesterday!).

Although it is wonderful to have a goal, such as posting a document for all to see, you might find that content owners have not thought about the format, placement, permissions, or other elements that are necessary for the website administrator to complete the task. If the content owner answers all those questions once, it also doesn't mean that he will think about it the next time he wants you to post a document. So what you do is provide content owners with a consistent format and the ability to do their own work, within the structure of a CMS. In general, a CMS separates the two camps—design and content—so that they can work independently of each other and still achieve their goals.

A worthwhile CMS should contain some of the following features, and Plone certainly does:

- **Page templates**—A good CMS has not only modifiable page templates, but also templates that are part of a hierarchy. In fact, the master page template should call several other templates that define different sections of a page. Plone uses this method, enabling designers to make changes to small portions of a template that then easily are rolled into the site itself. Templates should adhere to the latest web standards regarding end-user accessibility.

- **Style sheets**—Along with page templates, a crucial feature of a CMS is a comprehensive style sheet that separates elements of a site even further. Styles speak to the individual items such as element placement, color, fonts, and so forth. After templates have been set, designers still can modify numerous elements of site by making changes only to one file—the style sheet.

- **HTML knowledge not necessary**—Although HTML is the language of the Web, it should not be a requirement that content know HTML (or any other markup language) just to publish a document. A good CMS helps the user through the process by using a form with a series of questions regarding items such as the title, description, and content or file. The CMS then stores the user's answers in its database. When another user requests the information, it is displayed in the appropriate marked-up format. For example, the title of a document might be bold and might be a link, the description might be normal text directly below the title, and so forth. Even though the content owner didn't surround the title text with bold and link tags, the CMS handled it successfully because of the manner in which the content was added.

- **Record data about an item**—Making an item available for consumption is just one piece of the puzzle. Users should be able to add and review metadata regarding the item. Metadata includes the list of authors, the owner, the last update date and update history, the review date, the publishing date, keywords, and so forth.

- **Access roles**—Availability of content and the right to publish content should be available to only a specific set of users, and these users can be predefined. You wouldn't want just anyone to be able to edit your documents, and your CMS shouldn't allow that, either. Although you should be able to define a hierarchy of users and access roles to both the content stored in the CMS and the management of the CMS itself, the underlying factor should be that users can see and do only what you (the administrator) grant them permission to see and do.

- **Capability to undo**—People make mistakes, and a good CMS should supply a way for users to get out of their mistakes by providing a rollback feature. Plone utilizes the undo action not only at the user level, but also at the administrative level. If a user adds, modifies, or deletes the wrong item or does so incorrectly, the user can undo the action. If a manager provides the wrong permissions, installs the wrong add-on tool, or changes a setting incorrectly, the manager, too, can undo the action.

> **Technology integration**—A CMS with all the features listed previously will do you no good if it can't be integrated with your enterprise applications. If you're a Microsoft shop, your CMS should be capable of running on servers with a Microsoft operating system. Similarly, if your enterprise employs Linux, Unix, or Solaris servers, your CMS should fit nicely within that framework. Enter Plone. This application meets the requirements of all four types of workers described earlier—the designers, usability experts, content owners, and website administrators. Plone also has all the features listed earlier, which determines a worthwhile CMS. You'll learn more about these features as you follow along in this book.

As you saw through the Mars Rover and Southern Utah examples, the visual display of a Plone-based site can be as varied as any standard, static website. However, Plone is also based on a set of templates designed with the greatest levels of usability in mind, meeting the needs of usability experts. Their job now is to decide on the implementation of usable pieces instead of having to ascertain and modify the overall usability of a site created from scratch.

Ahead of the content owner sits the website administrator, who has implemented the content hierarchy and security settings based on the determination of internal business rules (for example, Sales and Marketing can see some Operations documents but not all of them, or the Human Resources manager can post documents in her section but not within the Production Department section).

As previously stated, a good CMS goes to great pains to separate content from design. This alleviates situations that often arise in corporate intranets in which the Sales and Marketing section has yellow links on a red background, and the Operations area has all of its documents listed in 8-point Courier with a fade-in effect when the page loads. These are drastic examples, but they come from real life.

Separating content from design essentially means that the administrators of the content need not know HTML, how to use any standard web creation tools such as HTML editors, how to FTP, and so forth. In fact, there are no "pages," per se: Content is stored, which then populates the predetermined templates.

For example, recall the Southern Utah example and the addition of links in the Shopping directory. Users do not need to know how to create an image tag for the icon preceding the link, how to create the tag for the link itself, how to add line breaks, and so forth. All they need to know is the title and the text that they want to enter. The template feeds that information into the proper predefined slots, and the Plone application displays the link appropriately when that page is called.

The separation of design and content, a predetermined information hierarchy, and business rules related to the storage of document histories (change logs) are all key selling points of a CMS. These features allow nontechnical workers, such as administrative assistants, to carry out basic production tasks, such as maintaining documents and other posted information, instead of requiring programmers to handle them. This alone cuts the costs associated with the dissemination of content to employees, external users, and so forth. If that's not enough to sway your boss, consider the fact that, by using predetermined templates, the intranet or extranet will have a consistent style—and what good are corporate guidelines if no one follows them? Using a CMS forces users to follow corporate style guidelines, often without even knowing what they are.

Anatomy of a Plone Site

The next chapter is all about installing Plone and getting your site up and running. Before that happens, it's important to become familiar with some of the core elements of a basic Plone site that we have discussed in this chapter. These elements are part of the overall template and help to provide the sense of community and interaction among your users.

As you saw in the Mars Rover and Southern Utah examples, there is great variety among the usage of standard elements. In the next section, we focus on familiarizing you with the items on the right and left sides of the template. These items are called slots, and their presence is completely customizable.

Plone Slots

Plone slots are small bits that are defined as part of the overall template. Slots contain dynamic information; in fact, the visibility of the slot itself is dynamically based on meeting certain criteria. For example, the Login slot will not appear if the user is already logged in—why does this user need to see the login form?

> **Note**
> The appearance, placement, and general presence of all slots are defined through the management interface, which you will learn about in Chapter 2, "Installing Plone."

The following slots are standard elements of a Plone site. The examples shown are from the Plone site itself, at http://www.plone.org/. The appearance of slots is completely customizable—blue boxes are not required, although they are mighty clean.

The About Slot
When viewing an object, the About slot (see Figure 1.5) shows information regarding its owner, its type, and its date last updated.

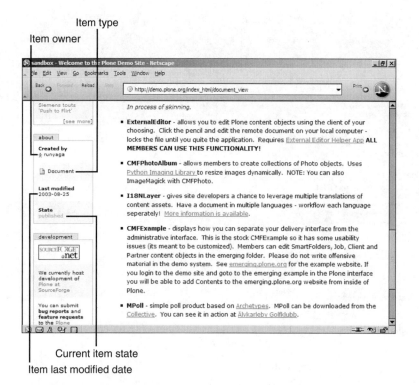

FIGURE 1.5   The About slot.

The Calendar Slot
Quite simply, the Calendar slot displays a calendar. It is completely customizable in display, but it often highlights the current day, as shown in Figure 1.6. Other highlighted information could be for days of the week that contain events.

The Events Slot
When a user publishes an event, it appears in the Events slot if it meets the preset criteria. You can set the Events slot to show the next *n* number of items, all items within a time frame, and so forth.

The Favorites Slot
If enabled, the Favorites slot shows a list of the favorite links for the user and a link to the management tool for them.

The Login Slot
If the user is not already logged in, the Login box appears. Along with the standard name/password form fields, links are present for help if the user has forgotten the password or needs to create a new account.

CHAPTER 1   Introduction to Plone and Content Management

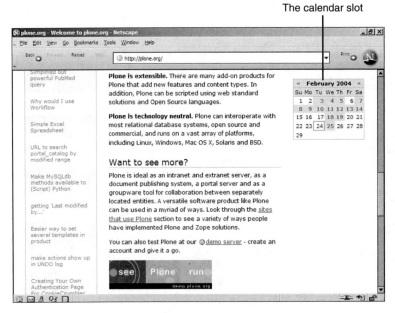

FIGURE 1.6   The Calendar slot.

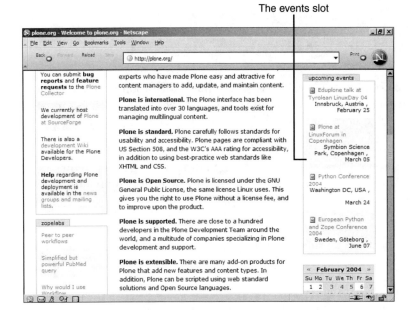

FIGURE 1.7   Items in the Events slot.

Anatomy of a Plone Site

The Navigation Slot
The Navigation slot shows a directory-like hierarchy of sections within the Plone site. Opening one directory shows any subdirectories within the tree.

The News Slot
Much like the Events slot, the News slot shows links to published news items that meet predetermined criteria.

FIGURE 1.8   The Navigation, Login, and News slots.

The Related Slot
When a page is viewed, any related items in the content repository is shown in the Related slot. Items are related to each other through matching keywords, which are added or assigned during the publishing process.

The Reviews Slot
Any bits of content that are awaiting review are shown in the Reviews slot. The Reviews slot is visible only to those who have permission to approve content for publishing, such as the Plone content administrator.

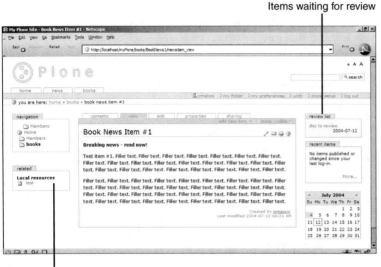

The related items slot

FIGURE 1.9 The Related and Reviews slots.

Creating Your Own Slots

You are not limited to the standard set of Plone slots. Just as you can remove and configure the base set of slots, you can create your own slots to hold static or dynamic content. You will learn to create your own slots in Chapter 5, "Customizing Plone."

Troubleshooting

This chapter didn't include any hands-on work, so there hopefully wasn't much to troubleshoot. If anything, you will want to know more about content-management systems in general, as well as the nuts and bolts of Zope. Both of these topics are extremely broad, and to go into any more detail than we have here would send this book off on a tangent. Use the links provided earlier to explore more about Zope, starting at http://www.zope.org/.

Summary

This chapter introduced you to the concept of a content-management system, and you learned how a Plone solution achieves the basic goals of an enterprise-class CMS. You took a look at some real-world examples of Plone, including how to customize the look and feel to fit the needs of your organization. Some of the basic elements of Plone were discussed, including the standard slotlike areas of the overall page template. This introduction helps ease you into the next chapter, in which you install and begin to configure your new Plone site.

Installing Plone

IN THIS CHAPTER

▶ Plone User Roles

▶ Installation and Access Requirements

▶ Obtaining Plone

▶ Installing Plone

▶ Where Do We Go from Here?

▶ Troubleshooting

With a basic introduction to content management behind you, it's time to jump right in and create your own Plone installation. Not only is Plone open source, but it's also available for numerous platforms, including Windows, flavors of Linux/Unix, and Mac OS X.

But before installing Plone, let's take a look at the numerous types of user roles you will encounter. Plone is a workflow-based CMS, so it is important to have a solid understanding of the different types of user roles before you try to create and manage content.

Plone User Roles

Two general types of user roles exist in Plone: global and local. Just like it sounds, global roles are in effect for the entire Plone installation, whereas local roles are in effect on only a folder-by-folder basis. Every user has at least one role: the standard role of member. But users can also have more than one local role, and many do.

Next, we take a moment to delineate the basic roles of Plone users.

The Manager Role

The manager is the highest role that a user can achieve, and this is a global role. The manager has "god" privileges to perform any task within Plone, including the following:

- Adding and modifying all users at any time
- Assigning (or revoking) local roles to users at any time
- Publishing, revoking, and modifying all content
- Adding keywords to pull together related content
- Modifying templates and other elements of the Plone installation

When you install Plone later in this chapter, your role will be that of manager.

The Member Role

As you saw in Chapter 1, "Introduction to Plone and Content Management," one of the standard elements of a Plone site is the ability to "join." Plone sites are intended as member-based communities; when you join a site, you become a user with a member role. When you are a member, your own space is created in the Plone system, where you can add, modify, and generally maintain your own documents.

The manager can promote users with simple member roles to additional levels within other members' spaces. For example, if you are the human resources manager and you have two employees under you in the corporate hierarchy, the Plone manager would provide the same hierarchy within the Plone workflow: You would be granted permission to work with documents that belong to members in the workflow beneath you.

You'll learn more about workflow roles in the next section, which describes these local roles in a bit more detail.

Workflow Roles

Within a Plone site, the basic workflow for content visibility goes like this:

1. A member adds content in his workspace. The member is the owner of this content.
2. A member who has been granted the role of reviewer for content in this particular folder reviews the content (as the name suggests).
3. The reviewer publishes the content, and it becomes visible for everyone.

By "basic workflow," I mean that there are no problems with the content or roadblocks that would keep the member or reviewer from publishing the content to the membership at large. In fact, other states in the workflow could block a clear path to publishing:

- **Private**—Marked by the owner, the Private status makes the content available only to the owner. Content also then is removed from the Plone search engine index so that no one will accidentally wander past it.

- **Retract**—The member might withdraw content from consideration for general publication. In this case, it reverts to being visible to its owner.

- **Reject**—The reviewer rejects the content for general publication, and it reverts to being visible to its owner.

We discuss workflow roles and states in much greater detail in Chapter 3, "Using Your New Plone Site," but an introduction to the concepts was necessary at this point.

From this brief glimpse into the world of user roles, you should take away the idea that one overall manager controls the assignments of the general user roles. This manager account is the one that was initially created during installation. It has immediate access to the configuration of the application and its users. With this in mind, move on to the next section to learn about the basic requirements for installing and running Plone; we then wrap up this chapter by showing you how to install Plone on your platform of choice.

Installation and Access Requirements

Because it sits on top of the Zope Application Server, Plone can run on anything that Zope runs on—and that's a long list that includes most flavors of Linux/Unix, Solaris, Windows, and Mac OS X. As with any software, the more powerful the machine is in terms of processor and RAM, the better the application will run.

For production usage, the minimum requirements should be at least a processor speed of 1.5Ghz, 1GB of RAM, and about 100MB of hard drive space. Zope and Plone will work just fine on a machine with 256MB of RAM or a processor less than 1Ghz, but those should be test machines only—you don't want tens of thousands of accesses sucking the life out of that little box.

If you do not meet the minimum requirements exactly, or if you have some interesting combination of a moderately fast processor but more RAM than you can shake a stick at, there are plenty of ways to fine-tune your installation to take advantage of the items at your disposal. You'll learn more about these techniques in Chapter 8, "Technical Administration."

When Plone is up and running, it becomes a client-based application, and the client used to access it is your web browser. The core Plone templates are based on current HTML standards, so all browsers that adhere to standards can be used. These include the following:

- Internet Explorer 5.0+
- Netscape 4.7, 7.0+
- Mozilla 1.0+
- Opera 7.0+

- Konqueror 2.*x*+
- Safari 1.1+
- Text-based browsers such as Lynx and w3m AWeb

In fact, any browser that handles basic HTML and form input, and that accepts cookies can be used with Plone, although the overall display might not appear as intended. In other words, your PDA or web-enabled mobile phone might be capable of successfully browsing a Plone-based site.

Obtaining Plone

You can't walk into a store and buy a copy of Plone off the shelf. Plone is open source and freely distributed, so the best place to go for obtaining current versions of Plone is the Downloads section of the Plone website, at http://www.plone.org/download. Here you will find prepackages installers, released source code, and instructions on accessing prerelease source code from the CVS repository.

> **Note**
>
> If you are experienced in installing pre-release snapshots, feel free to use the CVS repository. However, sticking to the official customer releases is the best way to go for the novice user, or even for the advanced user who doesn't want to deal with the esoteric bugs and other issues that untested snapshots sometimes produce.

The bundled installers are definitely the way to go. They make life especially easy for Windows and Mac OS X users: The wizard-based interface can get you up and running in 15 minutes or less. With these installers come the following components (in addition to Plone itself):

- Python 2.1.3. Win32 extensions are included in the Windows install.
- Python Imaging Library (PIL) 1.1.3, used in conjunction with CMFPhoto to manipulate images.
- Zope 2.6.1.
- Zope Controller 1.0.
- Content Management Framework (CMF) 1.3.1.
- CMF Collector 0.9b, a bug-tracking system.

- ReportLab 1.15, for the creation of PDFs with Python.
- CMF Quick Installer, used to install additional Zope-based products.
- CMF Wiki 0.1.
- CMF Photo, which enables you to view and resize image files within your Plone site.
- CMF Forum, used to create a simple bulletin board within Plone. It also forms the base of the commenting system for documents and other content items.
- External Editor 0.6, which enables you to edit objects and content.
- Zope Book 2.5.
- Localizer, which assists you in translating core elements of Plone into multiple languages.
- Placeless Translation Service, which provides ready-made templates for standard Zope and Plone elements. It works in conjunction with Localizer.

> The version numbers referenced here are for installation of Plone 2.0.3, the current release at the time of writing. Your specific Plone version might be different by the time you read this book, as will the items bundled with the installer.

Linux/Unix users have a variety of options, based on their distribution type. For example, Red Hat/Mandrake/SuSE users can obtain RPMs of required elements, while Debian users can use apt-get. All Linux/Unix users can build elements from the source code, although the RPM or apt-get method is most common.

Installing Plone

The next few sections outline how to install Plone 2.0 on your operating system of choice. The assumption is that you have never installed Plone or any of its corresponding elements, such as Zope. If you have, skip ahead to the section "Upgrading Plone."

For all other users, read the appropriate section for your operating system, and feel free to skip the section that does not apply to you. Be sure to rejoin the fray for the last section of the chapter, "Where Do We Go from Here?"

Installing on Windows

The prepackaged Plone installer for Windows should be used only on Windows NT, 2000, and XP. Before you begin, you should be logged in as the administrator, or the corresponding highest level of access for your system. When you're ready, go to the Downloads section of the Plone website, at http://www.plone.org/download, and follow the link for the Windows installer.

> Your Plone version might differ from that shown here, as will the Windows desktop and general environment shown in these screenshots. Installation wizards are meant to help you, so do not be alarmed by the differences. If you are in doubt about how to proceed, visit the Installation section of the Plone documentation, at http://plone.org/documentation/book/2.

After the installer has been downloaded to your hard drive, double-click it to begin the installation. You will see a screen like the one in Figure 2.1.

FIGURE 2.1 Beginning a Plone installation on Windows.

Click the Next button to continue. The installer goes through the usual steps for a wizard-based software installation, including asking you where you want the files to be installed. It selects a default location of `C:\Program Files\Plone 2`.

After you select the file installation location, you are asked to select the components to install. Three items are available:

- **Main Plone Installation**—This is required, obviously.
- **Client-Side External Editor**—Optional. When installed, this Zope-based product acts as the default editor for nonbinary content within Plone (HTML, structured text, plain text, and XML, for example).
- **Install Service**—Optional. When this is selected, it installs Plone as a service on your Windows machine. If it is not installed as a service, you manually must start Plone when you boot your machine.

Select the appropriate responses—only Main Plone Installation is required—and press the Next button to continue. You will see a screen as in Figure 2.2, prompting you to create the Plone Manager Account. This is the account used to access the Zope and Plone-management application, which is crucial for running a Plone site.

FIGURE 2.2 Creating the Plone manager account.

At the Enter a Password screen, you create the account for the Plone manager. It is extremely important that you retain this information for later use; otherwise, you will be unable to access the management interface. After you create the account, continue in the wizard until you see the Ready to Install screen, shown in Figure 2.3.

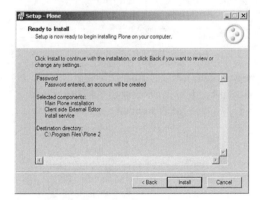

FIGURE 2.3 Plone is ready to be installed.

Select the Install button. The installer runs through its paces, eventually telling you that it has completed the installation. With the Launch Plone Controller check box checked, click the Finish button. The installation process cleans up after itself and then launches the Plone Controller application, shown in Figure 2.4. Press the Start button to start Zope and Plone.

CHAPTER 2 Installing Plone

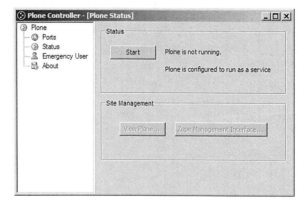

FIGURE 2.4   Plone has been started.

The Plone Controller provides access to basic setup information, such as the ports to use and the status of your Plone installation. You can start and stop Plone by using this controller or by right-clicking the taskbar icon. If you haven't already, use the controller to start Plone and then skip ahead to the "Where Do We Go From Here?" section at the end of this chapter.

Installing on Mac OS X

The prepackaged Plone installer for Mac OS X will get you up and running in no time flat. When you're ready to begin, go to the Downloads section of the Plone website, at http://www.plone.org/download, and follow the link for the Mac OS X installer.

> **Note**
>
> Your Plone version might differ from that shown here, as will the Mac OS X desktop and general environment shown in these screenshots. Installation wizards are meant to help you, so do not be alarmed by the differences. If you are in doubt about how to proceed, visit the Installation section of the Plone documentation, at `http://plone.org/documentation/book/2`.

After the installer has downloaded to your hard drive, double-click it to begin the installation. You will see a screen like the one in Figure 2.5, showing the installation steps that you will follow.

Installing Plone

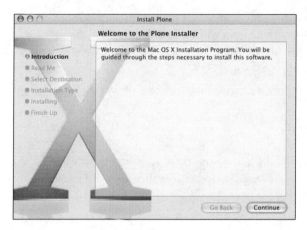

FIGURE 2.5   Beginning a Plone installation on Mac OS X.

Click the Next button to continue. The installer goes through the usual steps for a wizard-based software installation, pausing to ask where you want the files to be installed. At this point, you must select the partition on which Mac OS X is installed. Press the Continue button to move on to the next screen, and continue doing so until you see a screen like the one in Figure 2.6, prompting you to create the Plone Manager Account. This is the account used to access the Zope and Plone management application, which is crucial for running a Plone site.

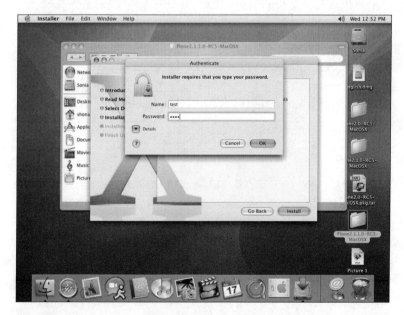

FIGURE 2.6   Creating the Plone manager account.

At this screen, you create the account for the Plone manager. It is extremely important that you retain this information for later use; otherwise, you will be unable to access the management interface. After you create the account, continue in the wizard; it runs through its paces, eventually telling you that it has completed the installation.

When Plone has been successfully installed, open a terminal window and type the following command at the prompt:

```
# sudo /Library/StartupItems/Plone/Plone start
```

Plone should now start. For additional command-line methods for starting and stopping Plone, view the `ReadMe.rtf` file located in your `/Applications/Plone` directory. If Plone has successfully started, you can skip ahead to the "Where Do We Go From Here?" section at the end of this chapter.

Installing on Linux/Unix

Although there are RPMs for various flavors of Linux/Unix, there's no all-in-one installer as there is for the Windows or Mac OS X folks. So, a little more work is required for Linux/Unix administrators.

Specific installation instructions will differ, depending on the exact flavor of your operating system and whether you choose to install via RPMs, use apt-get, or build from the source code. As such, this book provides only an overview of the process for installing Plone on a non-Windows/non–Mac OS X platform. During each general installation step, be sure to read the important documents, such as the `README.txt` and `INSTALL.txt` files, within the packages. These files invariably contain notes, tips, and specific instructions for adding the individual pieces of the puzzle to your system.

> **Tip**
> All major software installation should be performed as the root or administrator user.

The general steps follow:

1. Download and install the current version of Python (2.3.4 or later) from `http://www.python.org/download/`.

2. Download and install the current version of Zope (2.6.2 or later) from `http://www.zope.org/Products`.

3. Download and install the current version of CMF (1.3.2 or later) from `http://cmf.zope.org/download`; this should include DCWorkflow.

Installing Plone

4. Download and install the current version of Plone, called CMFPlone, from http://www.plone.org/download; this should include Formulator 1.4.0 (or later), CMFActionsIcons, CMFQuickInstallerTool, GroupUserFolder 1.32 (or later), BTreeFolder2, and CMFFormController.

If any of the items listed in steps 3 and 4 as "should be included" are not included in the tarball of the master product (for example, CMF and Plone), you should be able to download them separately from their respective locations.

The following instructions assume that you are familiar with the process of installing software either from RPMs or through a build process (`configure`/`make`/`make install`). As such, we'll just fly through these steps:

1. Unpack the Python tarball.
2. Install Python, using the instructions in `INSTALL.txt`.
3. Unpack the Zope tarball.
4. Install Zope, using the instructions in `INSTALL.txt`.
5. Start Zope via the command line (where */myzope/instance/* is the location of your Zope installation):

    # */myzope/instance/*bin/zopectl start

6. Test that Zope is running by opening a web browser and navigating to the Zope Management Interface (ZMI), at http://localhost:8080/Control_Panel/manage_main.

> **Tip**
> Debian users should use port 9673 instead of 8080. If you have changed the default port to use on your own, use it to access the ZMI as appropriate.

7. On your file system, locate the value of `INSTANCE HOME`. You will place all packages in the `INSTANCE HOME/Products` folder, so make a note of its location.
8. Unpack the CMF tarball.
9. Move all subdirectories, such as CMFCalendar, CMFCore, DCWorkflow, and so forth, plus documentation, to the `INSTANCE HOME/Products` directory.
10. Restart Zope so that these products are loaded. You can verify that they are loaded by logging in to the ZMI and looking the Products section of the Control Panel, as shown in Figure 2.7.

CHAPTER 2 Installing Plone

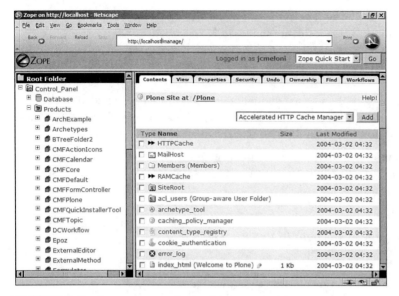

FIGURE 2.7 Items appear in the Products section of the Control Panel.

11. Unpack the Plone tarball. It should contain at least the following subdirectories:

    ▶ BTreeFolder2

    ▶ CMFQuickInstallerTool

    ▶ CMFActionIcons

    ▶ CMFFormController

    ▶ CMFPlone

    ▶ Formulator

    ▶ GroupUserFolder

    ▶ PlacelessTranslationService

12. Move these subdirectories to the INSTANCE HOME/Products directory.

13. Restart Zope so that these products are loaded. You can verify that they are loaded by logging in to the ZMI via your web browser and looking for an entry called Plone, as shown in Figure 2.8.

Installing Plone

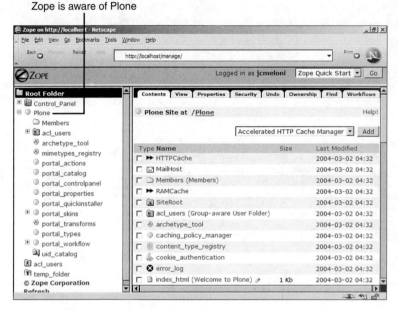

FIGURE 2.8 Plone appears in the ZMI.

Congratulations! You can now skip ahead to the "Where Do We Go from Here?" section at the end of this chapter, to add your Plone site.

Upgrading Plone

If you have an older version of Plone installed on your system, you can easily upgrade. You do not need to uninstall your existing Plone version; the installation process will overwrite all necessary files. This is especially true when upgrading within minor versions, such as Plone 2.0.2 to 2.0.3. If you are using Plone 1.0, which is almost an entirely different species than Plone 2.0, uninstalling it first is also not required—the Plone 2 installation will occur in a completely different place. However, you should uninstall Plone 1.0 after Plone 2.0 has been installed and is running, just because there's no need for unused files to hang around the system.

Follow these steps to migrate to the latest version of Plone; it is assumed that you have a working Plone site within the Zope architecture.

1. Back up your Plone site. You can simply back up the Data.fs file found in /plonehome/Data/var/, or you can make a copy of all files and directories, in case you want to revert completely back to your old version.

2. Stop Plone.

3. Begin the installation process of the new version of Plone, using the previous instructions appropriate for your operating system (for example, follow the instructions for using the Windows installer, using the Mac OS X installer, installing via RPM/apt-get, or building from source code).

4. Go to the Zope Management Interface, click on your existing Plone instance in the navigation frame, and then look for the tool called portal_migration in the workspace frame, as shown in Figure 2.9.

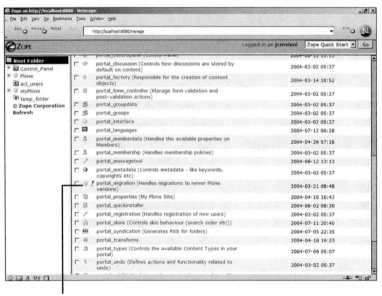

The portal_migration tool

FIGURE 2.9 The portal_migration tool is available to help with Plone migration.

5. Click the Migrate link, which is part of the sentence "If you wish to upgrade to a new Plone instance...."

6. On the migration screen, shown in Figure 2.10, you have two options: Upgrade and Force Upgrade. Usually, pressing the Upgrade button is all that is necessary to bring Plone up to speed. However, if you attempt to do so and are met with errors, you can select the old version of Plone (the one from which you are upgrading) from the drop-down list and then press the Force Upgrade button.

7. Repeat the process for each Plone site on your system, if you have more than one.

8. Shut down and restart Zope.

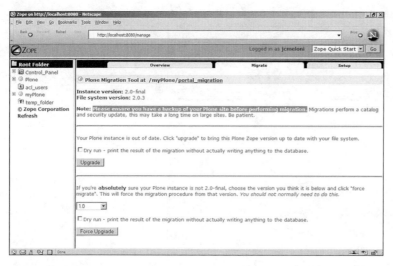

FIGURE 2.10   Plone migration options via the ZMI.

Where Do We Go from Here?

With Zope, CMF, Plone, and all sorts of other great products now installed on your system, you can add your first Plone site. Installing Plone, the software, is not the same as creating a Plone site; the latter requires performing tasks to specifically let Zope know that this new Plone object is now part of its world.

> **Note**
>
> If you used the Windows or Mac OS X installer, a default site called plone has already been created. But follow the next steps to create a Plone site on your own, to familiarize yourself with the process.

Follow these steps to add a Plone site to your Zope application server:

1. Log in to the Zope Management Interface and select Plone Site from the Add drop-down list, as shown in Figure 2.11.

2. Complete the form for adding a Plone site, see Figure 2.12. The ID is a short name in alphanumeric characters and becomes part of the URL to your Plone site (for example, an ID of myPlone means that the URL to your Plone site will be http://*yourdomain*/myPlone). The title will appear on all pages of your Plone site; Membership Source should be the default for now. The description field is self-explanatory.

CHAPTER 2 Installing Plone

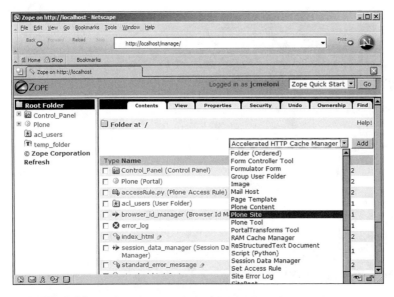

FIGURE 2.11 Select Plone Site from the drop-down list.

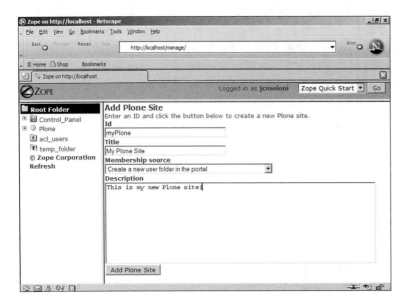

FIGURE 2.12 Completing the form to create your Plone site.

Troubleshooting

3. After you press the Add Plone Site button, your site is created and appears in the window. You can access it directly at its URL; you will see the following Figure 2.13.

FIGURE 2.13   Your new Plone site.

Congratulations, you're the proud owner of a brand-new baby Plone!

Troubleshooting

In a chapter filled with installation procedures, you would think that the troubleshooting section might be unwieldy. That's not the case here because the installation wizards are well built and usually run without fail. Issues arise for less spectacular reasons than installation software failure:

- **Installing as the wrong user**—Installation should occur as the administrator or root user, depending on which your operating system uses. Windows and Mac OS X users will be familiar with the administrator account, while Linux/Unix users will know this account as root. If you do not have the appropriate permissions for reading, writing, and creating directories and files during the installation process, the installation will fail. Using the top-level user on your respective operating system, at least during installation time, alleviates that issue.

▶ **Build issues**—These can vary greatly, from issues with your compiler to library mismatches. If you are familiar with building from source or installing from RPM or apt-get, you are probably familiar with these types of errors and how they are presented. Typically, the build or install process is halted midstream, and an error string is printed that will help you deduce which libraries might be missing or other issues that might have arisen. If your issues have to do with missing libraries, simply track them down from your operating system's installation CDs or FTP site, and install; when they are installed, try again. Depending on how antiquated your operating system libraries are, the process of updating your system could take longer than installing Zope and Plone.

If you have installation issues of any sort that do not fall into these general categories of pilot error, consult the documentation for the product in question. For Plone-specific issues, which would be the case with Windows or Mac OS X installers, or the specific Plone binary or source distributions for Linux/Unix platforms, visit the Plone site at http://www.plone.org/. Zope-related issues, which would be the case for those having to install Zope and the CMF separately, are addressed at http://www.zope.org/. Similarly, Python-related issues can be solved by reading the documentation at http://www.python.org/.

Summary

This chapter was all about installation, and unless you have three different servers running three different types of operating systems, you should have breezed right through. The chapter opened with a brief discussion of the types of roles utilized in the Plone workflow—these roles are discussed in greater detail as the book goes on. You learned about the requirements for running Plone and how to install Plone on various operating systems. Instructions for upgrading an older version of Plone using the migration tool were provided as well.

Finally, you learned how to add a brand new Plone site into the Zope application framework. In the next chapter, you start to work with your new Plone site, beginning with simply logging in, and then you move through working with the numerous standard content types.

Using Your New Plone Site

IN THIS CHPATER

- Joining a Plone Site
- Working with Content in Plone
- Publishing Content in Plone
- Utilizing the Content Discussion Feature
- Searching Content
- Troubleshooting

In the previous chapter, you created a management user and a new Plone site. In this chapter, you'll work within your new site as a manager, but you will also create a generic user account and perform tasks as a nonmanager. This will help you to gain an understanding of a Plone site and workflow from both points of view, which will help you to build a better environment for your users and the overall needs of your organization.

To get started, navigate to your new Plone site. If you're logged in with your manager account, use the Log Out link. If you haven't logged in yet, even better—in the next section, you'll join the site as a generic user and act as that user while performing some nonmanagerial tasks.

> **Note**
> Throughout this chapter and the next, the default Plone installation is shown in examples. You'll learn to customize the colors, styles, elements, and other aspects in Chapter 5, "Customizing Plone."

Joining a Plone Site

When visiting a Plone site, if you are not logged in to the site, you will likely see text such as "You are not logged in" displayed in the Plone toolbar. Next to this text usually are links to Log In and Join. Following the Log In link takes you to a page containing a form with Name and Password fields, as well as a link to follow if you have forgotten your password.

These elements are standard when it comes to logging in to a membership-based site. The fact that you can find these links from several different areas is an example of good usability.

> **Tip**
> In addition to the Log In and Join links in the toolbar, many Plone sites display a standard Plone login slot, which is omnipresent until the member has logged in. The standard Plone login slot is a box containing username and password form fields, which often are displayed in the left column but can be placed anywhere in the template.

To create a new, generic user, follow the Join link. You will see a form that contains the following fields, with red squares next to the field labels to indicate when a field is required:

- **Full Name**—Your full name. This is not a required field. You can change the value of this field at any time.

- **Username**—An alphanumeric username, without any spaces. This is a required field. Use the username to log in; you are identified by this name in numerous areas throughout a Plone site. Your username identifies you as a content owner and a member of the site, and is also used to create the URL to your personal page, such as `http://localhost/myPlone/Members/johnsmith`. The value of this field cannot be changed.

- **Email**—Your email address, used to validate the account and also used for contacting you if you request a new password. This is a required field. You can change it at any time.

- **Password**—Must be at least five characters long. This is a required field. You can change it at any time.

- **Confirm Password**—Re-enter the password, to confirm that you're typing the correct value.

Additionally, there is a check box titled Send a Mail with the Password. If you check this box, an email will be sent to the email address that you specified, containing your username and password information.

When you press the Register button, the user account is created and a welcome message is displayed along with a Log In button. Although your new account has been successfully created, you will not be automatically logged in. In the next few sections, you'll log in as this new user and see the different user preferences that you can modify.

FIGURE 3.1 A Plone user registration form.

Logging In

As mentioned previously, if you have not yet logged in to a Plone site, the links to doing so are plentiful. If you have just created a new user (as in the previous section), you will see a Log In button directly following the success message. As shown in Figure 3.2, the default Plone template also shows a login slot on the left side of the page and a link to Log In in the Plone toolbar in the upper right.

Whether you follow the links or head over to the slot and log in to the form provided there, you will see a link that says Forgot Your Password? or some text related to retrieving your password. This type of functionality is commonly found in member-based sites; following the link leads you to a form for retrieving your lost password.

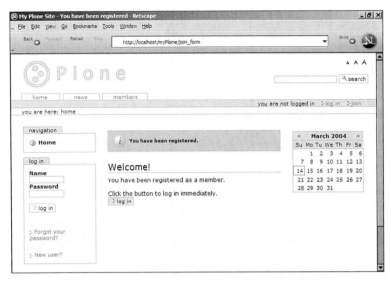

FIGURE 3.2 Many ways are presented for the new user to log in.

The Lost Password form requires you to enter your username, such as johnsmith. If a matching username exists, a message is sent to the corresponding email address for that user. Obviously, it behooves the user to enter a valid email address because a user cannot retrieve the password if a bogus email address is entered.

> **Note**
>
> The functionality for mailing a password requires an outgoing mail server (SMTP server) to have been set up for your Plone instance. This is covered in Chapter 8, "Technical Administration."

Assuming that you have remembered the password for the generic user you created, go ahead and log in to your Plone site. If you are successful, you will see another welcome message (the Plone Team was nothing if not polite when it created the default templates) that also points out various links that you can follow, such as going to your Member folder, setting user preferences, and so forth.

As you can see in Figure 3.3, the slot with the Login form has disappeared because you are logged in and no longer need it. The Navigation slot, the Recent News slot, and the Calendar slot are displayed; the toolbar in the upper right now has links to your member home page (you username is the link) and your Member folder, a link to your preferences, a link to the undo functionality, and a link for logging out of the Plone site.

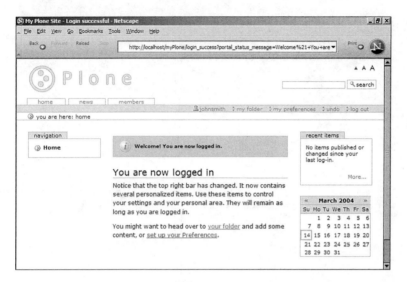

FIGURE 3.3 Now that you have successfully logged in, you can do several things.

In the next sections, we take a closer look at each of the items in the Plone toolbar that are available to logged-in members.

The Member Home Page

When a new member registers with a Plone site, a default member home page is created (see Figure 3.4). Acting as the member, you can get to your home page by clicking on your username in the Plone toolbar in the upper-right corner.

> **Tip**
>
> Your member home page is also accessible by a URL such as `http://localhost/myPlone/Members/johnsmith`. Also, any time your username appears within the Plone site, such as when you add a document or add a comment somewhere in the site, or when another member performs a member search, it is hyperlinked to your home page.

When you are viewing your own home page, you will see that it is part of a series of tabbed elements that only *you* can access. Any other user accessing this page will not see the action tabs—nor will you see them unless you have logged in to Plone. Because these tabs correlate to actions that only the content owner can perform, logging in validates that you do indeed have the proper permissions to perform the action.

CHAPTER 3 Using Your New Plone Site

FIGURE 3.4 A default member home page, viewed by its owner.

To view your own content while logged in, access the View tab. You will see the same content, in the same style and presentation, that other users will see. Additional action tabs available to you are Contents, Edit, Properties, and Sharing; other tools are the Add New Item and the State drop-down lists. All of these items make up the Member folder, which you are actually in by default because, after logging in, your home page is definitely part of your Member folder.

In the next section, you'll get a brief rundown of these elements, but first, here's one note about your home page: If your home page is in the visible state, any other member can view the contents of your page. Other members, however, will not see the Contents, View, Edit, and other tabs—those are available only to you. Other members will see only the content of the page, such as in Figure 3.5.

The Member Folder

The Member folder contains each member's home page, but it also contains much more—provided that you add much more to it! This area, accessible from the My Folder link in the toolbar in the upper right of the site, is your own space for items you have created and collected.

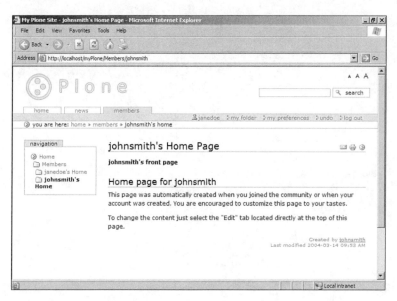

FIGURE 3.5   A default member home page, viewed by someone other than its owner.

When accessing the My Folder link, you first see the items listed under the Contents tab, as shown in Figure 3.6. As you add more items—web pages, documents, images, and so forth—they appear as line items in this view. As you can see, you can select an item by checking its check box, and then you can perform numerous tasks on that item:

- **Rename**—You can change the name of the file and the title of the item.
- **Cut**—This cuts an item to make it available for pasting. When you cut an item, the Paste option becomes available.
- **Copy**—This copies an item to make it available for pasting. When you copy an item, the Paste option becomes available.
- **Delete**—This removes an item.
- **Change State**—You can change the state of an item, such as to make it private, publish it, and so forth.
- **Order**—You can change the position of the item in the list, to move it up or down.

Also in this area, you will find two different starting points for adding a new item. You can use the drop-down menu and corresponding button directly above your file list, or you can use the Add New Item drop-down list from the upper-right portion of the tab. You have the same options available to you either way, and you'll work with these actions later in this chapter.

FIGURE 3.6 The Contents tab of the Member folder.

The next tab to the right of the Contents tab is the View tab. When selected, the View tab displays a list of items created or collected by the member, including the title and description of each item. When you add elements, as you will later in this chapter, you will see that Title and Description are editable properties.

The tab to the right of the View tab is the Sharing tab. Under this tab are tools you can use to assign local roles to other users. You might not want to give other people greater access to your own files, but suppose you were a member of a committee and you created a subfolder in your member area to hold documents relating to this committee. This would be a situation in which you could assign greater access roles to a folder within your member area. We take a look at additional role assignment later in this chapter.

The final tab is the Properties tab. If you are working in your Member folder, selecting the Properties tab enables you to modify the name and description of your folder. Similarly, when working with content or documents, selecting the Properties tab enables you to change the title and description of documents, files, and so forth.

Now that you are familiar with the core elements in the Member folder, you can take a look at the user preferences.

User Preferences

When you access the My Preferences link in the upper-right toolbar in the default Plone site, you will see two links in the body text. The first link takes you to a form that enables you to change your password. This simple form requires you to enter your current password, the new password of your choice, and a confirmation of that new password. After you submit the form, the new password takes effect, and you must use that password the next time you log in to your Plone site.

The second link in the preferences area is for Personal Preferences. These include the following:

- **Full Name**—This is your full name, which you entered during the registration process.
- **Email**—This is your email address, which you entered during the registration process.
- **Content Editor**—If the administrator of the Plone site has installed a content editor and made it available to members, you can choose to use it by setting this preference.
- **Listed in Searches**—The default value is Listed, indicating that your profile will be available to other members under the Members tab and when other members perform a search that results in a match to your profile.
- **Allow Editing of Short Names**—The default value is Yes (checked), which enables you to edit short names when editing items.
- **Portrait**—If you want, you can upload a 75 × 100–pixel image to your member profile. If uploaded, your portrait will be displayed in the member list and in member search results, as shown in Figure 3.7. This simply adds to the feeling of community, knowing that there is a real face behind a username.

FIGURE 3.7   Showing a member portrait.

Any changes that you make in your preferences will be available immediately. Making changes of any sort leads to the next item in the upper-right tool bar: the Undo feature.

Undo

Its name says it all: This tool enables you to undo any action that you have performed, and not just in the current session. When you click on the Undo link, you will see a table with headings such as Action Performed, Affected Item, Performed By, and Date and Time. An example of a member's Undo table appears in Figure 3.8.

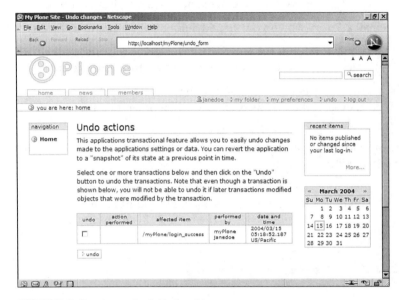

FIGURE 3.8 A member's Undo table.

Although this is not a particularly exciting list of Undo-able options, it does show that you could check the box next to an action and click the Undo button. The purpose of the Undo tool is to revert content, files, preference changes, and so forth to a previous incarnation. The only caveat is that you cannot undo a transaction in the past if more recent actions modified something that the original transaction modified. Other than that, you can roll back any transaction from the past that appears in your list.

With a good working knowledge of how to navigate around the member area, let's move on to actually creating and collecting items to fill up that area.

Working with Content in Plone

A member can add content only in an area to which that member has been given permission to do so, such as a shared folder or his own Member folder. All of the examples in this section use the Member folder as the content repository. To get to your Member folder, log in

Working with Content in Plone

to your Plone site and click on the My Folder link in the upper-right toolbar. This presents you with the content view of your folder, which you have seen before. Unless you've added things on your own already, the only item in the document list for this folder is a line item representing your home page.

As discussed earlier in this chapter, in this view you have two drop-down lists available for adding a new bit of content. In the next sections, you'll use this interface to add one of each of the different content types. Of course, feel free to add as many as you want during this introductory process.

Following are the most common content types, but as you'll learn in Chapter 7, "Advanced Content-Related Techniques," you can create your own types. When you use the Add New Item drop-down list, the entries will be ordered as in this list:

- **Document**—Although anything with text in it is usually generically referred to as a document, within Plone, a document is a web page. For example, the entry in your Member folder that holds the content for your home page is a document.
- **Event**—Anything that is added to a calendar is considered an event. When you publish an event, it also is displayed in the calendar view.
- **File**—Any content that isn't a web page document and that is in file format is a file. Microsoft Word documents and Adobe PDF documents are examples of files.
- **Folder**—Although it is not content in the strictest sense of the word, a folder is a container for content. You can create as many folders and subfolders as you want in your member area.
- **Image**—An image file—JPEG, GIF, PNG, and so on—is added as the image content type.
- **Link**—This content type holds local URLs or URLs to external websites.
- **News item**—When you want to call attention to something, add a news item. This item then is added to the news slot and under the News tab.

When you add any of these content types, there are some consistent themes. Each item has a name, a title, and an optional description, followed by attributes particular to the content type, such as the uploaded file and the URL. In the next few sections, you'll learn more about adding and modifying each of these basic content types.

Creating and Modifying Documents

In Plone, a document is what you would usually refer to as a web page, or any chunk of text that is not part of another file format. For example, if you wanted to write a blurb about something and make it available to other members of the Plone site, you would probably create a document containing just that text instead of opening a word-processing program, creating a new file, typing your text, and uploading the file to your member directory.

When a new user is registered within a Plone community, one document is automatically created and placed in the member's directory: the user's home page. Documents such as the home page (and any other document that you create on your own) can be composed in one of three different types of text:

- Plain text, with no visible or structural styles through any type of markup.
- HTML, which uses HTML markup for visible and structural styles.
- Structured text, which is the default setting for creating or editing a document. When you type in structured text, special formatting is used for visible and structural elements, which is rendered as HTML when viewed by the browser.

Next, you'll get an overview of the process of creating or modifying documents, followed by a brief primer on using structured text.

The processes of creating a new document and modifying an existing one start differently but end in the same place: working within a form that contains the same fields, representing the properties of the document. These fields are as follows:

- **Short Name**—This becomes part of the URL to the document. This short name should be relatively descriptive but should contain no underscores; it also should not be mixed case. For example, myvacation is an appropriate short name, but My Vacation_to_Alaska is not acceptable. If you do not input your own short name, Plone creates one for you. But beware: They end up like Document.2004-04-07.4992387560 when they're automatically generated, and that's not an easy-to-remember name!

- **Title**—Also required, this field is used to identify the content in a number of areas. The title is displayed at the top of the page and in the browser's title bar, as part of the navigational breadcrumb trail, as a link in search results and folder content displays, and so forth. Not surprisingly, then, this field is required.

- **Description**—Used to introduce the document, this is usually displayed underneath the title of a document when viewing a listing. The description is not required, but it should be used when the content is not discernable from the title of the document.

- **Body Text**—This is the actual content of the document. Although it is technically not required, what would be the point of having an empty document? In this text area, you can type plain text, HTML, or structured text—just be sure to select the matching format from the set of radio buttons that appears next in the form, or your content might look strange.

> **Note**
> If you're wondering about this "structured text" thing, have no fear. You'll learn the basics of structured text later in this chapter—and even then, you can still use HTML or plain text to create documents in Plone.

- **Format**—The default selection is Structured Text. You can also select HTML or plain text; the selected radio button should match the typed text in the Body Text field or, as you'll see, in the file uploaded via the Upload Content field.

  - **Upload Content**—If you already have a text file full of formatted content, you can simply upload this file via the Upload Content field instead of pasting or retyping your content into the Body Text field. Uploading content into a document is not the same as uploading a file to your member directory, as you'll learn later in this chapter. In fact, if you attempt to upload a binary file, such as a Microsoft Word document or another proprietary file format, you will receive an error message to the effect that you are placing a square peg in a round hole, and to please try again.

Uploading content is simply a shortcut for getting pre-existing, text-only content into a Plone document. When using this shortcut, remember to select the correct Format option. For instance, if you are uploading a file containing HTML markup, select the HTML radio button in the Format field. Similarly, structured text and plain text should be indicated appropriately. Although Plone will display HTML properly even if it is tagged as structured text, you will see only the raw code if you tag it as plain text.

When you are in the contents view of your member area and decide to add a new document, you will see a form such as the one in Figure 3.9, with all of the fields described previously. As you learned earlier, you can add a new document by using either of the two content-related drop-down lists available in that view; both get you to this same form.

You will notice immediately that Plone has already created a document and provided a short name in the Short Name field. Plone does not wait until you press a button to create a document; it creates a document when you initiate the creation process.

> **Tip**
> If you decide that you don't really want to add the new document after all and you either navigate away from the page or press the Cancel button, you must delete the document shell from your member area. You can also use the Undo feature to roll back the previous action.

Unless you are particularly attached to the Plone-generated short name, the first thing you should do is replace the contents of the Short Name field with your own text. Next, enter a title, followed by a description, if you want, and the body text of the document (leave this blank if you want to upload a file containing the text). Select the appropriate content format and press the Save button to retain your changes.

After you save the document, you will see a confirmation message and the contents of the document as they appear when viewed. In Figure 3.10, you can see this confirmation, plus the title, description, and contents of a poorly formatted document.

CHAPTER 3 Using Your New Plone Site

FIGURE 3.9 Adding a new document.

My bad formatting leads us directly into the next topic: modifying an existing document. Because the title of the document was already "Sports in the Springtime," there was no need for me to repeat it. Similarly, my structured text formatting was a bit off, so some text appears bold when it was intended to be a single paragraph of normal font weight.

Working with Content in Plone

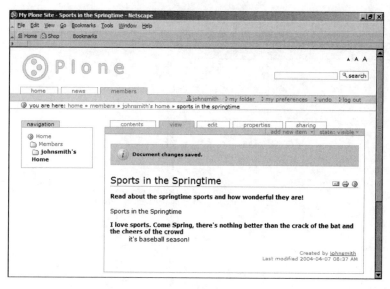

FIGURE 3.10 A new document has been added.

You can initiate the editing process by selecting the Edit tab when viewing the content in question. However, you will see the Edit tab only if you are the owner or otherwise have permission to edit the document. For example, a document created by user johnsmith will not be editable for user janedoe, unless johnsmith gave janedoe such permission. Assuming that he has not, janedoe will never see the Edit tab for that document.

Taking the role of johnsmith and initiating the editing of this document, the Edit form looks exactly like the Addition form, with the content already living in the appropriate boxes. You can see this in Figure 3.11. Also note the use of the document title in the navigational breadcrumb trail at the top of the page.

After you make the appropriate changes in content and formatting, press the Save button to see a confirmation and return to view mode. As you can see in Figure 3.12, the formatting has been fixed and the document appears as it should. If things still don't look right in your document, you can continue to go to the Edit tab, make changes, save the changes, view the changes, and so forth until you get the look you're trying to achieve. Or, you can go to your Undo area and selectively choose which editing action to roll back and choose which position you want to continue from.

When you have finished making changes to your document, you can place it in the publishing queue by selecting the Publish Item from the State drop-down list when viewing the item. Your item will be in the queue until the administrator decides to publish or reject it. Later in this chapter, you'll see how documents are published for public consumption.

FIGURE 3.11 Editing an existing document.

In the next section, you'll learn the basics of structured text before you move on to working with other content types.

Structured Text Basics

Structured text is the default text-formatting type when creating new documents in Plone. Structured text is a system of notation used when typing text that does not revolve around a set of tags or any proprietary software. Instead, following a simple set of rules helps you quickly produce a document that then is rendered in a specific structure (headings, paragraphs, lists) and displayed (bold text, italicized text, and so forth). This section provides you with the basics for working with structured text.

FIGURE 3.12 The document was successfully edited.

The simplest element in a document containing structured text is the paragraph. This text is rendered as a single paragraph:

```
This is my first sentence.  This is my second sentence.
```

In HTML, this would be:

```
<P>This is my first sentence.  This is my second sentence.</P>
```

However, if you separated your input with line breaks, Plone would interpret it as two separate paragraphs:

```
This is my first sentence.
This is my second sentence.
```

In HTML, these would be:

```
<P>This is my first sentence.</P>
<P>This is my second sentence.</P>
```

Headings and levels of text are achieved through indentation. A single line of text is rendered simply as a paragraph, as shown earlier. If you indent the next line, however, the first line becomes a Level 1 heading and the second line becomes the paragraph. If you continue the indentation by typing another line and then another paragraph indented further, the previous line becomes a Level 2 heading. This can continue for at least four levels of headings, as shown in Figure 3.13.

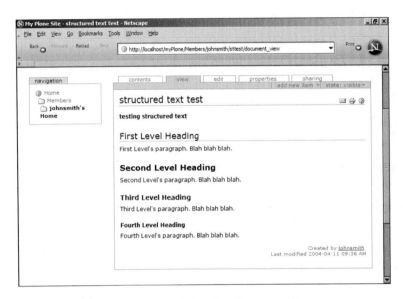

FIGURE 3.13 Showing multiple headings in structured text.

This display was achieved through the following structured text:

```
First Level Heading

        First Level's paragraph.  Blah blah blah.

    Second Level Heading

        Second Level's paragraph.  Blah blah blah.

        Third Level Heading

            Third Level's paragraph.  Blah blah blah.

            Fourth Level Heading

                Fourth Level's paragraph.  Blah blah blah.
```

Several other block-level formatting options are available in structured text, including lists. As in HTML, you can use three different types of lists in structured text: bulleted, numbered, and definition.

Bulleted-list items are simply preceded by an asterisk (*) and followed by a new line:

```
* first item

* second item

* third item
```

You can even make nested bulleted lists by using indentation:

```
* first item

    * first item in nested list

    * second item in nested list

* second item

* third item
```

Numbered lists are structured similarly to bulleted lists, except that the asterisk is replaced by a number. Nesting is possible with these lists as well:

```
1 first item

    1 first item in nested list

    2 second item in nested list

2 second item

3 third item
```

The third type of list is also quite simple; the definition is simply separated with two dashes (--) from the item that it is defining:

```
Item One -- definition of item one.
Item Two -- definition of item two.
```

You can see the output of these structured text list type examples in Figure 3.14.

CHAPTER 3   Using Your New Plone Site

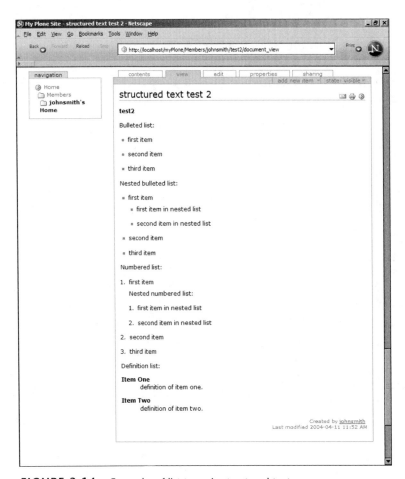

FIGURE 3.14   Examples of list types in structured text.

> **Note**
>
> You cannot nest various types of lists within each other. For example, it is not possible to nest a numbered list inside a bulleted list, or a bulleted list inside a numbered list.

You've seen examples of structurally formatted text—paragraphs, lists, and the like. Now you need the display formatting information to round out your knowledge. The very basic display markup elements are bold, italics, and underline. To render bold content, surround the text with double asterisks:

I am **bolded**.

Italicized text is surrounded by single asterisks:

```
I am *italicized*.
```

Text to be underlined is surrounded by underscores:

```
I am _underlined_.
```

Preformatted text, which is often used for code examples or other types of text that needs to preserve its line breaks and spacing, is preceded by double colons (::) and must be indented. When you break out of the indentation, normal formatting resumes. In the following example, only the two lines of code will be in preformatted text:

```
The following is a code listing::
    print "Hello World!\n"
    print "How are you?\n"
I am no longer a code listing.
```

You can also use inline preformatted text, such as when you want to show filenames or names of variables, or other code snippets. Inline preformatted text is achieved by surrounding the text with single quotations:

```
The names of the important variables are '$a', '$b' and '$c'.
```

The next set of display-formatting examples are of the functional sort; you'll see how to present links to URLs, email addresses, and images, and how to add footnotelike references in your text.

Links to URLs are created by presenting the text to be linked in quotes, followed by a colon, followed by the URL. For example, a link to Plone.org would be this:

```
"A link to Plone.org":http://www.plone.org/
```

Similarly, a mailto link would be this:

```
"Send me mail":mailto:joe@fakeplace.com
```

Linking to an image follows the same structure:

```
"thickbook.com logo":img:http://www.thickbook.com/images/tb_main_boringlogo.gif
```

> **Note**
>
> When displayed in Plone documents, linked items are accompanied by an icon representing the link type. URLs have a little globe icon, mailto links have a little envelope, and so forth. You can see this in Figure 3.15.

Footnotelike references are very useful elements in long documents such as whitepapers and technical essays. References are also quite simple to produce in structured text. To create a reference, simply place the number inside square brackets:

```
I am writing something very important, but I have a good tangent in mind. [1]
```

At the end of your document, in an area for all footnote text, place two periods, then repeat the number in the square brackets, and begin typing your text:

```
.. [1] This is my tangent.  I am sure it is fascinating.
```

You can see the outcome of the display-formatting examples used here in Figure 3.15.

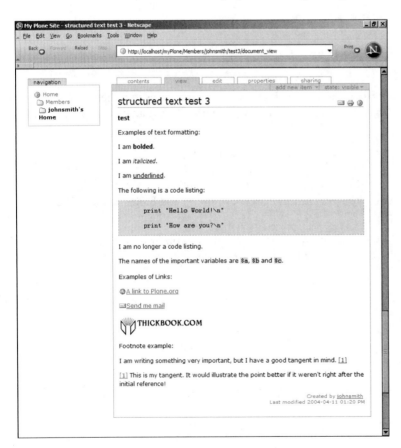

FIGURE 3.15 Examples of display formatting in structured text.

These examples have only scratched the surface of the possibilities when using structured text, but they certainly cover the basics. For more information and plenty of examples, visit `http://zwiki.org/StructuredText`.

In the next section, you'll see how to work with news and events elements, two content types similar to documents, which are also displayed in other areas of a Plone site besides your own Member folder.

Adding and Modifying Events and News

News and events are both text-based content types in Plone, which, when added, appear in your member area as well as in other areas of a Plone site. When adding or modifying a news item, the fields are as follows:

- **Short Name**—This becomes part of the URL to the news item. This short name should be relatively descriptive, but it cannot contain underscores or have mixed case.

- **Headline**—This is a required field and is used as the linked text in your member area, under the News tab, and anywhere else the link appears.

- **Lead-In**—Much like the `Description` field when adding a document, this is displayed under the headline.

- **Body Text**—This is the content of the news item. It can be structured text, HTML, or plain text; the default type is HTML.

As with adding a document, the news item is created when the new item is initiated. If you decide that you do not want to continue adding the item, you must manually remove the news item shell that already exists.

After you have added the news item, you can modify it by selecting the Edit tab, just as you did when editing a document. The same set of fields applies, as do the field requirements. When you have finished making changes to your news item, you can place it in the publishing queue by selecting Publish from the State drop-down list when viewing the item. Your item will be in the queue until the administrator decides to publish or reject it. Later in this chapter, you'll see how news items are published for public consumption. When published, news are available to all members, not just you.

An event is added and maintained similarly, but the form for adding or editing is much different. Because an event is essentially a news item or simple document that ties directly into a calendar, several calendar-related fields are used. The field list in the event addition/modification form is detailed here:

- **Short Name**—This becomes part of the URL to the event. This short name should be relatively descriptive, but it cannot contain underscores or have mixed case.

- **Title**—This is a required field. The title is used as the text for the link when the event appears in your member area, on the calendar, and so on.

- **Event Location**—This optional field describes where the event will take place. This can be a meeting room, an address to a hotel, or anything else you want to use.

- **Event Type**—This is an optional selection from a drop-down list of available types, such as an appointment, a meeting, and so on.

> **Note**
> You can modify the list of event types through the Zope Management Interface. This is discussed in Chapter 8.

- **Description**—Optional. This is a description of the event.

- **Event URL**—Optional. This is a URL for the event, such as registration information or just additional information.

- **Event Starts**—Required. Use the drop-down lists to select the day, month, year, hour, and minute of the start date of the event.

- **Event Ends**—Required. Use the drop-down lists to select the day, month, year, hour, and minute of the end date of the event.

- **Contact Name**—Optional. This is the name of the contact person for the event. Enter the full name of the person (or however you want the name to be displayed). This person does not have to be a member of the site, and no automatic linking from name to user home page occurs.

- **Contact Email**—Optional. This is the email address of the contact person for the event.

- **Contact Phone**—Optional. This is the phone number of the contact person for the event.

As with adding a news item, an event entry is created when the new item is initiated. If you decide that you do not want to continue adding the item, you must manually remove the event shell that already exists.

After you have added the event, you can modify it by selecting the Edit tab, just as you did when editing a document, news item, or anything else in Plone. The same set of fields applies, as do the field requirements.

The event item display is different from that of other content types you've seen so far because the form fields play an important role in placing items in appropriate areas of an event template. Instead of having one large body text field for typing, events contain specific types of information that are then placed in particular areas when displayed. You can see an example of an event that has been fully edited in Figure 3.16.

FIGURE 3.16 A completed event.

When you have finished making changes to your event, you can place it in the publishing queue by selecting Publish from the State drop-down list when viewing the item. Your item will be in the queue until the administrator decides to publish or reject it. When published, events are available to all members.

In the next section, you'll learn the process for adding another content type: files.

Adding and Editing Files

As you learned earlier in this chapter, any file that already exists in a proprietary format, such as Microsoft Word or Adobe PDF, is a file. Files have one of the simplest addition/modification forms in Plone because they have only three fields (you've seen all of them already):

- **Title**—Optional. The title is used as the text for a link to your file. If it is left blank, the name of the file becomes the default title.

- **Description**—Optional. This text appears below the title.

- **Upload File**—Required. Use this field to upload the target file from your hard drive to the Plone site.

After you have added the document, you can modify it by selecting the Edit tab, just as you did when editing a document, news item, or anything else in Plone. The same set of fields applies, as do the field requirements.

When a file is added and visible to a user, another tab is added: the Download tab. When you select the Download tab after viewing the description and link to the item from the View tab, a download is initiated. In other words, the Download tab functions as if you click on the Click Here to Get the File link under the View tab. Also available under the View tab is the file size and the MIME type of the file being viewed. For example, if the file is a 62K PDF, the following appears under the link to the document:

```
Size 62798 - File type application/pdf
```

When you have finished adding or modifying your uploaded file, you can place it in the publishing queue by selecting Publish from the State drop-down list when viewing the item. Your item will be in the queue until the administrator decides to publish or reject it. When published, the file is available to all members.

In the next section, you'll learn the process for working with the remaining standard content types in Plone: images, links, and folders.

Adding and Editing Other Content Types

This section introduces you to the remaining standard content types used in Plone: images, links, and folders. Given the earlier description of a file—any nondocument that is in a proprietary format—you would think that images would fall under this category. But images have their own content type in Plone because they are displayed differently than simple files. When an image is added to Plone, it can be viewed inline—if the type is supported by the user's web browser—and does not have to be downloaded to be viewed, as a file does.

These fields are used to add an image:

- **Short Name**—This becomes part of the URL to the image. This short name should be relatively descriptive, but should not contain underscores or have mixed case.
- **Title**—This is optional. The title is used as the text for a link to your file. If it is left blank, the name of the file becomes the default title.
- **Description**—Text that appears below the title, used to introduce and describe the image. The description is not required.
- **Image**—Use this required field to upload the target file from your hard drive to the Plone site.

After you have added the image, you can modify it by selecting the Edit tab, just as you did when editing a document, news item, or anything else in Plone. The same set of fields applies, as do the field requirements.

When a file is added and visible to a user, the image is viewed inline if the image type is supported. The file size also appears. Figure 3.17 shows an example of an uploaded image—in this case, a JPEG— appearing inline when viewed.

FIGURE 3.17 Viewing an image inline.

The next standard content type is a link. Just as it sounds, a link is a reference to a URL, on either the Internet or an intranet. These fields are used for adding a link:

- **Short Name**—Optional. This should be relatively descriptive but should not contain underscores or have mixed case.
- **Title**—Required. The title is used on the display page but not as text for the link.
- **Description**—Optional. This is a description of the URL to which you are linking.

- **URL**—Required. This is the URL itself. If you do not use a protocol prefix, such as `http://` or `https://`, Plone assumes that the URL is relative.

After you have added the link, you can modify it by selecting the Edit tab, just as you did when editing a document or anything else in Plone. The same set of fields applies, as do the field requirements.

The final standard content type in Plone is the folder. You have already worked with folders because your member area is, by default, a folder. But you can create additional folders within your member area, and you can provide others with access to add or modify the documents within it, as well as view the content. To add a folder, simply select it from the Add New Item drop-down menu. These fields are used for adding or modifying a folder:

- **Short Name**—Optional. This becomes part of the URL to the folder. This short name should be relatively descriptive but should not contain underscores or have mixed case.

- **Title**—Required. No default value is provided if you fail to create your own title. The title of the folder is used in directory listings and is clickable; selecting a folder link displays the contents of the folder to the user.

- **Description**—Optional. This is a description of the folder that you are creating (or modifying).

After you have created a new folder, it is ready and waiting for new items to be added to it.

When you have finished adding or modifying your images, links or folders, you can place these in the publishing queue by selecting Publish from the State drop-down menu when viewing the item. Your item will be in the queue until the administrator decides to publish or reject it. When published, the item is available to all members.

In the next section, you'll learn how the documents are published and made visible to other users.

Publishing Content in Plone

If the content that you store in your Plone Member folder is just for yourself, you might never need to participate in the publishing process. However, if you want your content—documents, news, events, files, and so on—to be visible to others, you must mark them for publishing and wait for the administrator to approve or reject your request.

When you create a new document, its default state is visible. This means that you can see it, and anyone to whom you give the direct URL can see it; it will not show up in the navigation, under the News tab (if it's news), in the calendar (if it's an event), or as a search result.

However, you can remove even this layer of visibility by selecting Make Private from the State drop-down list. When an item is private, only you can access it.

Assuming that you want to publish an item for public consumption, you can also edit its properties if it's a document, image, file, URL, or folder. These properties are standard for all types and include the following fields:

- **Allow Discussion on This Item**—The default is to inherit the default settings of the entire Plone site. Also available are Enabled and Disabled, which enable or disable discussion, respectively. You will learn more about item discussion later in this chapter.

- **Keywords**—This field is for search results and other uses of metadata. You can select none, one, or more than one, and you can also add new keywords appropriate to the item.

- **Effective Date** and **Expiration Date**—These are related to the visibility of your item. The effective date is the first day that your item will be visible, and the expiration date is the last day of availability. If this is blank, the item always is available.

- **Format**—The MIME type of the item. If you upload a file and Plone interprets the MIME type incorrectly, you can modify the MIME type using this field.

- **Language**—The language in which the item is written, as in English, German, French, and so on.

- **Copyright**—Any copyright and reprinting information that you want to include with your item.

- **Contributors**—The names of all those responsible for the creation of the item. Each name should be on a separate line. Enter the name of the person, as you would like the name displayed. This person does not have to be a member of the site, and no automatic linking from name to user home page occurs.

You can leave any and all of these properties blank or in their default state. However, if you are publishing content within a corporate intranet or other managed site, the administrators might have strict rules for publishing content. For example, an administrator might not approve a document that is missing an effective date range or copyright information. Before you place your items in the publishing queue, be sure that you are adhering to your site's requirements.

To place an item in the publishing queue, select Submit from the State drop-down list. The status of your document changes to Pending, and it appears in the administrator's review queue. When an administrator logs in, the review queue is available as a standard slot.

The links in the review queue take the administrator to the Member folder of the owner of the document in question, and the administrator can perform the same editing and viewing operations as the owner. In other words, the administrator can simply view and approve the item for publishing; view, edit, and then approve the item; change all manner of preferences for the item; or even reject the item. Figure 3.18 shows the administrator viewing a pending document and preparing to change the state to Publish, which makes it available to all members through navigation and searching.

FIGURE 3.18   Approving a document.

When you view the contents of the owner's Member folder, the published items are indicated as such in the State column. Other states include visible and private. After an item has been published, the owner can retract the item from public view. This changes the state back to visible. Additionally, the administrator can reject a pending document, which also sends the state back to visible.

In the State drop-down list, there is also an entry called Advanced. Selecting the Advanced entry displays a form filled with publishing details such as effective dates, comments, and a change of state selection button. If any comments have been posted or any actions have been taken on a document, they appear at the bottom of the form. For example, when the owner changes the state to publish, it is noted here. When the administrator approves the document or rejects it, it also appears here. If any comments are added during the action, such as "Your news item is bogus and I am rejecting it," they appear within the appropriate line item.

To recap, the three main states of an item are visible, published, and private. A visible item is available for viewing by other members but isn't officially part of any navigational or display element, such as in the calendar or under the News tab. A published item is visible to all members and guests, and it appears in the appropriate slot and tab and in searches. Private items are viewable only by the item owner and the administrator.

In the next section, you'll see how content discussion can add a forumlike quality to any item.

Utilizing the Content Discussion Feature

Before placing an item in the publishing queue, the owner might decide to enable content discussion. When the item is approved by the administrator, content discussion is enabled and an Add Comment button appears on the item page. The ability to discuss content is available to all members of the Plone site. Selecting this button takes you to the Add Comment form, which contains the following fields:

- **Subject**—The subject line of your comment
- **Body Text**—The actual bulk of your comment

No other fields are present, but your identification and a time stamp are added to the comment. Figure 3.19 shows an item with a comment added.

FIGURE 3.19 Content discussion in action.

After a comment has been added, a new button appears: Reply to This. A member now has two options for continuing discussion on an item: add a new comment or reply to a comment. Adding a new comment places a new comment at the same hierarchical level as the first comment. Replying to an existing comment places the reply one level lower in the hierarchy, as is commonly seen in threaded discussion.

The text of comments is automatically indexed and is used when a general search is performed. Any keywords or matching search terms that appear in a comment, no matter what hierarchical level in the threaded discussion, result in a search results match.

Speaking of search results, that leads to the last general topic covered in this "getting started" type of chapter: searching content.

Searching Content

In Plone, you can perform a simple keyword search, or you can try to pinpoint your search results by using the Advanced Search feature. The simple Keyword Search field is found in the upper-right corner in the standard Plone template. Type your keyword and press the Search button to display your results. On the results page, you will either see matching results or a message that no results were found. With either message, you also are presented with a link to the Advanced Search form.

All types of Plone content, including comments attached to items, are searchable. Even if a keyword is not found in a main item, such as a news item, if a comment has been added to the item and it contains the keyword used in the search, the comment is returned as a matching item. Figure 3.20 shows sample search output. As you can see, the identification icons are used to show the type of item in which the keyword was found. Additionally, the title of the item is used as the link, and any description or lead-in text is used in the search results display.

The search results page is structured exactly the same, regardless of whether you're using the simple search or the advanced search. The next section details the elements of the Advanced Search form.

Using Advanced Search

The Advanced Search form enables you to find more precise results because you can enter search criteria for specific areas of an item, such as its title and description. You also can select only specific item types to search, and you can filter results by author. Additionally, you can look for items that were added only within a certain time frame, such as the last week or the last month. Any combination of these search criteria is possible; the more precise the combination of search criteria is, the better the overall search results will be.

Searching Content

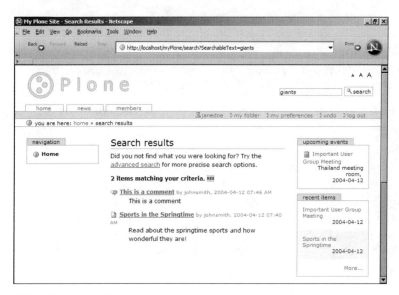

FIGURE 3.20 Successful search results.

These are the fields on the Advanced Search form:

▶ **Search Text**—Text entered here is the text for which you want to search. If you enter more than one term, you can use the Boolean AND or OR, such as "important AND memo" instead of just "important" and "memo"; the first search would return items that match both terms, while the second search would return anything with *important* and anything with *memo*, regardless of whether they're together in the same searchable content.

▶ **Title**—Text entered in this field is used to match text in the item's Title field. For example, if you are searching on the term *memo* in the Title field and it appears only in the body text, that is not a successful search. The term must appear in the Title field for the search to be successful.

▶ **Keywords**—If you select one or more keywords from this select list, they must all be present in the keywords elements of the item. Keywords are added via item properties at the time of publishing. Any keywords that have been added for any items in the Plone installation are available for selection in this select list.

▶ **Description**—Text entered in this field is used to match text in the item's Description field. This field works much like the Title field described earlier: If the term is present in this field, you're in luck; otherwise, the search fails.

▶ **New Items Since**—Use this field to limit your search to items added since your last login, in the last day, the last week, in the last month, or ever.

- **Item Type**—Check one or more check boxes, to limit your search to items of a specific type. The number of check boxes corresponds to the number of content types available in your Plone installation and, thus, varies. For example, if you install Plone add-ons that create their own content types, such as photo albums and message boards, these types are represented in this list.

- **Author**—Select a Plone user from the drop-down list, to limit your search to items published by this user.

- **Review Status**—Check any combination of All, Published, or Visible to limit your search to items that are in these states.

The Advanced Search form allows for great customization in your search. However, this can be a blessing or a curse. The more search criteria are used, the more specific the search is and, thus, the likelihood increases that you might inadvertently filter out some results. If you use the Advanced Search, you might want to start with your ideal set of filtering criteria and then remove some filters to see if your results change.

Troubleshooting

All of the activities described in this chapter take place within the installed Plone site, not the management interface. In other words, you are limited to utilizing the tools that are part of the Plone application itself—forms, tabs, links, and so forth. This includes helpful error messages when mistakes are made. For example, if you forget to complete a required field in a form, Plone returns an error message describing how to fix your error and continue with your desired action. Similarly, if you attempt to perform an action that is disallowed, such as attempting to undo an action that cannot be undone, Plone simply tells you that it can't be done—it doesn't halt your program and send it spinning out of control.

Summary

In this chapter, you learned a great deal about how members work with content in their member areas and make it available to other members. You learned about the interaction between the administrator and the general user as it applies to content publication. At this point, you should have a good grasp of the basic elements of a Plone site, and you should be ready to add more elements to it, to enhance the user experience and make the site do more things. In the next chapter, you'll learn where to find the best Plone add-ons, and you'll get specific instructions for adding some of the most popular elements, such as Zwiki, into your Plone site.

Additional Plone Elements

IN THIS CHAPTER

- Using the CMF Collective
- Working with CMFBoard
- Working with CMFMessage and CMFUserTrackTool
- Working with CMFPhoto and CMFPhotoAlbum
- Working with SimpleBlog
- Working with Wikis
- Troubleshooting

In the previous chapter, you navigated through the default Plone installation and became familiar with all of the content types that can be used and the actions that a user can perform. This chapter shows you how to take advantage of the freely available add-on products created by Zope and Plone developers around the world. For the majority of this chapter, you will be using the Plone manager account because a greater level of permissions is required to add elements to your Plone installation. However, the functionality of these elements is demonstrated for the member user as well.

Using the CMF Collective

The CMF Collective is a collection of freely available open-source products created by developers for use with the Zope CMF and, thus, Plone. These items range from packages of skins to installation utilities, to full-fledged shopping carts, photo albums, and messaging applications—and that's really naming just a few. You can access the CMF Collective at http://sourceforge.net/projects/collective. A list of elements in the CMF Collective is maintained as part of the Plone documentation at http://plone.org/documentation/howto/ProjectsInCollective.

> **Note**
>
> Not all CMF-related open-source software is found in the CMF Collective. Zwiki, a product that is discussed later in this chapter, is found at its developer's website. This is not uncommon: Thousands of developers worldwide have products just as useful as those in the CMF Collective but want to house them internally instead of within the CMF Collective framework.

Each element in the collective comes packaged with its own instructions, such as an INSTALL.txt or README.txt file, which you should read before attempting to install and integrate anything within your Plone site. In some cases, elements that you download are dependent on having other elements already installed. This makes it even more important to read the installation instructions in each downloaded package.

Items available in the collective have been tested for functionality and meet or exceed the standards for software releases to the public. In other words, you won't get a bunch of strange files that lack instructions when you download an item from the CMF Collective. Installation of most elements is as simple as extracting elements of a package into a particular directory structure and utilizing the Plone setup menu to complete the process. Throughout this chapter, the installation procedures for the elements are described in further detail.

> **Note**
>
> You can also install Plone add-ons through the Zope Management Interface. This is covered in Appendix B, "Introduction to Zope and the ZMI."

The remainder of this chapter is devoted to obtaining and installing numerous elements from the CMF Collective that will enhance your Plone instance. The more elements you provide to your users, such as the capability to participate in message boards, send instant messages, or keep and share photo albums, the more popular your community will become. You also might enable your users to read and write personal blogs with a blogging tool, or install Zwiki for an entirely new web experience.

Working with CMFBoard

CMFBoard is a standard message-board application that integrates smoothly into the Plone architecture and workflow. Message boards are designed to contain topics, messages, and replies to messages in a hierarchical flow. Just as books contain chapters and chapters contain paragraphs, message boards contain topics, topics contain posts, and posts are followed by replies (at least, you hope that your topics are exciting enough to contain posts and replies).

Working with CMFBoard

Using a message-board application such as CMFBoard differs from just adding a comment to a published document, in that it fosters discussion among users on a wide array of topics and in a structured form. The forum owner or administrator can create forums with custom names and descriptions, targeting potential discussion accordingly. As you'll see in the next few sections, installing CMFBoard and setting up a few forums for use on your Plone site is an absolute breeze.

Installing CMFBoard

CMFBoard is one of those aforementioned elements whose installation process is as simple as extracting files from a package and pressing a button. After the CMFBoard package has been downloaded from the CMF Collective, use your unzip utility of choice (perhaps WinZip on Windows, gunzip on Linux/Unix) to extract the files into a subfolder within the Data/Products folder in the Plone installation directory.

> **Note**
> The installation example uses CMFBoard 2.1.2, but if a more recent version is available, you certainly can install that one.

To finish the installation of CMFBoard, you can use the Add/Remove Products option in the Plone setup section, available to the Plone administrator user only. For CMFBoard to show up as an element to be added, you must restart Plone. After restarting, log in as the Plone administrator and follow the Plone Setup link in the navigation, then follow the Add/Remove Products link. You will see a list of available products to install, all selectable by check box. An example is show in Figure 4.1.

Select the appropriate check box to install CMFBoard, and press the Install button. The installation actions occur, and you should see a message similar to this on the screen:

```
Installed Products
====================
CMFBoard:ok:
```

> **Note**
> You might see more than one item in the Products Available for Install section of the Add/Remove Products page. For instance, in Figure 4.1, you can see several other items available for installation besides CMFBoard 2.1.2. In this case, you could have checked as many items as were available and then pressed the Install button; Plone would have installed all of the selected items at the same time.

CHAPTER 4 Additional Plone Elements

FIGURE 4.1 CMFBoard is available as an installation option.

After they are installed, some products such as CMFBoard have configuration options that the administrator can set. If so, links to these customization elements can be found on the Plone setup page, in a section called Add-on Product Configuration, shown in Figure 4.2.

Configuration options specific to CMFBoard

FIGURE 4.2 CMFBoard has additional configuration options.

Customizable CMFBoard options range from activating the capability for users to create their own signatures to accompany their posts, to replacing the standard Plone content discussion with CMFBoard. You can set all or none of these options; CMFBoard works perfectly well without making any configuration modifications.

Creating a CMFBoard Forum

When CMFBoard is installed, the only change that members of a Plone site see is their capability to add an element with a new content type: a forum folder. In other words, adding a discussion forum to a Plone site is no more difficult than adding a document or a file.

When added, a forum folder appears in the member folder of its owner, and it can be edited just like any other item in the member folder. To edit a CMFBoard forum folder, select it from the member folder content view and then select the Edit tab. These are the editable items:

- **Id**—This becomes part of the URL to the forum, much like the short name field used in other content types. This short name should be relatively descriptive but should not contain underscores or be mixed case. If you do not input your own Id, Plone creates one for you.

- **Title**—This required title is used as the text for a link to your forum folder.

- **Description**—This optional text appears below the title.

- **Forum Folder icon**—If provided, this custom icon precedes the forum name when referenced in body text or in navigation menus.

- **Predefined Skin**—Select the radio button appropriate to your selection of the default skin, either the Plone skin (the default selection)_or the CMFBoard 1.*x* skin.

- **Use Custom Skin**—Check this box if you intend to use another custom skin.

- **Custom Skin**—If the previous box is checked, enter the value for the custom skin you want to you.

> **Note**
> You will learn about creating custom skins in Chapter 6, "Creating and Implementing a Custom Skin."

Of these fields, only the `Title` field is required for the forum folder instance. You can now move on to editing the forumNB instances, including adding or removing instances as you see fit.

> **Note**
>
> *ForumNB* is the name the CMFBoard creators gave to the actual structural elements that make up a forum. According to the creators, "forumNB stands for 'nothing in particular' but could stand for 'forum notice board,' if you like."

Setting Up ForumNBs

When a forum folder is added, two *forumNBs* are automatically created: a public test forum and a member test forum. These two forumNBs are created to give you a head start on using your forum. However, you can immediately remove, rename, or add forumNBs to meet your goals. When creating a forumNB, these are the possible states:

- **custom**—In this state, the Plone manager can assign specific permissions via the Permissions tab.

- **members**—In this state, only Plone members can read or create topics and posts; no anonymous access is allowed. The default member test forum has this state.

- **open**—In this state, Plone members can create topics and posts, and anonymous users can also read posts, reply to posts, and start topics of their own.

- **public1**—In this state, Plone members can create topics and posts, but anonymous users can only view the topics and posts. The default public test forum has this state.

- **public2**—In this state, Plone members can create topics and posts, and anonymous users can read and reply to posts or add posts in a topic.

After a forumNB has been added to a forum instance, topics, posts, and replies can be added to it, according to the rules of its selected state. Assume for a moment that the default forumNBs were kept and not renamed, and the discussion forum was published and is now ready to be used. When a member navigates to the discussion forum URL or clicks the link that will be visible in the Recent Items slot on the main page of the Plone instance, they will see something like Figure 4.3.

This new forum is empty: The number of topics, replies, and views is 0. Clicking on the name of a forum—in this case, either Public Test Forum or Member Test Forum—displays the topics in the forum, as well as drop-down menus for adding topics, changing views, and performing other navigational options. Adding a new topic is the next step in populating your forumNB.

Adding Topics and Posts

When adding a topic to a forumNB, you are actually adding the topic plus the first post in the thread. As such, the form for adding the topic contains all of the available text-format-

Working with CMFBoard

ting options, and in CMFBoard there certainly are plenty. (Figure 4.4 shows the Topic Addition form.)

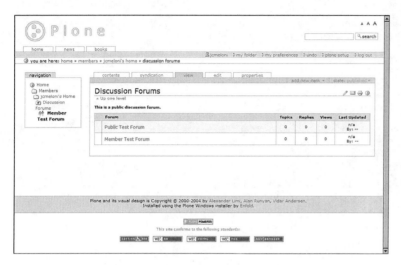

FIGURE 4.3 An empty discussion forum, ready for topics and posts.

- ▶ **Title**—The topic title is required.

- ▶ **Body Text**—Enter the text of your message in this field, up to a limit of 10KB.

- ▶ **Text Format**—As with adding a document in Plone, you can use plain text, structured text, or HTML in your post.

- ▶ **Emotion Icons**—While typing in the Body Text field, clicking an emoticon places it within your typed text.

- ▶ **Wizards**—Clicking any of these wizards launches a JavaScript alert box that takes you through the required steps to add a link, an image, or text formatted as italic, bold, big, or code. Figure 4.5 shows an example of how a wizard functions for adding big-formatted text. Some wizards, such as this one, are single-step wizards; others have two steps, such as adding a link. In the two-step wizard for adding a link, you are asked first for the URL and then for the text for the URL you provided.

- ▶ **Message Icons**—Selecting a message icon is optional, but when selected, it appears next to the topic title in all views.

- ▶ **Image**—You can add an image of up to 150KB, which appears scaled in your message but also is clickable to display its full size.

- ▶ **File**—You can add a file of up to 100KB that appears as a link within the message text. The filename and file size are displayed as part of the link.

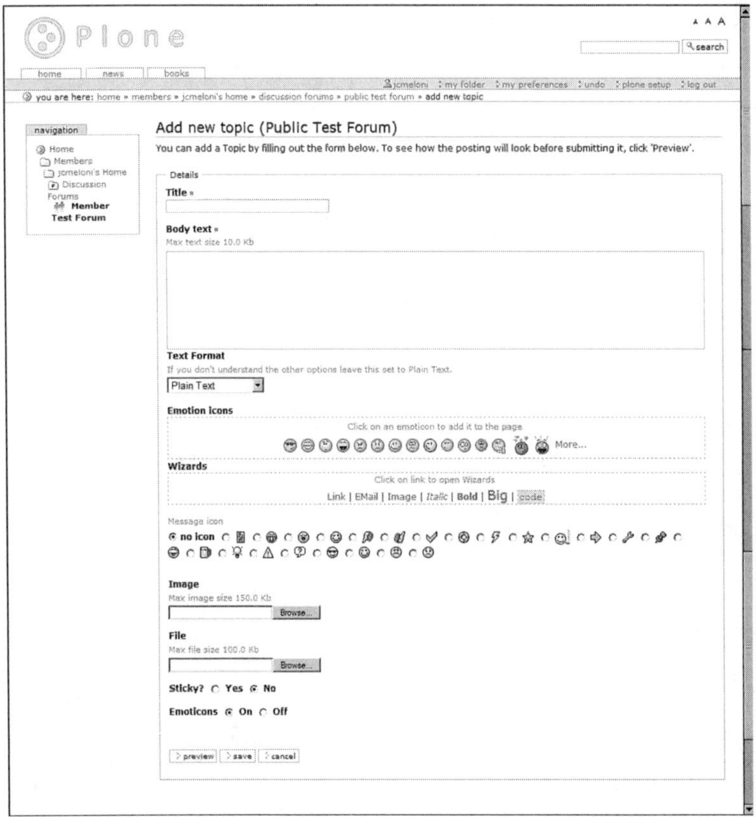

CHAPTER 4 Additional Plone Elements

FIGURE 4.4 The form used to add a topic to a forumNB.

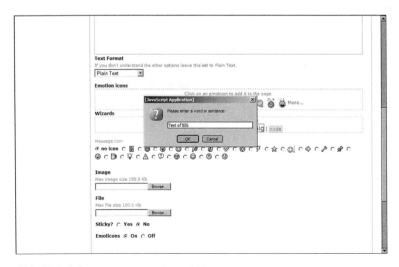

FIGURE 4.5 Using a wizard to add big text in your post.

▶ **Sticky**—A sticky topic is one that always appears at the top of the topic list. The default is No.

▶ **Emoticons**—You can opt not to show any emoticons in your post by selecting Off. The default is On.

After completing the form, you can preview it without saving. That way, you can immediately see changes that you need to make and then make them before your content becomes available to the community. After it is added, a topic immediately appears in the forumNB menu along with its content. There is no need to publish a topic as you do a document, a file, or even a discussion forum. Within the CMFBoard structure, topics and posts immediately become viewable and are searchable elements within the Plone architecture.

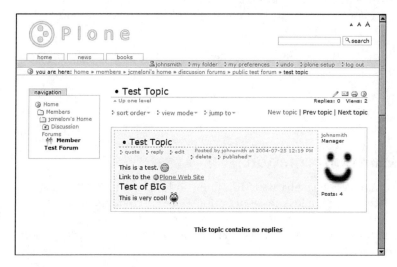

FIGURE 4.6 A topic has been added.

Users with the appropriate permissions can add replies to any topic or post, or add new topics of their own within a forum. The form for posting replies is remarkably similar to the form used for adding a topic, except that the Title field is not used. Additionally, users replying to a post can quote the previous text by pressing the Quote link in the topic to which they are replying. The text automatically is placed within their text field, formatted as a quote.

Owners of topics can also edit or delete their own posts by clicking the appropriate link within their post. One possible reason for editing the first post in a topic is to "stickify" it, meaning to keep the topic at the top of the forum's topic list at all times. Deleted posts are removed from the hierarchical list of posts, and the number of posts is decremented appropriately in the forum menu.

Member Preferences for CMFBoard

When CMFBoard is installed, another option, Forum Preferences, appears in the Plone preferences for each member. In this area, members can customize numerous options to enhance their CMFBoard experience, including these:

- **Forum Details**—In this section, members can toggle check boxes for displaying information such as full name and email when forums posts are made. Members can also select the capability to automatically subscribe to their own topics, which emails all replies to them. Default forum display preferences, such as setting the forum and topic view mode and sort mode, can also be set.

- **Contact Details**—Members can choose to enter all sorts of additional contact information to be displayed with other contact information when posts are made. Options include the member's home page URL; instant messenger nicknames for Yahoo!, AIM, MSN; and more.

- **My Information**—In this section, members can enter personal information, such as location, occupation, and interests.

- **Signatures**—Members can enter up to three signatures that can be used to sign their posts.

Additional CMFBoard Information

The previous sections have shown you the basics of installing and using the CMFBoard application, which is a rich application that adds plenty of options to your Plone member community. For more information on CMFBoard, visit its website at http://www.cmfboard.org/. Here you will find discussion on the CMFBoard application, including support forums for any problems or questions.

Working with CMFMessage and CMFUserTrackTool

When you download the CMFMessage package from the CMF Collective, two actual elements are present: CMFMessage and CMFUserTrackTool. Each of these elements performs very different tasks, but they work in tandem to enhance the value of the other. CMFUserTrackTool simply displays the usernames of all currently logged-in members of your Plone site, in a slot on the right side of the template, underneath the standard calendar. CMFMessage also adds a slot to the right side of the template that displays links to instant messages sent to a member, along with a link allowing members to send a message of their own.

Working with CMFMessage and CMFUserTrackTool

Instant messaging is a very popular form of communication. Integrating it in this way within your Plone community helps foster a sense of a "living" community, providing members with even more reasons to continually participate in discussions, document sharing, and other community activities. As with installing CMFBoard in the previous sections, adding CMFMessage and CMFUserTrackTool is a very simple process.

Installing CMFMessage and CMFUserTrackTool

The CMFMessage package is part of the CMF Collective, and CMFUserTrackTool is included in the CMFMessage package. To install it, first download this package from the CMF Collective and use your unzip utility of choice (perhaps WinZip on Windows, gunzip on Linux/Unix) to extract the files into a subfolder within the Data/Products folder in the Plone installation directory.

To finish the installation of CMFMessage and CMFUserTrackTool, use the Add/Remove Products option in the Plone setup section, available to the Plone administrator user only. For CMFMessage and CMFUserTrackTool to show up as an element to be added, you must restart Plone. After restarting, log in as the Plone administrator and follow the Plone Setup link in the navigation; then follow the Add/Remove Products link. You will see a list of available products to install, two of which are CMFMessage and CMFUserTrackTool. Check the boxes for both, and press the Install button. The installation actions occur, and you should see a message indicating the successful installation of each package.

Unlike CMFBoard, there are no additional options to configure, so no elements are added to the Add-on Product Configuration section of the Plone setup menu. After CMFMessage and CMFUserTrackTool are installed, their functionality is available to you upon your next login.

Viewing the CMFMessage and CMFUserTrackTool Slots

The default location of the CMFMessage and CMFUserTrackTool slots is the right side of the standard template, beneath the calendar, as shown in Figure 4.7.

> **Note**
> In Chapter 5, "Customizing Plone," you'll learn how to change the location of slots.

In this example, two members—janedoe and jcmeloni—are currently authenticated within the Plone site. No messages have been sent to the particular user who was logged in at the time of the screenshot—in this case, janedoe. The usernames in the Active Users slot are clickable; the links lead to the member home page of the user. The Mail icon next to the username is also clickable and leads to the form for sending an instant message to the user.

CHAPTER 4 Additional Plone Elements

FIGURE 4.7 Showing the CMFMessage and CMFUserTrackTool slots.

Sending an Instant Message

The form for sending an instant message is invoked by clicking the Mail icon next to a username in the Active Users slot or by clicking the New Message button in the Messages slot. This is a very simple form, as you can see in Figure 4.8.

In this example, user janedoe completes the form to send an instant message to user jcmeloni. The simple form contains only these fields:

- **To**—Enter the Plone username of the user to whom you want to send the message.
- **Subject**—Enter the subject of your message.
- **Message**—Enter the text of your message, in plain text.
- **Attach URL of Current Location**—If this is checked, the URL of the page you are currently browsing also is sent. This is useful if you are viewing content and want to send a message to its owner without utilizing the content discussion feature, or if you want to alert another member to a piece of content.

When the instant message is sent, its subject, sender, and date sent appear in the recipient user's Messages slot. This is shown in Figure 4.9.

Taking Action After Receiving an Instant Message

Clicking on the subject of an instant message in the Messages slot takes the user to the message-display screen, as shown in Figure 4.10. Additionally, all instant messages are stored in a member's Personal Messages subfolder, inside a Personal Items folder within the member's master folder.

Working with CMFMessage and CMFUserTrackTool

FIGURE 4.8 Sending an instant message.

FIGURE 4.9 The user has received an instant message.

CHAPTER 4 Additional Plone Elements

> **Tip**
> This set of folders is automatically created the first time an instant message is received. The folders remain as long as a message is kept inside them. If you delete all your instant messages, the folders also are removed, but they reappear the next time a message is received.

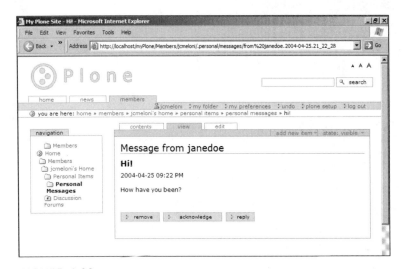

FIGURE 4.10 Viewing an instant message.

The recipient has several options when reading the instant message, but no action is required:

- **Remove**—Clicking the Remove button deletes the message from the Personal Messages folder and the entry from the Messages slot. In other words, it's really removed.

- **Acknowledge**—If this button is clicked, the message remains in the Personal Messages folder of the recipient, but the entry no longer appears in the Messages slot.

- **Reply**—The same actions are performed as when clicking the Acknowledge button, but the user is also shown a prefilled instant-message form for sending a reply to the original message sender.

The CMFMessage and CMFUserTrackTool elements are simple but useful items that enable members to see that they're not the only ones hanging out in your Plone community. They also enable members to interact with each other outside of more structured elements such as content discussion or discussion forums.

Working with CMFPhoto and CMFPhotoAlbum

Similar to the instant-messaging application installed previously, the capability to have a photo album content type in your Plone community requires two packages: CMFPhoto and CMFPhotoAlbum. Both are required to achieve the goal of allowing members to create and share photo albums, and, as such, are downloaded as separate packages.

Installing CMFPhoto and CMFPhotoAlbum

To install CMFPhoto and CMGPhotoAlbum, first download the packages from the CMF Collective and use your unzip utility of choice (perhaps WinZip on Windows, gunzip on Linux/Unix) to extract the files into a subfolder within the Data/Products folder in the Plone installation directory.

To finish the installation of CMFPhoto and CMGPhotoAlbum, use the Add/Remove Products option in the Plone setup section, available to the Plone administrator user. You must restart Plone for CMFPhoto and CMGPhotoAlbum to show up as elements to be added, after extracting them into the folder described earlier. After restarting, log in as the Plone administrator and follow the Plone Setup link in the navigation; then follow the Add/Remove Products link. You will see a list of products available for installation. Check the boxes for both, and press the Install button. The installation actions occur, and you should see a message indicating the successful installation of each package.

With CMFPhoto and CMFPhotoAlbum, there are no additional options to configure, so no elements are added to the Add-on Product Configuration section of the Plone setup menu. After you have installed CMFPhoto and CMFPhotoAlbum, their functionality is available to you upon your next login.

Creating a Photo Album with CMFPhotoAlbum

After CMGPhotoAlbum has been installed, a new content type is available to members: a photo album. A photo album is essentially just a folder that is specifically designed to hold photos. To add a photo album, select Photo Album from the add new item drop-down in your member photo. The form for adding an album is quite simple, as shown in Figure 4.11.

The fields in this form are as follows:

- **Short Name**—This becomes part of the URL to the photo album, much like the Short Name field used in other content types. This short name should be relatively descriptive but should not contain underscores or be mixed case. If you do not input your own short name, Plone creates one for you.
- **Title**—The title is used as the text for a link to your photo album. It is required.
- **Description**—This is optional text appearing below the title.

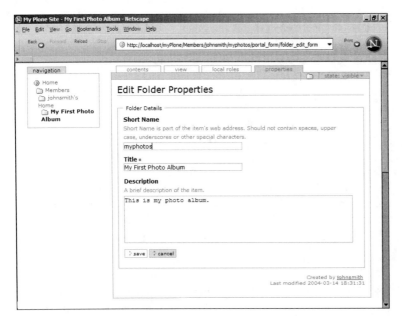

FIGURE 4.11 Adding a photo album.

These three fields are the only editable items for a photo album. Now you can move on to adding photos to your album and publishing it.

Adding Photos to a Photo Album

Just as a photo album is really just a folder that holds photos, adding photos is not dissimilar to adding other content types inside a specific folder. After your album has been added, navigate to the View tab for this item. The Add New Item drop-down list contains two entries: Photo and Photo Album. You can add another photo album inside the current one, but for our purpose of introducing you to the process of adding photos, select the Add New Photo entry to add a photo and invoke the Edit form.

This is another simple form:

- **Short Name**—This becomes part of the URL to the specific photo, much like the Short Name field used in other content types. This short name should be relatively descriptive but should not contain underscores or be mixed case. If you do not input your own short name, Plone creates one for you.
- **Title**—This is used when viewing the photo on its own page.
- **Description**—This is used when viewing the photo on its own page.
- **Image**—This is required. Use the Browse button to find the file on your filesystem that you want to upload.

Working with CMFPhoto and CMFPhotoAlbum

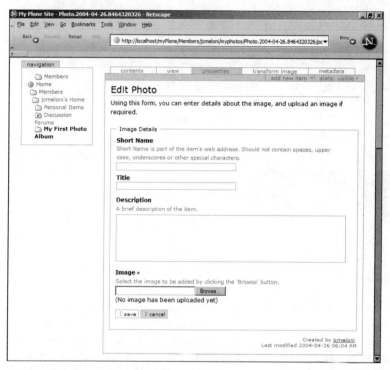

FIGURE 4.12 The Edit Photo form.

After you have added the image, you can do all sorts of things with it. Of course, you can edit the short name, title, and description, but you can also rotate your images. When viewing an image in your photo album, select the Properties tab to revisit the Edit Photo form, and select the Transform Image tab to find the Photo Rotation tool.

To delete entries from your photo album, simply select the Contents tab when viewing the photo album itself. This view shows the line items (photos) in the folder (photo album), just as if you were viewing the contents of your member folder itself. Check the check box next to the item that you want to delete, and press the Delete button. Your photo is removed from the album and from the Plone site in general.

The End-User View of a Photo Album

When you have finished adding items to your photo album, be sure to publish it (or place it in the publishing queue for approval, if you are not the administrator) so that others can enjoy it. When a member navigates to the initial view of another member's photo album, that member sees a set of thumbnail images, such as those shown in Figure 4.13.

FIGURE 4.13 End-user view of a photo album.

Each of these thumbnails is clickable; clicking on one displays the photo page with a larger image, the title of the image, and the image description. The end user can resize the view of the image without changing the size of the original file, by selecting a size from a drop-down menu on the photo page. The available sizes range from thumbnail (128 × 128 pixels) to Xtra Large (1,024 × 1,024 pixels). Additionally, the user can navigate the album linearly by selecting Next or Previous, as appropriate, in the album view. Or, the user can jump to a specifically numbered image using the same album view.

Photo albums definitely lend a sense of personality to your members' areas, and using CMFPhoto and CMFPhotoAlbum is as simple as adding any other content type in Plone. Next, you'll discover two more useful Plone add-ons: The first is one of many available blogging tools. The second is Zwiki, which is not a blog, but a whole different animal unto itself.

Working with SimpleBlog

The popularity of blogs has exploded, both for reading blogs and actively updating one's own blog. A blog is simply a web-based journal that is updated frequently by the owner. Blog postings are usually arranged in chronological order, with the most recent appearing first in the list. The primary attraction of blogging software is that it removes the need for the user to know anything technical about maintaining web-based content. The user simply has to type within a form field, something that even the newest of web surfers can handle with ease.

SimpleBlog is a Plone add-on that enables users to maintain a blog within their member area of your Plone community. Providing a blogging tool to your members is yet another reason for them to actively participate in your Plone community and encourage others to join in. The process of installing SimpleBlog is similar to installing the other items described previously in this chapter, so you should have no problems.

Installing CMFWeblog

SimpleBlog is available in the CMF Collective, so the first step toward installation is to download the SimpleBlog package. The current version is 1.2.1, but if you see a newer version in the Collective, by all means, install it. Next, use your unzip utility of choice (perhaps WinZip on Windows, gunzip on Linux/Unix) to extract the files into subfolders within the Data/Products folder in the Plone installation directory.

To finish the installation of SimpleBlog, use the Add/Remove Products option in the Plone setup section, available to the Plone administrator user only. For SimpleBlog to show up as an element to be added, you must restart Plone. After restarting, log in as the Plone administrator and follow the Plone Setup link in the navigation, then follow the Add/Remove Products link. You will see a list of available products to install, one of which should be SimpleBlog. Check its check box and then press the Install button. The installation actions occur, and you should see a message indicating a successful installation:

```
Installed Products
====================
SimpleBlog:ok:
```

That's all there is to it. Upon successful installation, three new content types are available to users:

- **Blog**, which will be the container for all postings and subfolders
- **BlogEntry**, individual posts within a blog
- **BlogFolder**, a folder that can exist within the blog and contain postings

To create your Blog, navigate to your member folder and select Blog from the drop-down menu of available types, then press the Add New Item button. You will see a form like in Figure 4.14.

The fields for the blog creation form are straightforward, and only the `Title` field is required:

- **Short Name**—This becomes part of the URL to the blog, much like the `Short Name` field used in other content types. This short name should be relatively descriptive but should not contain underscores or be of mixed case. If you do not input your own short name, Plone creates one for you.
- **Title**—The title is used as the text for a link to your blog. It is required.

- **Description**—This is optional text that appears below the title of your blog.
- **Display mode**—The options are Full, Description Only, and Title Only; select the one that corresponds to how the front page of your Blog should be displayed.
- **Blog Entries to Display**—Enter a number corresponding to the maximum number of items to display on the front page of your blog. The default value is 20.
- **Possible categories**—Free text field in which you can enter one or more categories that can be used for subsequent blog entries.

FIGURE 4.14 Creating your blog.

When you have configured your blog to your liking, press the Save button to save changes. You will then see and have access to the main page of your blog, as shown in Figure 4.15. In this case, I have also configured some categories into which future posts might go.

With a structure now in place, you're ready to add witty and informative blog entries—within blog folders, if you want.

Working with SimpleBlog

FIGURE 4.15 Blog main page.

Adding a Blog Folder

If you created any categories during the configuration of the blog, you might want to add corresponding blog folders for those categories, just to keep items in order. However, this is not required because the association of blog entry to category is done during the creation of the entry and is independent of blog folders. In this section, you'll just add a simple blog folder called musings, which will eventually hold some blog entries.

From the blog main page, or within your member folder, select Blog Folder from the Add New Item drop-down menu. The form is quite simple, and only the `Title` field is required:

- **Short Name**—This becomes part of the URL to the blog folder, much like the `Short Name` field used in other content types. This short name should be relatively descriptive but should not contain underscores or be of mixed case. If you do not input your own short name, Plone creates one for you.

- **Title**—The title is used as the text for a link to your blog folder. It is required.

- **Description**—This is optional text that appears below the title of your blog folder.

- **Additional Categories**—You can create categories in addition to the ones defined for the blog itself that will be available only when adding a blog entry within this blog folder.

When you have configured your folder, press the Save button. You're now ready to populate this blog folder with blog entries.

Adding a Blog Entry

To add a blog entry, first determine in which blog folder you want to add it—within the master blog folder or within a subfolder such as the musings folder you created earlier. After you make your selection, use the Add New Item drop-down list within the folder to add a new blog entry item. When you press the Add button, you will see a form containing the following fields:

- **Short Name**—This becomes part of the URL to the blog entry, much like the Short Name field used in other content types. This short name should be relatively descriptive but should not contain underscores or be of mixed case. If you do not input your own short name, Plone creates one for you.

- **Title**—The title is used as the text for a link to your blog entry. It is required.

- **Description**—This is optional text that appears below the title of your blog entry.

- **Body**—This is the contents of your blog entry. You can type in plain text, HTML, or structured text.

- **Text Format**—Select the format that corresponds to the text typed in the body—for example, text/plain, text/structured, or text/html.

- **Upload a File**—If you wrote the contents of your blog entry in a text file, you can upload the file here; you should still select the corresponding text format.

- **Categories**—Select one or more categories to which your entry should be assigned.

- **Entry Is Always Listed on Top**—If this is selected, this blog entry will always appear at the top of the list, regardless of the date.

When you have finished creating your blog entry, press the Save button. Your entry is now created but is in the draft workflow and is not yet published for all users (just like other content types). In the next section, you'll publish your blog entries and also see how user commenting works.

Publishing Your Blog Entries

Your blog entries are not available to all users until you change their state to publish; until published, blog entries are only drafts. To change the state of a blog entry, view the entry and then select the State drop-down menu. Select the published item from the drop-down list, and the status automatically changes.

After you publish your blog entry, any member can view it. In addition, elements within the Blog slot are updated: The recent entries area shows a link to this entry, and the category to which it was assigned shows a 1 instead of a 0, representing the one item within it. Figure 4.16 shows a published blog entry, including these changes to the Blog slot.

FIGURE 4.16   A published blog entry.

Readers can also comment on published blog entries. Commenting is an important part of blogs because it allows discussion to take place between readers and the blog writer. When users click on the Add Comment button, they see a simple form containing two fields: subject and body text. The user completes these fields using plain text and then presses the Add Comment button. The comment is immediately added to the blog entry, with the personal attributes attached, as shown in Figure 4.17.

Other users can add their own comments or can reply to the comment just posted, resulting in a threaded discussion. Or, the site owner can remove the discussion altogether, if it becomes unsuitable for public viewing.

Additional SimpleBlog Configuration

SimpleBlog is one of my personal favorites when it comes to Plone add-ons. Not only does it work well, but the author of the tool provides a good deal of documentation in the installation package. You can find this documentation in the readme.txt file within the installation directory.

FIGURE 4.17 Commenting within a blog entry.

Use the instructions in the readme.txt file to learn more about the portlets that are available to users of SimpleBlog and how to configure the resulting slots. Additionally, this file explains some of the properties available for configuration within the SimpleBlog control panel, within the Zope Management Interface. As you've seen in this chapter, however, an out-of-the-box installation works quite well; you might find that you don't want or need to modify any core configuration.

Working with Wikis

People often have difficulty grasping the concept of a wiki, and this is not helped by the fact that there's no single definition of a wiki. Basically—and I do mean *basically*—a wiki is a collection of pages in a website that anyone can modify. The websites that come out of wikidom are primarily text based because wikis are designed as ways to communicate, not ways to impress people with graphical ingenuity and style. A wiki is somewhat like a discussion board, except that there is no forum/topic/post hierarchy. A wiki is also somewhat like a blog, except one that anyone can use, edit, or add pages to.

If you're still scratching your head, don't worry. Many people do. So, here's a practical example. Suppose that your Plone site exists for the purpose of collaboration among a development team of 10 programmers, managers, and writers, all of whom are responsible for different aspects of the project. Perhaps this group has a project roadmap that you are trying to follow. Now imagine that you have installed a wiki in your Plone site (which you will in a moment) specifically regarding this project roadmap.

Now, any one of the members of your group can edit the content of the roadmap, add comments to it, pose questions, and even create different types of documents. Perhaps one of

Working with Wikis

those documents is the release notes document for the product, which anyone can add content to, edit before the writer, or make it into some proprietary document format. Think of the time saved and the productivity increased just by making all the content available to all members of the team in a nonproprietary and quickly editable format. Such is the goal of a wiki.

With that in mind, let's get on to installing a wiki in your Plone site using the Zwiki software.

Installing Zwiki

Zwiki is one of several wiki software packages freely available, but this one integrates quite well with Plone and appears to be rather stable. However, Zwiki is not part of the CMF Collective. To install it, you must visit http://www.zwiki.org/ and download the package. From that point, the installation is similar to what you have already seen in this chapter. When you have the Zwiki package, use your unzip utility of choice (perhaps WinZip on Windows, gunzip on Linux/Unix) to extract the files into a subfolder within the Data/Products folder in the Plone installation directory.

The remainder of the installation occurs through the Zope Management Interface (ZMI) instead of the Plone setup screen because adding a wiki is slightly different than modifying something that is already part of Plone, such as a content type. Using the management login, go to the ZMI on your server (http://zopehost/manage/) and click on the name of your Plone instance in the directory tree. Next, click on the portal_quickinstaller option to see the list of available packages for installation. Select the check box for the Zwiki package, and press the Install button.

> **Note**
>
> This portion of the installation process is actually similar to what occurs in the Plone setup area for adding and removing products, but you will be doing a few more tasks related to management that require you to be in the ZMI.

After Zwiki has been installed, click on the name of your Plone instance once more to return the contents list. Next, you need to add a Zwiki instance. This occurs through the drop-down list of available instances to add, as shown in Figure 4.18.

After you select a Zwiki instance to add, you are presented with a form to complete. This form asks you for the ID and title of your Zwiki instance, as well as the Zwiki type, which should be left as Basic. After you complete the form, a folder appears in the directory listing for your Plone instance; its name is the ID you supplied for your wiki. For example, if you gave an ID of wiki1, your Zwiki instance is called wiki1 and is accessible via URL at http://zopehost/ploneinstance/wiki1/ (as with the sample wiki I've created for use in the remaining screenshots, accessible to me at http://localhost/myPlone/wiki1/).

CHAPTER 4 Additional Plone Elements

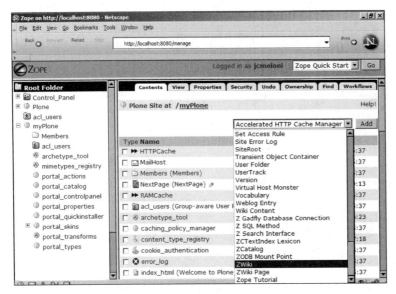

FIGURE 4.18 How to add a Zwiki instance.

> **Tip**
>
> The And Enter check box, next to the Create Wiki button, drops you into the front page of the newly created wiki as soon as it is created. Otherwise, you would be returned to the ZMI.

You're not finished yet: Zwiki requires that some permissions be specifically set so that members can participate in the editing of wiki pages. To access these security settings, click on the folder icon with the name of the new wiki. You will see some line items such as FrontPage, HelpPage, and WikiWikiWeb, but above the directory contents are the very important action tabs. Click on the Security action tab and scroll all the way to the bottom, where eight different permissions exist for using Zwiki. For each of these items, such as Zwiki:Add Pages, Zwiki:Delete Pages, and most important, Zwiki: Edit Pages, check the check boxes next to the user types that should be able to perform these tasks. For example, you can allow users of the Member user type to add or edit pages, but only those of the Manager user type to delete pages.

> **Note**
>
> Don't be alarmed by the numerous entries in the ZMI. Many of these items are explained in detail in Appendix B.

When your security settings have been saved, you can return to your Plone instance and log in to the site. After logging in, navigate to the first page of the wiki (`http://zopehost/ploneinstance/wiki1`) to see what it's all about. The next sections provide you with a brief primer on working with wikis. You'll see that it's more of a conceptual issue than a technical one.

Wiki Basics

You should understand a few bits of terminology and wiki-related concepts before moving on to working in your wiki. Potentially the most common question, and one that I asked myself first, is "Why don't people just wipe out wikis?" I suppose this question comes from years of watching script kiddies and other malicious types attempt to deface, defraud, spam, and just generally cause mayhem among all things online.

The thing to remember about wikis is that, in general, they are placed within a Plone community site or are standalone sites that require authentication of their own. In other words, no one has anonymous access. Second, anyone who does have access probably has had it specifically granted to them. There's no faking of usernames and what not—and in the wiki-using community, real names are preferred to usernames (for instance, Julie Meloni is preferred to jcmeloni). With all of these points being true, would you then want to be the one who stepped up and wiped out a community of work, a community that you belonged to? As I read on one wiki, among the musings of people who asked this same question to themselves (and others), one person put it like this: Members don't deface wikis, just like you never see graffiti on art. Some semblance of social responsibility still remains in the wiki community.

On to the basic structure of a wiki. It starts out as a single page, a singleton. Pages have titles, usually mixed-case words called *WikiWords*, such as WikiWord itself or FrontPage or JuliesHomePage. As pages are added, other pages can link to them, and people can start editing the content. Edits do not go into some black hole—you can always see what has been edited by checking the history and contents of the page you are viewing.

The rule of thumb for adding or editing content is very simple: If you think that what you have to say adds more value than what is already there, edit it. Remember, all edits and additions are attributed to their creator.

For more information on wikis in general, visit `http://c2.com/cgi/wiki?WikiWikiWeb`. In the next section, you'll see how to perform some of these user actions in your Zwiki wiki within your Plone community.

Working with Your Zwiki Wiki

Assuming that permissions have been granted to members in your Plone community, these members can add and edit content in the wiki that you created through the ZMI. When navigating to `http://zopehost/ploneinstance/wiki1`, you are greeted with the default Zwiki front page, called FrontPage. Clicking on the Edit tab enables you to change its content by invoking the editing form, shown in Figure 4.19.

FIGURE 4.19 Editing a wiki page.

Make all the edits you want in the body text area of a document, and add any comments you want in the history area. Similar to documents, Zwiki pages can be structured text, plain text, or HTML. In Figure 4.20, you can see how important the History tab is for a wiki document. This figure shows part of the original text crossed out and the new text at the bottom.

When viewing a Zwiki page, the Add New Item drop-down list is always available to an authenticated member. To add a new page in your Zwiki wiki, select Wiki Page from the drop-down list. You will see a form quite similar to the editing form. You need to add a page title, the body text, and any comments for the history. You also need to select the text type.

Working with Wikis

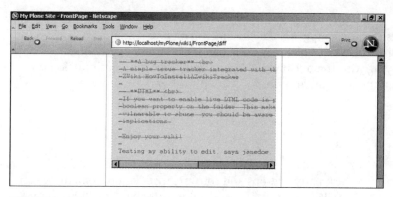

FIGURE 4.20 The history of an edited wiki page.

> **Note**
>
> Whether they are new pages or an edited version of existing pages, wiki pages are automatically published and never become part of the request queue.

When your page has been published, it is listed under the Wiki Contents tab, as shown in Figure 4.21. Wikis appear in a hierarchy if they are linked to or contain links to other pages in a wiki.

FIGURE 4.21 Showing wiki contents.

This section has shown you the very basics of working with wikis, but, in general, they're no different than documents that are simply editable by anyone in your community. Most of the knowledge that exists regarding working with Zwiki is hands-on knowledge attained by simply diving in and playing with them. However, if you would like more information on Zwiki, such as FAQs, support questions, and tips for use, visit the Zwiki website at http://www.zwiki.org/.

Troubleshooting

Anytime you are working with third-party add-ons and software installation, something can go wrong. However, using the installation methods described in this chapter will help you — items will either install or they won't. If the installation fails, a complete error message will be shown, along with links that enable you to quickly search for similar errors or report your bug to Plone developers.

It's important to remember to restart Zope after you add something to the Products directory, in anticipation of installing it. This directory is not read in real time, so if you simply place the program files in the Products directory and navigate to the QuickInstaller (or Plone setup screen), you'll find that these new items are not in the list of available products. Zope must be restarted for these items to appear. However, you do not need to restart Zope after you successfully install a product, nor do you need to log out and log back in again to see changes. If you feel that your screen should be showing different items, reload the page or clear your browser's cache.

Summary

This chapter showed you where to find Plone add-ons and explored the general manner of installing these items. Some of the more popular and useful add-ons were singled out, and their installation, configuration, and usage were explained in more detail. If you installed all of the items in this chapter, your Plone site now has discussion forums, the capability for users to add and maintain photo albums and blogs, and a platform on which users can send and receive instant messages.

In the next chapter, you'll learn how to customize the overall Plone template, including slot location and the implementation of custom tabs and graphics. Additionally, you'll learn a bit about internationalization and localization of websites, and you'll apply this knowledge to your Plone site.

Customizing Plone

The previous chapter introduced you to some of the more useful add-on products for Plone and showed how to integrate them into your system. This chapter takes you further down the customization path: You will learn to add, remove, and modify Plone slots, and you begin the process of customizing the user interface templates. This chapter also touches on the internationalization and localization aspects of a Plone site, including how to work with the Placeless Translation Service and the PloneLanguageTool.

Working with Standard Slots

In Chapter 1, "Introduction to Plone and Content Management," you learned that Plone slots are defined as part of the overall template, and you were introduced to the standard Plone slots that appear when viewing an out-of-the-box installation. In this section, you'll learn how to move those slots around, disable them for certain user types, and remove them altogether.

Changing the Location of Slots

The location of the left-side and right-side slots within the standard Plone template is controlled via a simple form in the Zope Management Interface (ZMI). To get started, log in to the ZMI with your manager account and select your Plone instance from the navigation frame. The contents populate the workspace frame, and you will see several tabs across the top of that frame. Click the Properties tab; a form is displayed that controls various overall properties for your Plone site, including what elements populate the left side and right side of the templates (see Figure 5.1).

IN THIS CHPATER

- ▶ Working with Standard Slots
- ▶ Creating and Maintaining Custom Slots
- ▶ Customizing Tabs and Graphics
- ▶ Internationalization and Localization of Your Plone Site
- ▶ Troubleshooting

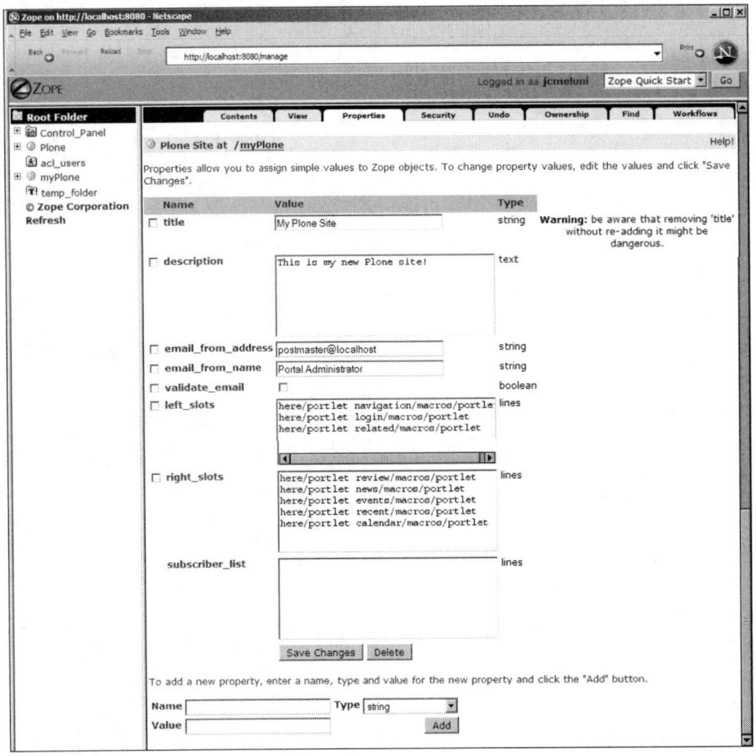

FIGURE 5.1 Viewing the properties of the Plone site.

The two form fields of most interest here are `left_slots` and `right_slots`. Each line in the content of these form fields represents a call to a specific Plone portlet, which displays the appropriate information in the template. For example, the `left_slots` field calls the following:

here/portlet_navigation/macros/portlet
here/portlet_login/macros/portlet
here/portlet_related/macros/portlet

These items correspond to the content displayed in the Navigation slot, the Login slot, and the Related Information slot, respectively. Similarly, the `right_slots` field calls the following:

here/portlet_review/macros/portlet
here/portlet_news/macros/portlet
here/portlet_events/macros/portlet
here/portlet_recent/macros/portlet
here/portlet_calendar/macros/portlet

Working with Standard Slots

These items correspond to the Review slot, the News slot, the Events slot, the Recent Items slot, and the Calendar slot, respectively. The order in which the calls to portlets are entered in the form fields corresponds to the order in which they are displayed in the Plone template. For example, on the left side of the template, the Navigation slot always appears at the top, followed by the Login slot, based on the previous entry.

> **Note**
>
> The information that you see in your Properties form might differ, depending on what add-on modules you have installed. For instance, if you installed CMFMessage and CMFUserTrackTool, you will see the following in the right_slots field, at the end of the list:
>
> here/message_list_slot/macros/messagesBox
>
> here/activeusers_slot/macros/activeusersBox

Removing and reordering the appearance of standard slots is as simple as modifying the entries in this form. For example, to remove all slots on the right side, simply delete the entries in the `right_slots` form field and press the Save Changes button. The change occurs immediately, and the right side of your template then is empty, as shown in Figure 5.2.

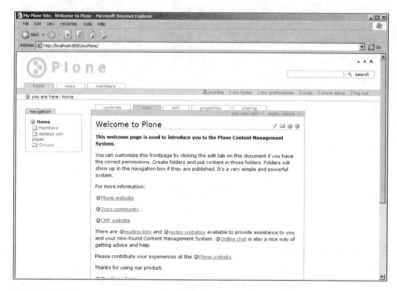

FIGURE 5.2 All right-side slots have been removed.

You can use this same process for moving around the location of your standard slots, not simply removing them from your template. For example, if you wanted the Calendar and

Events slots to appear under the Navigation slot, and you wanted the Login slot to be at the top of the right-side slots, your `left_slots` field would look like this:

here/portlet_navigation/macros/portlet
here/portlet_calendar/macros/portlet
here/portlet_events/macros/portlet
here/portlet_related/macros/portlet

Similarly, the `right_slots` field would contain this:

here/portlet_login/macros/portlet
here/portlet_review/macros/portlet
here/portlet_news/macros/portlet
here/portlet_recent/macros/portlet

Using the handy Undo function, you can immediately revert to the previous usage of right-side slots by clicking the Undo tab in your ZMI, selecting the check box of the last action you performed, and pressing the Undo button. Figure 5.3 shows an Undo screen, complete with selectable entries.

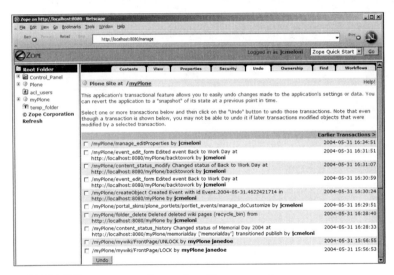

FIGURE 5.3 How to undo an edit to Plone properties.

After you roll back the edit to Plone properties, the right-side slots reappear throughout your template. Next, you can take this concept one step further and modify the behavior of the template at the folder level.

Modifying the Visibility of Standard Slots

The modifications discussed earlier were to the Plone template as a whole, meaning the front page and all subsequent pages, pages inside member directories, directories for add-ons, and so forth. In this section, you'll learn how to modify the appearance of standard slots on a per-directory basis. The sample directory in this case is for an installed ZWiki living in the mywiki directory within the sample Plone site.

Using the ZMI and looking at the contents of your Plone site, select the folder in which you want the changes to occur—in this case, the mywiki folder. After you view the contents of this folder in the workspace frame, click the Properties tab, just as you did in the previous section. The properties for this directory look different than the properties for the overall Plone template. The properties for the mywiki folder are significantly fewer, as shown in Figure 5.4.

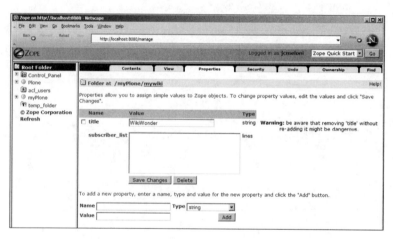

FIGURE 5.4   The properties of the mywiki folder.

> **Note**
>
> The brevity of the properties page for the `mywiki` folder is not tied to the fact that it is a folder holding a wiki. Any folder in the Plone hierarchy has fewer properties than the overall Plone properties.

In this case, there are no form fields called `left_slots` or `right_slots` because those areas are controlled by the master Plone properties seen previously. Thus, to modify these areas of the template, within this individual folder, you must make new form fields that will override the master settings.

CHAPTER 5 Customizing Plone

To remove the standard right-side slots, within the `mywiki` folder, follow these steps:

1. At the bottom of the properties page, look for the text "To add a new property...," followed by three form fields.
2. In the `Name` field, enter **right_slots** as the name of the new property.
3. In the `Type` field, select Lines as the type of the new property.
4. Press the Add button, leaving the `Value` field blank.

The changes are saved, and you no longer have right-side slots on any pages in the mywiki folder, as shown in Figure 5.5.

FIGURE 5.5 The mywiki display, without right-side slots.

You succeeded in replacing the value of the `right_slots` property within the `mywiki` folder with blank values—no slots. Because no slots are present, you can see in Figure 5.5 that the page content expands to fill that now-empty space.

If you wanted to keep content in the right side of the template within the `mywiki` folder, the previous instructions are still valid. After you create the `right_slots` property, you can give it a value (or enter a value during creation). If you assigned the following value to the `right_slots` property, for example, the only slot present in the right side of the template within the `mywiki` folder would be the Calendar slot:

```
here/portlet_calendar/macros/portlet
```

Working with Standard Slots

In the next section, you'll see how to modify the template so that only members of the site see particular slots.

Making Slots Visible to Members Only

Perhaps you have a Plone site that caters to registered, logged-in members, but it enables anonymous users to browse some freely available content. You can modify your Plone template so that certain slots are shown for only logged-in members. For example, perhaps you do not want to show the Events slot until a user is logged in. This requires a few different modifications to Plone properties and templates, but when you get the hang of it, the task won't seem so daunting.

The first step is to add a new property within the site_properties object. To access this object, log in to the Zope Management Interface and click on your Plone instance in the navigation frame. Then click on the portal_properties object in the workspace frame and then the site_properties object in the workspace frame. You should see a form like Figure 5.6 that scrolls for a bit because it's quite long.

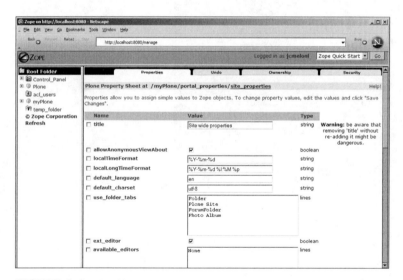

FIGURE 5.6 Modifying the site_properties object.

At the bottom of this form, you can add a new property, much as you did in the previous section. In this case, the new property is a true/false option specifically for viewing the Events slot as an anonymous user.

1. In the Name field, enter **allowAnonymousViewEvents** as the name of the new property. You can call it anything you like, but this makes sense.

CHAPTER 5 Customizing Plone

2. In the Type field, select Boolean as the type of the new property.

3. Press the Add button, leaving the Value field blank.

Now that you have added this property (and it is unchecked, which means that it is false), you have completed the first part of the process. Next on the list is to modify the Events portlet itself, to make it aware of this property and act accordingly. In the ZMI, navigate to your Plone instance in the navigation frame, then to the portal_skins object in the workspace frame, and then to the plone_portlets object in the workspace frame. You will see a list of available portlets, as shown in Figure 5.7.

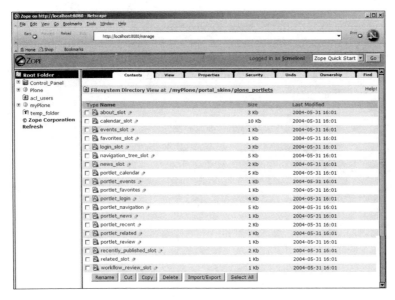

FIGURE 5.7 Portlets available for modification.

Tip
The only portlets that you should work with are those that begin with portlet_*. The rest are deprecated but remain part of the installation for any backward-compatibility issues.

Because you need to modify the functionality of the Events slot, you need to work with the portlet_events portlet. Click on this object to view the existing code and to make a custom copy for your purposes. To make a custom copy, press the Customize button. This makes a copy of the portlet, which will be shown in edit mode, as in Figure 5.8.

Working with Standard Slots

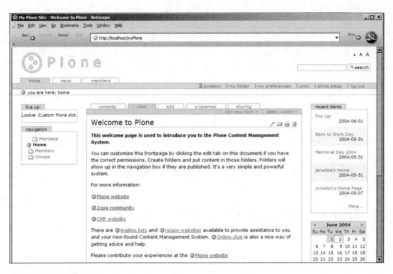

FIGURE 5.8 Custom version of portlet_events.

The code, written in Plone template language, has a tag at the top that defines this portlet:

```
<div metal:define-macro="portlet"
    tal:define="results python:here.portal_catalog.searchResults(
        portal_type_operator='or', portal_type=('Event', 'ATEvent'),
        end={'query': here.ZopeTime(), 'range': 'min'},
        sort_on='start', review_state='published')[:5];"
    tal:condition="results">
```

Replace the last line of the tag, the one with the tal:condition statement, with the following:

```
tal:condition="python:test(not site_properties.allowAnonymousViewEvents
and site_properties.portal_membership.isAnonymousUser(), 0, 1)">
```

The tag should now read:

```
<div metal:define-macro="portlet"
    tal:define="results python:here.portal_catalog.searchResults(
        portal_type_operator='or', portal_type=('Event', 'ATEvent'),
        end={'query': here.ZopeTime(), 'range': 'min'},
        sort_on='start', review_state='published')[:5];"
    tal:condition="python:test(not site_properties.allowAnonymousViewEvents
        site_properties.portal_membership. is Anonymous User (7,0,1)">
```

This new condition says that if the `allowAnonymousViewEvents` property is not checked (that is, you do not want to allow anonymous viewing) and the viewer of the page calling the object is anonymous (that is, not yet logged in), do not show this slot. If you want to allow anonymous viewing of this slot, you can simply go back to the `allowAnonymousViewEvents` property in `site_properties`, check the box (Boolean `true`), and save the change. No further changes would have to be made to the portlet because it is already customized to react to the value of `allowAnonymousViewEvents`.

You can repeat the process of creating a Boolean property and then modifying the portlet to check for this value for any standard slot—or any slot of your own creation. In the next section, you'll learn how to create your own slot using tools you've already seen.

Creating and Maintaining Custom Slots

Moving around and modifying the standard Plone slots is important, but adding your own slots will further your ability to customize your site for your audience. In this section, you'll learn how to create a portlet that will contain static content housed in a Plone document. You then can place the custom slot in any position in the Plone template or use your newfound skills to utilize folder- or user-specific settings.

To create the foundation for your portlet, which we'll call `portlet_announce`, log in to the Zope Management Interface and navigate to your Plone instance. Then select the `portal_skins` object and the custom folder. This folder might or might not be empty, depending on how much you've played around with custom instances of portlets. From the drop-down menu, select Page Template and press the Add button. You'll see a form containing two fields: `id` and `file`. The `file` field is relevant only if you want to upload the content of an already-created file containing your page template. Because that's not the case in this instance, you can leave it blank. Enter an ID of `portlet_announce`, and press the Add and Edit button. This creates a basic page template and places you in the editing screen. You should replace the content in that generic template with the code found in Listing 5.1.

LISTING 5.1: The portlet_announce Code

```
1: <html xmlns:tal="http://xml.zope.org/namespaces/tal"
2: xmlns:metal="http://xml.zope.org/namespaces/metal"
3: i18n:domain="plone">
4: <body>
5: <!-- The annoncements box -->
6: <div metal:define-macro="portlet">
7:     <div class="portlet" id="portlet-announce">
8:         <h5><tal:block replace="here/announce/Title">Replace</tal:block></h5>
9:         <div class="portletBody">
```

Creating and Maintaining Custom Slots

LISTING 5.1: Continued

```
10:             <tal:block replace="structure here/announce/CookedBody">Replace</tal:block>
11:          </div>
12:       </div>
13: </div>
14: </body>
15: </html>
```

Lines 1–3 are the basic document-definition lines that you'll see for any Plone template. They specify that although it is technically an HTML document, several other Zope- and Plone-specific attributes must be set. Line 4 opens the body tag, while line 5 is simply a comment that reminds you this is going to be an announcement box.

In line 6, the macro is defined. This is an important definition because it enables you to use the following line in your `left_slots` or `right_slots` field, for slot placement:

`here/portlet_announce/macros/portlet`

Line 7 gives the portlet an `Id` of `portlet-announce`. Line 8 begins the content display and places an H5 heading tag around a template tag. The template tag, with the attribute of `replace`, looks in your Plone document root for a document with an `Id` of announce. When it finds this document, it looks for the title of the document and replaces the placeholder text—`Replace`—between the template tags.

Line 9 begins the body of the portlet, which loads the styles that are associated with the `portletBody` class. Line 10 is another template tag that performs the same replacement action as the template tag in line 8, except that it looks for the body of the Plone page, not the title. The keyword `structure` in the template code tells the portlet to render all formatting found in the Plone document; in this case, the use of `CookedBody` tells the portlet to interpret the structured text of the document.

In addition to the template text area itself, the template contains several other modifiable elements and actions:

- **Title**—Use this field to specify a title for your template.
- **Content-Type**—Use this field to specify the content type of the document you are creating or modifying. The default value is `text/html`.
- **Expand Macros While Editing**—If selected, METAL macros will be expanded while editing the source code, to help you.
- **Taller, Shorter, Wider, Narrower**—These buttons modify the appearance of the text area in which you are typing.

▶ **File**—Use this field to upload the contents of a complete HTML or XML file into the text area instead of typing the contents.

When you have completed your modifications, press the Save Changes button. You can then add the name of your custom slot in the `left_slots` or `right_slots` field of your choice within the Plone properties screen. Next, log in to your Plone site and create the document called by the portlet. Simply create a document with the `Id` of `announce` in the root of your Plone site. Be sure to complete the workflow and publish the document for all members. When your document is published, your custom slot should be displayed in the side of the template you chose. The title and the body of the Plone document should be seen in the title bar and body box of your new static slot. An example of a custom slot that loads a Plone document is shown in Figure 5.9.

FIGURE 5.9 Sample static slot in use.

Although it's not the most fascinating use of a custom slot, the process described enables you to add whatever static slots you want. You can modify the placement and accessibility of these slots just as you can any standard Plone slot. In the next section, you'll leave slot-land to learn how to customize the tabs and graphics that make up your Plone site.

Customizing Tabs and Graphics

An out-of-the-box Plone installation contains several standard tabs and a whole set of supplementary graphics that are placed throughout the template. In this section, you'll learn how to add, modify, and remove the standard tabs, and also how to modify the basic images used in the template. The majority of these actions occur within the Zope Management Interface, so log in to the ZMI to get started.

Changing the Tabs

When you first view your Plone installation, you might see tabs across the top of the template for Home, News, and Members. If you are using Plone as a corporate intranet, you might want these tabs to represent departments within your organization, such as Sales and Marketing, Human Resources, IT, and so forth. Similarly, if you are using Plone within an educational department, you might want to have tabs that represent sections for faculty, for students, for general information—the list goes on. In other words, the tabs should represent the content architecture of your site.

Tabs are created and maintained as part of the `portal_actions` object, which is visible in the ZMI when you click on your Plone instance. When you view this object, you'll see a form containing a repeating series of entries; each entry corresponds to an action within your Plone site. An example is shown in Figure 5.10. You should see several entries in your `portal_actions` object, including the standard entries for News and Members. Scroll for the length of the page to familiarize yourself with the various entries.

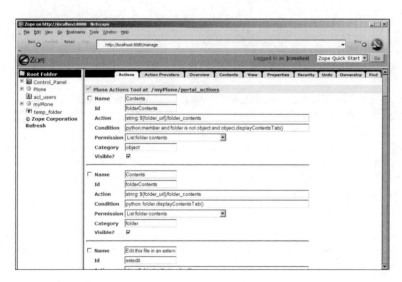

FIGURE 5.10   The `portal_actions` object contains many form entries.

Each entry has the following elements:

▶ **Name**—A text field containing the name of the item.

▶ **Id**—A text field containing the ID for the item.

CHAPTER 5   Customizing Plone

- **Action**—A text field describing the action of the item, such as where the contents of a tab are located.
- **Condition**—A text field containing any conditions for the item, such as restricting the visibility of the item to logged-in users only.
- **Permission**—A drop-down list containing numerous permissions types relevant to actions.
- **Category**—A text field describing the type of action, such as portal_tabs, folder, document_actions, and so forth.
- **Visible**—A check box that controls the overall visibility of an item.

For the remainder of this section, the goal is to display tabs across the top of the Plone template that represent folders for the following departments within a corporate intranet: Finance, Human Resources, IT, Legal, Product Management, and Sales and Marketing. Because the existing tabs in the standard Plone site are Home, News, and Members, this means removing two tabs and adding six new ones.

First comes the easy part—removing two tabs, News and Members. Because News and Members are already nicely defined in the ZMI, there's no reason to completely remove the entry—you might one day want to display these tabs. As such, instead of removing these tabs, simple uncheck the Visible check box and press the Save button at the bottom of the page. If you log in to your Plone site, you will no longer see these tabs—it's as easy as that. If you want to undo your action, you can, through the Undo tab in the ZMI or by simply checking the Visible check box and saving the form again.

Adding a tab is nearly as simple, but there is one extra step in the process: adding the Plone folder that you want to represent with the tab. To do this, log in to Plone and use the Add New Item drop-down list to add your folders in the Plone root. For instance, I've created folders with the following Ids, matching the tabs I want to add: finance, hr, it, legal, pm, salesmkt. Each of these items has a title, such as Sales and Marketing, and a description, such as Folder for Sales and Marketing Documents. After they are created, all of these folders must be published, so be sure to change their name.

With the target folders created within Plone, go back to the ZMI and navigate to the portal_actions object. Scroll to the bottom of the form; you will see a blank entry where you can add the first of your new tabs. The form fields match the fields described earlier, only without content. The first tab to add is the Finance tab because it is first in the alphabetical list of departments.

1. In the Name field, enter **Finance**.
2. In the Id field, enter **finance**.
3. In the Action field, enter **string:$portal_url/finance**.

Customizing Tabs and Graphics

4. In the Condition field, enter **python: member**.
5. In the Permission field, select **View**.
6. In the Category field, enter **portal_tabs**.
7. Check the Visible check box.
8. Press the Add button.

If you log in to your Plone site—or reload the page you're viewing, if you're already logged in—the Finance tab should appear at the top of your template. Clicking on the tab should display the contents of the Finance folder, as shown in Figure 5.11.

FIGURE 5.11 The Finance tab shows the Finance folder.

Continue adding new portal actions to represent the remaining tabs, and your Plone template will have all departments listed across the top, as shown in Figure 5.12.

The tabs are displayed in the order in which they are entered. However, that doesn't mean you can't change the order after they're in the system. The portal_actions form contains two buttons at the bottom: Move Up and Move Down. When the check box next to the Name field of a particular block is checked, this block becomes the active item. When it is active, you can move the block up or down. An example of a selected entry is shown in Figure 5.13, in which you can also see the Move Up and Move Down buttons.

CHAPTER 5 Customizing Plone

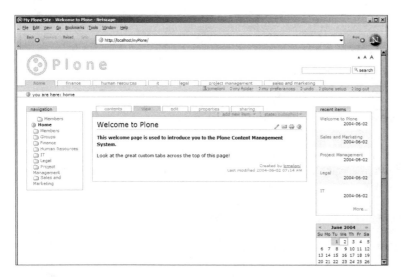

FIGURE 5.12 All the new tabs, neatly in a row.

Once checked, this becomes the active entry

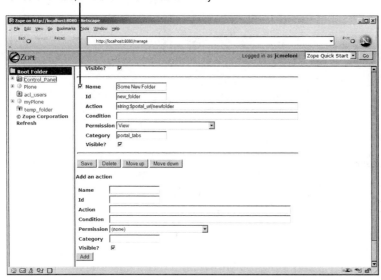

FIGURE 5.13 A selected and activated entry.

Suppose that you want to rearrange the order of your department-related tabs, such as having the Sales and Marketing and Project Management tabs switch places in the display. To achieve this, you would check the box next to the Name field of the Sales and Marketing tab and then press the Move Up button. The Sales and Marketing tab and the Project Management tab switch positions because their positions have been switched in the portal_actions display.

These up and down actions are not limited to adjacent form blocks—you can check the box next to the Name field for the Home tab and press the Move Down button several times until it is at the very end of the list. The Home tab then becomes the last tab across the top of your template, although that's not usually where one would find it. You'll also note that the position of the tabs is represented appropriately in the Navigation slot. As the order of tabs change, so does the order of the folders in the Navigation slot.

Customizing Logos and Other Images

The Plone logo in the upper-left corner of the template is nice and clean, but if you're creating your own site, you will want your own branding. Completely customizing the look and feel of your site is covered in Chapter 6, "Creating and Implementing a Custom Skin." This section gets your feet wet with asset replacement.

In the Plone template, the logo referenced in the template has an ID of logo.jpg. This does not mean that you need to use a JPEG or that your image file needs to be named logo.jpg; it simply means that there's an object with an ID of logo.jpg whose contents you will be replacing. For example, the file called tb_main_boringlogo.gif is used as a logo image file.

To customize your logo, navigate in the ZMI to your Plone instance and then through the portal_skins object to the custom directory. Using the drop-down list, select Image and press the Add button. You will see a form with three fields: ID, Title, and File. Enter logo.jpg as the ID; add a title, if you want; and then browse your file system for the new logo image that you want to use. When the form is complete, press the Add button. You have placed this object in the custom folder, so Plone looks for the custom version of the logo.jpg object instead of the standard logo.jpg object (the Plone logo).

As you can see in Figure 5.14, the new logo is now used instead of the standard Plone logo. The same concept can be used to replace any image asset used in Plone. You can see a list of most image objects used in Plone templates by looking in the portal_skins object for portal_images within the ZMI.

> **Note**
> Assets that add-ons use appear in other places within the portal_skins object. For example, if you install CMFBoard, the assets used in CMFBoard are in an object called cmfboard_images.

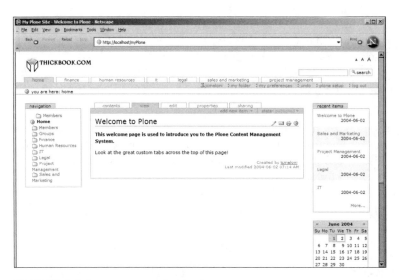

FIGURE 5.14   New Logo, Thickbook.com, in use.

Each image asset listed in `portal_images` is clickable; by clicking on an object, you can see its information, an example of the image, and a button that enables you to create a custom copy. Creating a custom copy produces the exact same result as going to the custom folder and adding a new image with the same ID as an existing image. Creating custom copies of image assets—that is, assets with the same ID but different source files—enables you to quickly modify the images used by Plone, without performing any customizations to Plone template code. Try it on your own—you can always use the Undo feature or simply delete the items placed in the custom folder.

Internationalization and Localization of Your Plone Site

Internationalization and localization are very different beasts, and neither is akin to translation, which is a common misconception. For example, you can have a translated website, but it might not be an internationalized or a localized site—just a translated site. Internationalization occurs at the application level as a preparatory step toward possible application localization. During the internationalization phase of application development, the primary occurrence is that all strings, icons, graphics, and any other modifiable elements are *externalized*. To externalize means to separate these elements from the core of your application so that they can be easily changed per locale, which is the process of localization.

Internationalization and Localization of Your Plone Site

A *locale* is essentially a grouping of the translated strings, graphics, text, and formatting conventions that are used in the application or website to be localized. These groupings are usually referred to by the name of the pervasive language of the application, such as the German locale. Although it might be obvious that the German locale includes text translated into German, it does not mean that the website is applicable only to people in Germany: Austrians who speak German would probably utilize a localized German website, but it would not be referred to as the Austrian locale.

Plone is already an internationalized application, meaning that it is ready and waiting to be localized. This application also ships with an add-on (installed by default) called PlacelessTranslationService, which handles the interplay between localized strings, images, and other items, and the base Plone templates. The "translation" in this case is the interpretation by Placeless Translation Service of the matching ID and strings in a message map file. The list of standard message map files includes numerous languages, from Afrikaans to Turkish and everything in between. You can view the list of installed message maps in the ZMI by selecting Control Panel from the navigation pane and then clicking on the Placeless Translation Service icon.

> **Tip**
> Message map files are modified and new languages are added all the time. To get the newest versions of files or add new languages to your Plone installation, visit the Plone Collective at `http://sourceforge.net/projects/collective`. If you are a language expert and want to create your own message maps or contribute to those already in the collective, see `http://plone.org/documentation/howto/PlacelessTranslationService/` for information on how these files are created and compiled.

In the next section, you install the PloneLanguageTool and learn how to localize your Plone site.

Localizing Your Plone Site

The PloneLanguageTool is an exceptional add-on that enables you to set the base language and character set, customize the available localizations, and provide easy access for users to view localized content. The PloneLanguageTool is found in the Collective and can be installed as you learned in Chapter 4, "Additional Plone Elements," or via the ZMI. You've worked in the ZMI for most of this chapter, and you can use it to install the PloneLanguageTool as well.

First, download the latest version of PloneLanguageTool from the Collective, and extract the contents of the zipped file to the `Data/Products` subfolder in your Plone installation directory. Restart Zope and Plone by going to the Control Panel in the ZMI navigation pane and

CHAPTER 5 Customizing Plone

pressing the Restart button. Wait for Zope and Plone to restart, and then access your Plone instance, also in the navigation pane of the ZMI.

Next, click on the `portal_quickinstaller` object in the workspace pane of the ZMI. You will see a list of add-ons that can be installed and that have already been installed. PloneLaguageTool should be in the list of items ready to be installed; select its check box and press the Install button. Assuming that it installs without a hitch and displays the "OK" text, you can use this tool to localize your Plone site.

Click on your Plone instance in the navigation pane to see the objects in its root folder. One of these objects should be called `portal_languages`. Click on this object to see what is essentially a localization menu, shown in Figure 5.15.

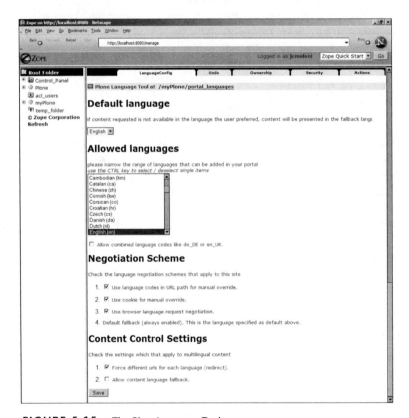

FIGURE 5.15 The PloneLanguageTool menu.

The first item is a drop-down menu that represents your selection of a default language. In this example, English is the default language used for the localized elements. The drop-down list of default languages changes, depending on the languages you select in the next form field, `Allowed Languages`. The `Allowed Languages` field displays all the different languages in

Internationalization and Localization of Your Plone Site

which character encoding or message strings are found. If you check the box beneath the `Allowed Languages` field to allow combined languages, the list becomes even longer.

> **Note**
>
> Combined languages include all the variations per country of a given language. For example, en_us represents English as used in the United States, whereas en_uk represents English as used in the United Kingdom. Other languages have variations as well, all of which are listed in the Allowed Languages drop-down list.

The remaining form fields on this menu are various check box options related to content negotiation and control. The default settings are appropriate for a standard Plone site, but feel free to select options that you feel are appropriate to your installation. After you have configured your options, press the Save button. You will see your changes immediately in your Plone site. Figure 5.16 shows an example of localization in action; Japanese is selected here as the working language.

FIGURE 5.16 Localized Plone site, Japanese style.

As you can see, all of the standard Plone tabs, links, actions, footnote text, and so on—items in the core Plone template—are presented in Japanese. A Language slot is present at the left side of the template and contains a drop-down list of the Allowed Languages selected from the PloneLanguageTool menu.

> **Note**
>
> If you select a small number of languages (five or less, usually), the languages are displayed as text-based links with a corresponding flag icon. The user-selected language is bold. In this example, the drop-down list is used because a larger number of allowable languages was chosen via the ZMI.

The user is in control of selecting the localized site to use, so you can imagine that the user would select one that his or her web browser can actually interpret. However, if you are testing your localization selections and notice that your language isn't changing when you make a selection, it's for a simple reason: Your browser does not contain the language accessories needed to view the translated text. For example, if you select Japanese but your operating system and browser are in English and you have not installed Japanese fonts or selected support for Japanese character sets, you won't see a Japanese Plone template. You'll learn more about character sets in the next section.

International Character Sets

Character sets are referred to as single-byte or multibyte character sets, corresponding to the number of bytes needed to define a relationship with a character that is used in a language. English, German, and French are examples of single-byte languages: Only 1 byte is necessary to represent a character such as the letter *a* or the number 9. Single-byte code sets have, at most, 256 characters, including the entire set of ASCII characters, accented characters, and other characters necessary for formatting.

However, multibyte code sets have more than 256 characters, including all single-byte characters as a subset. Multibyte languages include Chinese, Japanese, Korean, Thai, Arabic, Hebrew, and so on. The common thread is that these languages require more than 1 byte to represent a character. For example, consider the word *Tokyo* (the capital of Japan). In English, it is spelled with four different characters, using a total of 5 bytes. However, in Japanese, the word is represented by two syllables, *tou* and *kyou*, each of which uses 2 bytes, for a total of 4 bytes used.

The relevance of this information is that, to properly interpret and display the text of web pages in their intended language, the application needs to tell the web browser which character set to use, using content headers. When a language is selected via the PloneLanguageTool, the proper headers are sent for the selected language.

In the localized Plone site, you'll notice that plenty of content is not translated. This is content added by the user, in the user's language (in this case, English). Custom content does not appear in message map files and, thus, is not translated. However, if you are creating content in the language that you have chosen, your content is displayed as such. For example, suppose that your Plone site is for a German company, and the allowed languages are German and English. It's quite likely that any content added to the Plone site—folders, documents, events, and so on—will be in German. Your custom tabs would say Startseite instead of Home and Informationstechnologie instead if IT. When the folder and tab are created for IT, if you're in Germany and your audience is German, you'll name it something in German! Thus, when the localized site is viewed in English, all of the standard Plone elements will be in English, but the content entered in German—such as the custom tabs and folders—will remain in German.

Troubleshooting

When working within the ZMI, you have opportunities to make mistakes that have rippling effects within your Plone site. However, as with all Zope and Plone actions, any settings that you modify or template that you add can be removed using the omnipresent Undo action. For example, if you are modifying the location of slots and, while cutting and pasting, accidentally enter the name of the slot twice, you can simply undo the action and try again. Similarly, if you accidentally change the visibility of slots via the ZMI and find when you log in to Plone that all your slots are gone, you can simply return to the ZMI and either undo the action or just try again. The ZMI is designed to make it difficult for a manager to lose data or settings because previous versions are only an Undo action away.

As you're working with Plone add-ons such as PloneLanguageTool, it's a good idea to stop and start Zope after installing the product. This way, if you have an error when Zope restarts, you can pinpoint it to the item recently added or the setting recently modified. At the very least, if you are logged in to your Plone site as a member, log out and log back in after the new item has been installed and configured. Doing so provides an opportunity to start with a clean slate as both a manager (in the ZMI) and a member (in the Plone site); you can be sure that you have access to the current add-ons and settings of your application.

Summary

This chapter provided numerous hands-on activities to get you started down the path of customizing your Plone site. Using the Zope Management Interface for the majority of the customization, you learned how to work with standard slots and tabs, and how to create and modify the text and placement of custom slots and tabs. You were introduced to the concepts of creating custom copies of standard template elements, such as a logo and other image assets. In the last section of this chapter, you were briefed on the differences among internationalization, localization, and just simple translations. You also installed the PloneLanguageTool in anticipation of configuring a localized Plone site.

In the next chapter, you'll spend the majority of the time working with Plone skins and related elements. You'll learn how to create your own skin and develop a display appropriate to the content architecture of your site.

Creating and Implementing a Custom Skin

IN THIS CHAPTER

- What's a Skin?
- Elements of a Plone Skin
- Working with the Plone Base Properties File
- Working with the Plone Style Sheet
- Pulling It All Together
- Troubleshooting

In the previous chapter, you learned some of the basics for Plone customization, such as moving and renaming tabs and replacing images. In this chapter, you'll learn more about the customizable portions of the underlying Plone template and how to make modifications that result in a useful yet completely customized Plone site.

What's a Skin?

The term *skin* might appear strange for the uninitiated. In software development, a *skin* is the general term for the elements that make up the graphical appearance of software. For example, if you have a software application that appears as a window, that window may have the following components:

- A title bar background color
- A font color and style for text in the title bar
- A body background color
- A font color and style for text in the window body
- A toolbar containing action-related icons
- Buttons within the body of the window

All of these elements (and many others) make up the skin of the application. To use the term *skin* in reference to a piece of software, that software must be *skinnable*, meaning that the end user must be able to change these elements and, thus, the outward appearance of the application itself. For end users to be able to do this, the software developers must have designed the application specifically with skinning in mind. This means that the developers would have separated the visual elements of the application from the inner workings of the software itself. If you have used an instant-messaging application such as Yahoo! Messenger or AOL Instant Messenger, or the Mozilla family of web browsers, you have encountered the ability to change application skins. Other types of software, such as media players for audio and video files, allow skinning as well.

You might also be a member of a web-based community that enables users to select a custom skin to enhance their browsing experience. An example of this is the My Yahoo! portal, where registered users can customize the colors, fonts, and even content shown to them when they log in to the site. Skinned sites such as this exist only because of the careful way in which the website developers built their functional and display templates. The developers of Plone have done just that: A Plone site administrator can change myriad elements related to the display of the Plone site without ever touching the code that drives it.

Beyond the administrative simplicity of maintaining display elements in a nice, neat package such as a skin, another feature of a skin is the ease with which a user can change his or her browsing experience. When browsing a skinned site, the user is often presented with a drop-down menu or other quick selection mechanism. With one click of the mouse, a user can apply a completely new set of colors and graphics to the site. Elsewhere, you might see the term *theme* used interchangeably with *skin*, but they're not exactly synonymous. If you think of a skin as a basket of goodies—action-related icons, font styles and colors, background colors, supplementary images, table and link styles, and so forth—then the theme is the thought process that put them all together. For example, if you tell your designer that you want a blue theme, you will probably get a skin that contains blue-tinted icons, styles that utilize blue and contrasting colors, and so forth.

Some of the changes you made in Chapter 5, "Customizing Plone," are precursors to developing your own Plone skin. For example, if you swapped out a few of the default icons for images of your own design, you can continue the trend and develop an entire set of thematically related icons as part of your own skin. In the next section, you'll learn about the modifiable elements that make up a Plone skin.

Elements of a Plone Skin

Creating a new Plone skin involves a few different elements:

- The base properties
- The style sheet
- Images

Elements of a Plone Skin

In the previous chapter, you learned how to swap out image files so that objects reference your own custom files. For example, the object called logo.jpg could actually hold the your-logo.gif graphic file. By the end of this chapter, you'll have a better understanding of how the properties and style sheet files work within Plone. As you go through this chapter and learn about the customizable pieces, you might find that you do not want to customize every single element that makes up a Plone skin. In fact, it is quite common for Plone administrators to simply change the color scheme—a thematic change—and be done with it. Creating a completely new skin is a time-consuming task that evolves from internal discussions with team members and mock-ups from a design team. When you are finished with this chapter, you should understand the elements and the process of skinning a Plone site, and you will have the necessary skills to develop and apply a new Plone skin.

Preparing to Use a Custom Skin

Many aspects of creating your custom skin will take place via the Zope Management Interface, but to get started, you'll make a few modifications on your actual file system. Within your file system, navigate to the Data directory within your Plone installation directory. Continue traversing your directory structure until you reach Products/CMFPlone/skins/plone_styles. In this directory, create a new directory to hold your custom style-related information. In this example, I've called the directory custom_plone, but you can use any name you want.

Still within your file system, copy the files base_properties.props and plone.css.dtml from the Products/CMFPlone/skins/plone_styles directory to the new directory you created (custom_plone, for example). In a text editor, open the base_properties.props file and look for a line similar to this:

plone_skin:string=Plone Default

Change this line to this:

plone_skin:string=Custom Plone

> **Note**
> You can name your new skin anything you want; this example uses Custom Plone as its name.

Save and close the file; you're finished working with your file system and will now go back to work within the ZMI. The next step in your preparation is to add the name of your custom skin to the list of available Plone skins. In the ZMI, click on your Plone instance in the navigation frame, and then click on the portal_skins object in the workspace frame. Click on the Properties tab; you will see a form containing the installed skins, as well as a place to add a new skin (see Figure 6.1).

CHAPTER 6   Creating and Implementing a Custom Skin

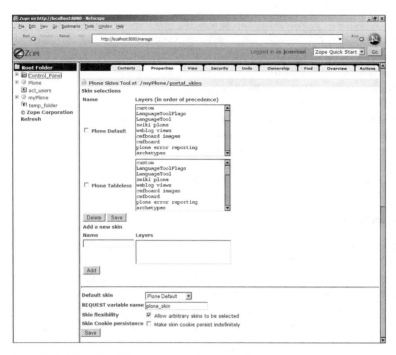

FIGURE 6.1   Modifying `portal_skins` properties.

To add a skin called Custom Plone, first enter Custom Plone in the Name field. In this instance, you'll want to use this skin for all the layers for which the Plone Default skin is used. In the Layers field next to the Plone Default entry, select and copy all of the entries, and then paste them in the Layers field for the Custom Plone entry. Press the Add button to add this new skin to the list of available skins.

The next step in the process is to prepare custom versions of the base properties file and Plone style sheet so that you can select Custom Plone as a skin and actually have it display something that has been customized. Navigate to the `portal_skins` object and click on it in the Workspace pane. Then select the `plone_styles` object, followed by the `custom_plone` object. The `custom_plone` object contains the two items you placed there via the file system: `base_properties` and `plone.css`. Click on the `base_properties` object and press the Customize button/ An editable version of this file now exists in your `plone_styles/custom` folder. Repeat this process with the `plone.css` object, and navigate to `plone_styles/custom` to ensure that copies are available to you.

To verify that everything is in order, select the `base_properties` object. You should see an editable form such as the one in Figure 6.2.

Elements of a Plone Skin

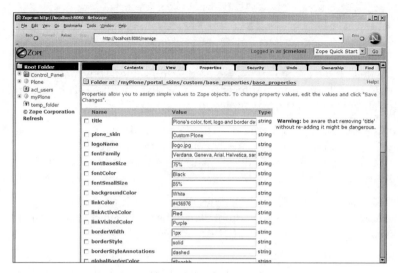

FIGURE 6.2 Modifying the base_properties object.

Follow the next few steps to ensure that your system is prepared to handle skin-related change:

1. Change the value of fontColor to Red.
2. Change the value of backgroundColor to Black.
3. Press the Save Changes button to save the form.
4. Navigate to the portal_skins object and click on the Properties tab.
5. Scroll to the bottom of this form and select Custom Plone from the Default Skin drop-down menu. Press the Save button to save your changes.
6. In your control panel, restart Zope.

After Zope has been restarted, navigate to your Plone site. You should see red text on a black background instead of the standard black text on a white background. Unless you're particularly fond of this color scheme, follow the same steps detailed previously, and change fontColor back to Black and backgroundColor back to White. With your system ready and waiting to accept changes, the next section explains the contents of base_properties and plone.css in more detail.

Working with the Plone Base Properties File

In this section, you'll learn more about the individual entries found in the base_properties file. All of the entries in the default base_properties file hold string values, so whatever you type in the value field should be a string, not an integer or some other data type. This section describes each of these default entries and shows you how to create an entry of your own.

- **title**—This field simply describes the properties file. If you are creating a custom file, you could give it a title, such as My Custom Blue Theme, to differentiate it from the standard properties file. The value of this field is not shown in your Plone site, but a value is required for this field.

- **plone_skin**—This field is used to attach the properties file to skin. If you change the value from Plone Default to something like Custom Skin, when you select Custom Skin from the portal_skins properties tab in the ZMI, this properties file will be used.

- **logoName**—The value of this field should be the value of the object that will hold your logo. You learned in Chapter 5 that the object called logo.jpg does not have to hold an image called logo.jpg; the image can be named mylogo.gif, for all it cares. The entry in the properties file simply tells Plone which object to look for. If you want your logoName to be mylogo.gif, you must also create an object called mylogo.gif that holds the image file of your choice.

- **fontFamily**—This value determines the list of fonts to be used for the body text in your site. The default value is Lucida Grande, Verdana, Lucida, Helvetica, Arial, sans-serif, which means that the designers really want the font to be Lucida Grande, but if that font is not present, the content should be displayed in Verdana. If Verdana is not present, use Lucida, and so on down the line. If none of the named fonts is listed, the site will be rendered using the default sans-serif font in the end user's browser. If you wanted to run a serif-based site, your fontFamily entry could look like Times New Roman, Times, Book Antiqua, serif, for example.

- **fontBaseSize**—This percentage value represents the base font size, from which all increases or decreases in font size will occur. The default fontBaseSize is 70 percent of the end user's default display font size; if the end user changes the Plone-viewing preferences to use the "bigger" font, the selection really means "add to the fontBaseSize." Similarly, selecting the "smaller" font results in a subtraction from the fontBaseSize.

- **fontColor**—This value is the font color used for all displayed text, whether body or header text. The value can be either a color name, such as Black, which is the default, or a hexadecimal representation of the RGB color.

- **fontSmallSize**—This percentage value represents the size of the small elements; its default value is 85 percent. This might seem strange at first glance because the default value of `fontBaseSize` is 70 percent. However, `fontSmallSize` is 85 percent of the `fontBaseSize`, not 85 percent of the end user's default display font size.

- **backgroundColor**—This value is the background color used throughout your Plone site, unless it is overwritten by the background color of another element, such as a tab. The value can be either a color name, such as `White`, which is the default, or a hexadecimal representation of the RGB color.

- **linkColor**—This value is used to color all hyperlinks that have not yet been visited or are not in the process of being clicked. The default value is `#436976`, which is sort of a dark blue-green color. You can use either color names or hexadecimal RGB notation.

- **linkActiveColor**—A hyperlink is this color when it is in the process of being clicked. The default value is `Red`; you can use either color names or hexadecimal RGB notation.

- **linkVisitedColor**—A hyperlink is this color after it has been visited. The default value is `Purple`; you can use either color names or hexadecimal RGB notation.

- **borderWidth**—If something has a border within your Plone site, this is its default width (1px). Examples of items with borders include tabs, slots, the horizontal rule, boxes around content, and drop-down menus. You can use a measurement in pixels (as in 1px and 2px), or you can use the generic `thin`, `medium`, or `thick` notations.

- **borderStyle**—Borders not only have widths; they have styles as well. The default style is Solid; if you keep the default `borderWidth` and default `borderStyle` values, all of your bordered elements will have 1-pixel-wide solid lines as their borders. Changing these two styles, in particular, can have dramatic effects on the appearance of your Plone site because nearly every element has a border of some kind. In Figure 6.3, you can see how changing the `borderWidth` to Thick and `borderStyle` to Dotted will make your Plone site look terrible—but now you should have a better picture of just how many elements have borders!

> **Note**
> The standard border styles are None, Hidden, Dotted, Dashed, Solid, Double, Groove, Ridge, Inset, and Outset.

- **borderStyleAnnotations**—When you add comments to a page in a Plone site, they are set apart in their own comments box. This box has a border, which uses the `borderStyleAnnotations` style. The default value is Dashed, but you can use any of the standard border styles. The `borderWidth` value is used to determine the width of the border here as well.

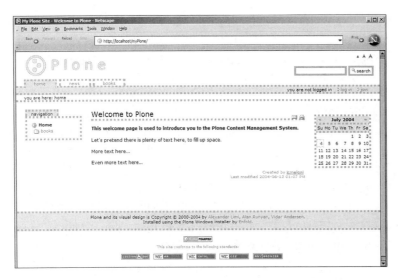

FIGURE 6.3   Terrible use of `borderWidth` and `borderStyle` modifications.

- **globalBorderColor**—This color is used as the actual border color for all bordered items. The default value is #8cacbb, which is a pleasant sort of light slate blue color. This element goes hand in hand with `borderWidth`, `borderStyle`, and `borderStyleAnnotation`; borders need widths, styles, and colors to be visible. This value can be a color name or hexadecimal RGB notation.

- **globalBackgroundColor**—If you put four borders together, you have a rectangular or square item—a tab, for example. The `globalBackgroundColor` sets the color for this area. The default value is #dee7ec, which is a very light blue color; the value can be a color name or hexadecimal RGB notation. Not all boxed-in items use the `globalBackgroundColor`. You will learn which default items do in the upcoming section on style sheets, "Working with the Plone Style Sheet."

- **globalFontColor**—This value, which happens to be the same value as `linkColor` (#436976) in the default Plone properties, is used to color the text that sits on anything colored by `globalBackgroundColor`. Using a tab as an example, it is filled in by `globalBackgroundColor`, and its text is colored by `globalFontColor`. Obviously, you want these two colors to be different and to contrast. You can use either color names or hexadecimal RGB notation.

- **headingFontFamily**—This value determines the list of fonts to be used for all headings in your site (H1 through H6). This list of fonts likely will be similar to, if not exactly the same as, the list used for `fontFamily`. Similar fonts for body and heading text help maintain a consistent look and feel throughout your site.

- **headingFontBaseSize**—Much like the `fontBaseSize` property, `headingFontBaseSize` represents the percentage value of the font size used in all headings (levels H1 through H6). The default value is 100 percent; any change you make should also be in percentage format.
- **contentViewBorderColor**—This color is used as the border color of items in the content view—that is, anything under the Contents, View, Edit, Properties, and Sharing tabs. The default color is `#74ae0b`, which is a dark green. This value can be a color name or hexadecimal RGB notation.
- **contentViewBackgroundColor**—This color is used as the background color for the bordered items in the content view. The default color is `#cde2a7`, which is a light green. This value can be a color name or hexadecimal RGB notation.
- **contentViewFontColor**—This value is used to color the text that sits on anything colored by the `contentViewBackgroundColor` property. The default color is `#578308`, a dark green. This color should contrast with `contentViewBackgroundColor` and can be a color name or hexadecimal RGB notation.

> **Note**
> Figure 6.4 provides sample elements controlled by `globalBorderColor`, `globalBackgroundColor`, and `globalFontColor`, compared to those controlled by `contentViewBorderColor`, `contentViewBackgroundColor`, and `contentViewFontColor`.

- **inputFontColor**—This value is the font color used in form fields; any text that the user types will be in this color. The value can be either a color name, such as `Black`, which is the default, or a hexadecimal representation of the RGB color.
- **textTransform**—This property is used to transform text into a specific case—for example, lower case (the default), upper case, or capitalized. Regardless of the case used by the user when providing titles of objects such as portlets, the `textTransform` property renders the text in the selected case.
- **evenRowBackgroundColor**—This color is displayed as the background of even-numbered rows in generated listings. The default value is `#f7f9fa`, which is a very light gray. This value can be a color name or hexadecimal RGB notation.
- **oddRowBackgroundColor**—This color is displayed as the background of odd-numbered rows in generated listings. The default value is `transparent`, so it takes on the background color of the elements it is displayed within. This value can be a color name or hexadecimal RGB notation, and it should contrast with `evenRowBackgroundColor` if you want users to be able to tell the difference in rows.

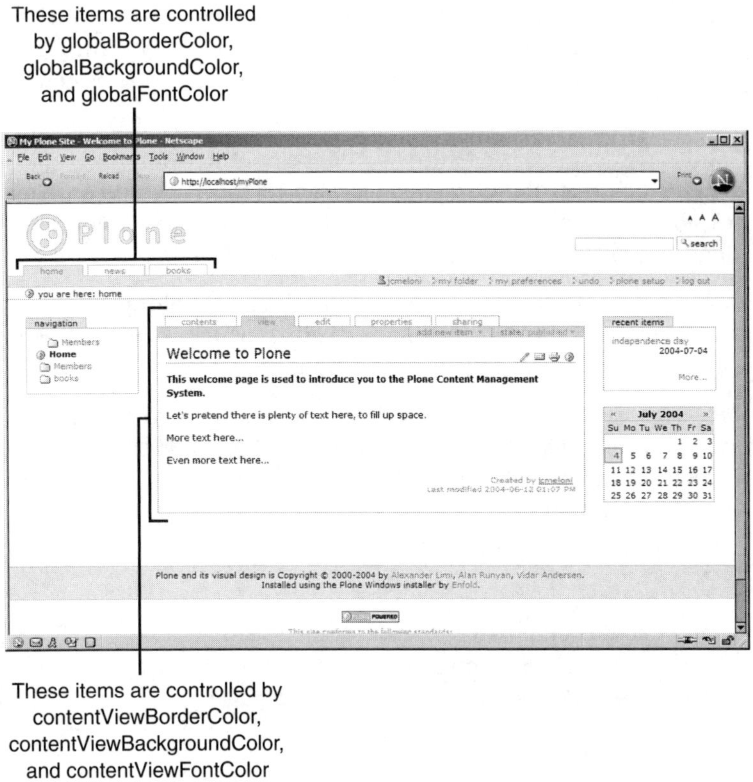

FIGURE 6.4 Display items controlled by the `global*` versus `contentView*` properties.

- **notifyBorderColor**—When performing actions within Plone such as logging in, adding or modifying content, setting preferences, and so forth, a notification box containing a status message usually appears upon completion of your action. This property defines the border color of this message area. The default value is `#ffa500`, a dark orange, but it can be a color name or hexadecimal RGB notation. The current day is also highlighted in this color, in the default Plone calendar.

- **notifyBackgroundColor**—This property defines the background color of the box containing messages, outlined by `notifyBorderColor`. The default value is `#ffce7b`, a light orange, but it can be a color name or hexadecimal RGB notation.

- **discreetColor**—This color is used to display helper text, such as that used near form fields. The default color is `#76797c`, a dark gray, but it can be a color name or hexadecimal RGB notation.

- **helpBackgroundColor**—In the standard Plone calendar, when a day has an event attached to it, a pop-up is visible when the user places the mouse over this link. The `helpBackgroundColor` property is used to color this box. The default value is `#ffffe1`, an off-white, but it can be a color name or hexadecimal RGB notation.
- **portalMinWidth**—This property is used to define the minimum width of the Plone display. The `portalMinWidth` property, as well as the `columnOneWidth` and `columnTwoWidth` properties that follow, are measured in *ems*. The default `portalMinWidth` is 70em.

> **Note**
>
> An *em* is a unit of measurement, the size of which is relative to the size of the font used in the page rather than an actual measurement taken by a ruler. For example, if you use a 10-point base font, the width of an em would be the approximate width of the letter *m* at that font size. If your base font size is 14-point, the value would be relatively larger. So, when the `portalMinWidth` value is 70em, that means approximately 70 letter *m*'s can fit on one line, which could represent anywhere from 70 to 80 or more actual characters (an *i* is skinnier than an *m*).

- **columnOneWidth**—This property is used to define the width of the left column. The default is 16em, but you can make this column width anything you want (still measured in ems). For example, if you want the left column to be noticeably wider than the right column, make this value something like 32em while keeping the value of `columnTwoWidth` at 16em.
- **columnTwoWidth**—See `columnOneWidth`, earlier, except that this property controls the right column, not the left.

The items previously described are all of the default Plone properties. You can add your own, using the fields at the bottom of the editable form. These are the fields:

- **Name**—The name of your new property, such as `fancyFontColor`.
- **Value**—The value of the new property, such as `Pink`.
- **Type**—The type of the new property, selected from a drop-down of available types. `String` would likely be the type used for a new property.

When these fields are complete, press the Add button to add the property to those available in your Plone site. After they have been added, you can reference this property within your Plone style sheet. You will learn about this in the next section.

Working with the Plone Style Sheet

In this section, you'll learn more about the items found in the `plone.css` style sheet file, and how and where to add your own styles. The Plone style sheets use the items found in the `base_properties` file as a sort of shorthand, which is why modifying properties is often much simpler than editing the default style sheet. For example, a style sheet might define several classes, all of which build on a base font size. Instead of repeating the value of the base font size throughout the style sheet and then having to modify every entry in the style sheet in which this item occurs, a property is referenced: `fontBaseSize`. One change to `fontBaseSize` in the properties files will cause the change to cascade through every variation of its usage in the style sheet, resulting in less work for you and confidence that each entry will be modified appropriately.

Quick Style Sheet Primer

Style sheets are used to separate the design elements of a site from the underlying code of a site. Using a style sheet greatly reduces the number of files you need to edit if you decide that you really don't like the base font of your site. That's just an example because a style sheet includes many more design elements than just the name of the font in use: Colors, text weight and decoration, and padding are among the attributes used in style sheets.

In HTML, you have tags pairs such as `<P></P>` to surround a paragraph, `<H1></H1>` to surround a level 1 heading, and so forth. Without a style sheet, your web browser renders the content surrounded by these tag pairs in some default font and size. Web designers want a bit more control than that and use style sheets to tell web browsers the specific way in which they want some text to be displayed. The `P` element, used for the `<P></P>` tag pair, could be defined in a style sheet as regular-weight, 10-point, sans-serif font. Or, it could be defined for whatever reason as bold, 12-point Wingdings. Regardless, any content within the `<P></P>` tag pair in that website would be displayed the same way.

The structure of a style-sheet entry follows this pattern:

`selector.class {property: value}`

The *selector* is the name of the element you want to define. For example, if you want to define the `<P>` tag, then your selector would be `P`. The selector is optional; you can leave it blank to define a *class* that can be used with any HTML element. The selector can be used in these possible ways within a style sheet:

- P {**property: value**} can be used to define the content within the `<P></P>` tag pair.
- P.someclass {**property: value**} can be used to define the content within the `<P></P>` tag pair when the attribute `class="someclass"` is used in the tag, as in `<P class="someclass"></P>`.

- **.someclass {property: value}** is used to define the `someclass` class, which can be used within any tag pair, such as `<P class="someclass"></P>`, `<H1 class=someclass></H1>`, and so forth.

The property and portions of the definition depend on the tag being used and what is valid per the HTML specification you are using (see http://www.w3.org/MarkUp/ for information on the various HTML specifications). The following are some examples of properties and values for various tags:

- To ensure that the background color of your site is white, you would use this:

    `body {color: white}`

    or

    `body {color: #FFFFFF}`

- If you want all of your paragraph containers to be Arial, 10 point, normal weight, you would use this:

    `P {font-family: Arial; color: black; font-size: 10pt}`

In many style sheets, including the ones used in Plone, you will see property/value pairs on individual lines, but still within the curly braces:

```
P {
    font-family: Arial;
    color: black;
    font-size: 10pt
}
```

This display makes your style sheets more readable, which is useful when you're searching through a long file for one particular element.

This section has provided the briefest of introductions to the structure of style sheets, but if you would like to know more, visit http://www.w3c.org/Style/CSS/ for learn more about the standards to use.

Structure of the Plone Style Sheet

The Plone style sheet is a very readable document, and its creators have provided numerous comments within it to help you understand the elements being defined. As an element is defined, it might include one or more of the properties from the `base_properties` file. You will find these properties referenced like this:

CHAPTER 6 Creating and Implementing a Custom Skin

```
&dtml-propertyname;
```

So, if the element being defined references the `fontBaseSize` property, it would look like this:

```
&dtml-fontBaseSize;
```

Here's an example:

```
body {
    font: &dtml-fontBaseSize; <dtml-var fontFamily>;
    background-color: &dtml-backgroundColor;;
    color: &dtml-fontColor;;
    margin: 0;
    padding: 0;
}
```

> **Note**
>
> The use of the double semicolons in lines such as
>
> `background-color: &dtml-backgroundColor;;`
>
> is not accidental. The first semicolon terminates the reference:
>
> `&dtml-backgroundColor;`
>
> The second semicolor terminates the style sheet directive itself.

In this example, the body element references four distinct properties from the `base_properties` file: fontBaseSize, fontFamily, backgroundColor, and fontColor.

> **Tip**
>
> If you wanted to use the `fancyFontColor` property used as an example in the previous section, you could add it here, replacing this line:
>
> `color: &dtml-fontColor;;`
>
> with this:
>
> `color: &dtml- fancyFontColor;;`
>
> This is simply an example; I don't advocate pink body text throughout an entire website.

The body element described earlier is the first stylistic element you encounter in the Plone style sheet, and it is preceded with the comment the `basic elements`. The "basic elements" consist of just that: specific definitions of core HTML elements such as P, H1 through H6, UL, OL and LI, and so forth. In addition, form elements are defined; you will find specific definitions for text fields, text areas, drop-down menus, and other form-related elements.

After the basic elements have been defined, comments are used to introduce additional definitions:

```
/* searchbox style and positioning */
```

This comment precedes the definition of the search box, which is found in the top right of the default Plone template:

```
#portal-searchbox {
    position: absolute;
    top: 45px;
    right: 1.5em;
    background-color: transparent;
    margin: 0;
    padding: 0;
    text-align: right;
    text-transform: &dtml-textTransform;;
    width: 50%;
    white-space: nowrap;
    z-index: 2;
}
```

As you can see, the style sheet is used to precisely place this item within the template; the `position: absolute` and `top: 45px` attributes tell the browser to render the search box exactly 45 pixels below the top of the viewable area of the browser window. The `plone.css` style sheet continues for many pages—it's a 30K file. Virtually all aspects of design are included in the `plone.css` style sheet; this allows for a highly accessible and usable underlying structure, customizable without touching any of the actual page templates that drive Plone. You'll learn more about the page templates themselves in Chapter 7, "Advanced Content-Related Techniques." In the next section, you'll see how to bring together properties and styles into your own custom skin.

Pulling It All Together

Modifications to the `base_properties` will have rippling effects within the Plone style sheet, which, in turn, will have an effect on the Plone templates, resulting in a change that is visible to the user. This can be a good thing, if the modification was planned for, or it can be a horrible misstep if you did not mean to change all of your body text to the color pink (for example). However, if you inadvertently change your body text to pink, you can use the Undo feature to roll back the `base_properties` to its previous form.

As noted earlier in this chapter, implementing a custom skin is a project that begins with a design team. If you are a site administrator for a corporation, an educational institution, or even a secret society of some sort, chances are good that there are design guidelines, logo usage rules, and so forth that must be followed. If you're just Joe User with your own Plone site, you have more freedom, but that doesn't mean you should do less planning.

The design process includes several factors, many of which have little to do with Plone but have everything to do with the message you are trying to send to your users. However, if you expect to be able to implement any of your plans within the Plone infrastructure, it is highly recommended that you traverse the planning process, to ensure that fewer (if any) items fall through the cracks.

Define Your Goals

Even if your site is only for you and a few friends, you should have some goals. If you are developing a site that is corporate, commercial, educational, or any combination thereof, you should seriously plan out your goals because your responses will determine where and how content is placed within the site, from hierarchy to aesthetic display. For example, if your goal is to provide information about an educational department, you won't be leaving a space in your design for the presence of a shopping cart and checkout button, as you would if you were designing a retail site. Your overall goals will have lasting effects on the design and architecture of your site, and those are not elements that you want to change often—it's best to get it right the first time and make only minor adjustments down the line.

Developing the Overall Site Architecture

Despite its name, you shouldn't actually build anything during the architecture phase. Instead, you should be thinking about the content that will be going into your site and how to organize it in a manner that makes sense to the user. For example, a very flat structure would have numerous sections with very little information in each one, while a tall structure would have only a few sections but a great depth of content. Usually, the "right" place is somewhere in the middle—four to six sections, with a similar number of subsections. Because sections will map to tabs in a Plone site, you can see where this decision is an important one.

Determining the content architecture is usually the most difficult step in the design process for a corporation or information-based institution; retail sites tend to have a ready-made site architecture, in that the sections of their online store tend to mimic the departments of a brick-and-mortar store. You can apply the same idea to a corporation if you're designing an intranet site because the sections could be the internal departments: Legal, Human Resources,

Sales and Marketing, and so forth. But if you're creating an external corporate website, your decisions get a lot more difficult.

For example, you first have to determine whether you're going to allow your users to choose their own path through your content or whether you are going to select it for them. You might have visited websites that ask "What type of user are you?" and then send you into a specific architecture if you answer with Individual User or Enterprise User. Although this does allow the company to subdivide its content and target it for the selected user type, it has its drawbacks: How do you ensure that you've presented the proper content? Is the information you want to present really mutually exclusive—that is, can you be sure that no individual user will ever want to read some bit of content you've chosen to place in the section for enterprise users?

Deciding not to target your content per user type also has its drawbacks because companies tend to create very broad sections for their content, often with ambiguous names. For example, what does the Press section of a corporate website really contain? Is it information *for* the press, or information *by* the press? In the ubiquitous Company section, what really belongs there? Information for investors, one might argue, but wouldn't that warrant its own section full of financial press releases, filings, executive team information, and so forth? Another frequent categorization issue is the debate between Products and Services. How do you present information for products—things you can buy in a box—and services—things you can buy but that don't come in a box? Fundamentally, they're both offerings from a company, usually in exchange for money. But just because you can make a differentiation between the two internally doesn't mean that the end user knows where to look. If your goal is to show the end user the items you offer in exchange for money, you want to make that as easy as possible; you don't want the user to have to determine whether it's a product or a service before selecting a section to visit because if the user selects the wrong one and doesn't see the item he thinks he wants, it's quite possible that he'll miss out on the sale.

Obviously, one could write an entire book on the thought processes that go into creating a site architecture, but the point is this: It's a crucial step and should not be taken lightly. All subsequent design decisions hinge on the architecture decided upon in this step. After the architecture has been mapped out, you can move on to the next step, which is determining the overall navigational presentation.

> **Tip**
>
> For more information on the concepts of site and content architecture, some helpful books include *Information Architecture: Blueprints for the Web*, by Christina Wodtke (Pearson Education, 2002), and *Practical Information Architecture*, by Eric L. Reiss (Pearson Education, 2000).

Determine Your Navigational Elements

Using a Plone site, this step is handled for you: Tabs represent sections, and the Navigation slot can be used to display the individual pages within a section. Because Plone is template driven and fundamentally well designed, you don't have to spend time worrying about your navigational elements being consistent or your users getting lost in your site. Unless you decide to turn off tabs, the Navigation slot, and the breadcrumb trail, your users will always know where they are and how to get to where they're going. Your biggest concern during this phase of the development process is determining how closely you want to stick to the default Plone style. This leads us to the next step, developing the overall look and feel, or theme, of your site.

Developing the Look and Feel

If you've made it this far, you probably have a content architecture in mind, corporate guidelines in hand, and a design team in tow. Now is when the fun begins: You'll select a color scheme and start mocking up graphical representations of pages. It is crucial that everyone on the design team understand the basics of Plone templates, not because you can't completely customize a Plone site (you can), but because some decisions will require far more customization than others.

For instance, suppose that your design team comes to you with a mockup that includes extremely stylized, curvy tabs to delineate your sections. Although you can certainly implement such a feature using partially transparent table cell background images, the design team should understand the trade-off: Any page laden with graphics will take longer to load than a page that is not. Similarly, suppose that the design team wants the top-level heading of all body content to be in some obscure font that users are unlikely to have on their system. Because users are unlikely to have the font, team members have determined that they want to use a graphical title for all content pages. Again, although this can be easily done, the process might outweigh the potential rewards. Instead of all H1 headings being 160 percent of the base font used throughout the site, which requires no additional work from the content administrator, now all H1 headings will be replaced with graphics, which must be created and then added into your Plone site so that you can link to it within the page body. Add to that the additional 3K of page weight, and you really have to ask yourself whether that special font is really worth the hassle.

The development of the look and feel should not be a contentious experience, but it should be a series of compromises that results in a set of web guidelines and assets for use throughout the site. Because one of the primary reasons for using Plone is to maintain content separately from design and to provide a consistent user experience, the last thing you want to do is nullify those positive aspects by selecting a design that simply doesn't work within a structured templatized environment.

Fitting the Pieces Together

After you and your design team have determined the overall look and feel, you can begin the process of customizing the `base_properties` and making any changes to the Plone style sheet that you feel are appropriate. As you've learned in this chapter, making modifications to the `base_properties` goes a long way toward customizing your Plone site because modifications to these properties have cascading effects throughout the style sheet. For example, if you and your design team have settled on a primary font family to use, you can see an immediate change throughout your site just by modifying the `fontFamily` property.

If you find that you need to fundamentally change the definitions of elements in the style sheet, do so via the `ploneCustom.css` file rather than the default `plone.css` master file. Any customizations made in `ploneCustom.css` override like-named items in `plone.css`; if you need to revert back to the original, you can simply remove your entry instead of trying to remember how the entry looked in the master file. If you want to add definitions of your own, you can also do this in the `ploneCustom.css` file; Plone templates look for this file first and then the standard `plone.css` to determine how pages should be rendered.

When you've worked out the basics of properties and styles, you can begin to collect custom assets—graphical headers, icons, and so forth—to replace the files that the standard objects reference. For example, if you change all of your supplemental images to red-tinged graphics to match your logo or corporate colors, you simply have to go into the `plone_images` area of the `portal_skins` section of your Plone instance with the ZMI and create custom versions of the referenced objects. As you learned in Chapter 5, you can attach a file of any name to an object called `arrowBottom.gif` (for example). While `arrowBottom.gif` is the ID used in Plone templates, it could display `myRedArrowBottom.gif`, if that's what you've uploaded as your custom asset. Continue the process for all custom images you want to use, and you will soon see your theme emerging.

The final step in a basic Plone customization is to move around or disable slots and other Plone-specific structures. In the next section, you'll see an example of an actual Plone-powered site that contains numerous customizations but retains enough of its inherent Plone-ness that you can see how and where the derivations occur.

Plone Customization Example

Plone customizations abound; you saw a few of them in Chapter 1, "Introduction to Plone and Content Management." An entire page at the Plone website (http://plone.org/about/sites/) is full of links to such sites. Some site designers have chosen to use the standard Plone template, not even changing the color scheme, while others have replaced almost all traces of standard elements with structures of their own. But the website for the current governor of Texas provides an example of a customization that embraces the fundamental structural and usability aspects of Plone, while applying its own look and feel to the elements. In other words, the design team for the Perry site has skinned the Plone installation.

CHAPTER 6 Creating and Implementing a Custom Skin

> **Tip**
> Figures 6.5 and 6.6 are used to illustrate some skinned portions of the Perry site. To see the full-color site, visit http://www.governor.state.tx.us/.

Figure 6.5 shows the majority of the Perry home page.

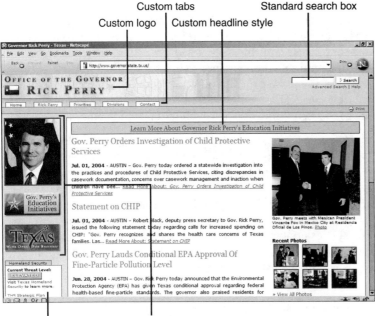

FIGURE 6.5 Main page of Gov. Rick Perry's Plone-based website.

At first glance, this site looks nothing like your out-of-the-box Plone installation because there are significantly more color fields and graphics used. But if you ignore the color and instead look at the structural elements within the template, the similarities become quite visible:

- The logo in the upper left of the page.
- The search box in the upper right of the page.
- The tools strip underneath the logo but above the body of the page. Although it does not include the Log In or Email links, it does include the Print link, and this area is used for the breadcrumb trail on subsequent pages.

- Sections are delineated using tabs.
- The left column contains slots, including the standard Plone calendar.

Even the standard Plone items, such as the slots and tabs, have custom colors. You learned previously in this chapter that the `globalBackgroundColor` property is used to fill tabs; in this case, the value has been set to #CBCFE0.

You can see instances in which other properties have been modified, such as `fontFamily`, `fontColor`, and `linkColor`. Continuing on to a subpage, even more customized Plone items are visible, as shown in Figure 6.6.

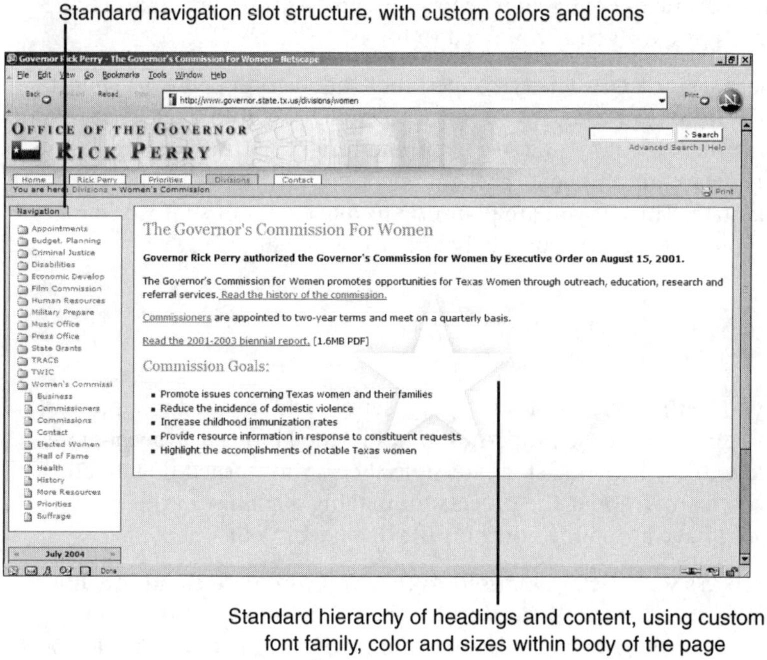

FIGURE 6.6 Subpage within Gov. Rick Perry's Plone-based website.

In Figure 6.6, you can clearly see the Navigation slot. This slot holds the secondary and tertiary navigation; the selected section is Divisions, and the secondary page selected was Women's Commission. In the Navigation slot, this secondary page is shown with all its attached tertiary files beneath it. If the selected secondary page had been Human Resources, its tertiary files would have been shown as links. The items in the Navigation slot are representative of the content hierarchy, as stored within the Plone database. The standard Plone breadcrumb trail is also seen in the color field under the heading. Utilizing this design, users can see where they are and also can access the navigational routes to other information, both above it and below it in the hierarchy.

Although it is common for templatized websites to all look the same, the Perry site and those on display at http://plone.org/about/sites/ show that customization is indeed possible. By studying Plone properties and the style sheets, and by carefully planning the elements of your design, you, too, can create skin for your site that will set it apart from all others.

Troubleshooting

The majority of this chapter is conceptual rather than hands-on, so the opportunities for missteps are fewer than if this were a chapter focused on technical administration. Just remember that anytime you work within the ZMI, you have opportunities to press the wrong button or change the value of a field, giving your entire site pink text, for example. The omnipresent Undo action is there for you if you need to use it.

For modifying base_properties or a custom style sheet, the Undo action will work, but it will roll back the entire file. In other words, if you make 10 changes within base_properties, apply the changes, and then decide that you don't like something, the Undo feature will return you to the previous incarnation of base_properties—with all 10 modified items reverting to their previous state. Thus, if you are planning to make a lot of stylistic changes, you might want to make your changes incrementally rather than all at once.

Summary

This chapter introduced you to the concept of a skin, or a set of styles applied to a piece of software. You then learned about all of the properties found in the Plone base_properties file and how they are used within the Plone standard style sheet. You learned how to add your own property, and you learned about the process for making a change in the base_properties that would have a rippling effect on the display of your site.

Additionally, the design process was briefly discussed so that you can understand the differences between creating a template for a static website and creating individual styles and elements that will fit into the Plone template. A good example of a Plone customization was shown, and you saw where standard Plone elements were customized to fit the goals of the example site.

In the next chapter, you'll learn about some varied topics, all related to working with content inside your Plone site. You'll learn about the underlying Plone templates, content syndication, and even how to create additional content types besides the common ones you've been using all along.

Additional Content-Related Techniques

IN THIS CHAPTER

- Working with Plone Page Templates
- Implementing Content Syndication
- Creating and Using New Content Types
- Troubleshooting

In the previous chapter, you learned all about the fundamental display elements used in a Plone site, and how to prepare for and create a custom display for Plone. In this chapter, you are introduced to a few different concepts related to the content stored in your Plone site: syndicating your content and creating custom content types to store and display data. First, in a continuation of the concepts addressed in the previous chapter, you'll learn a little more about the underlying templates used to piece together a Plone site.

Working with Plone Page Templates

In general, a template is anything that acts as a guide and assists you in completing a repetitive task. A document template might have its styles and general format already present, resulting in an easy path to completion because all you have to do is place your text where the template shows you, such as "Place document title here." When creating a static website, you can use HTML templates consisting of a general shell—the header, navigation elements, and footer might already be there, so your only job would be to type content in the space marked "Body content goes here."

Plone templates are used in much the same way as these other types of templates, but without the static content placement. Instead, Plone templates serve as models for the content that is dynamically generated from the application, but no static content is ever held within them.

Also, Plone templates do not represent the entire page that you see when you visit a Plone site. Individual areas of a Plone site each have their own template. These templates include references to Plone styles, which, in turn, reference the Plone `base_properties`. The elements you learned about in the previous chapter play an integral part in the templates you'll learn about next.

The Zope Template Language

Plone templates are actually Zope templates used within the Plone application. If this book were specifically about Zope and not Plone, the discussion of templates would still be the same. Zope templates use their own Template Attribute Language (TAL), which, as with HTML, DHTML, XML, and any other language you can think of, comes with its own set of tag attributes, called TAL statements. Some common statements are listed here, just as an introduction to the concept:

- **tal:attributes**—This statement calls for a dynamic change in element attributes.
- **tal:define**—This statement defines variables for use within the template.
- **tal:condition**—This statement is used to test a condition before continuing.
- **tal:content**—Use this statement to replace the content of an element.
- **tal:repeat**—Use this statement to repeat an element.

For example, the HTML `<title></title>` tag pair might look like this in a Zope template:

`<title tal:content="here/title">Page Title</title>`

Within the opening tag, you see the use of the `tal:content` statement. This statement is telling Zope (and, thus, Plone) to grab the content from `here/title` and use it for the page title—for example, replace the `Page Title` placeholder text with whatever value is in the `here/title` object. The closing `</title>` tag is provided, and all is right with the world.

These types of statements might seem completely foreign to you, and they should unless you've spent a great deal of time working with Zope. The point here is just to be familiar with the concept of TAL as its own language, which is used within Zope templates, which are used within Plone. The next section specifically shows you where these templates live, what some of these elements mean, and the types of modifications you can make to existing templates. For a complete discussion of TAL, visit Appendix C of the Zope Book, "Zope Page Templates Reference," at `http://zope.org/Documentation/Books/ZopeBook/2_6Edition/AppendixC.stx`.

Working with Existing Templates

To see the standard set of Plone templates, log in to the Zope Management Interface and click on your Plone instance in the navigation pane. Then navigate to the `portal_skins` object and click on it in the Workspace pane, and select the `plone_templates` object. You will see a list of files, as shown in Figure 7.1.

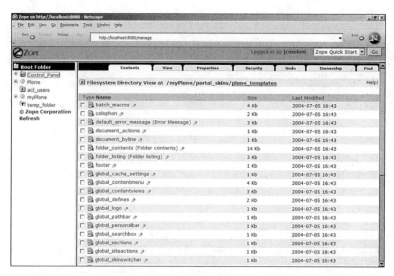

FIGURE 7.1 Contents of the plone_templates directory.

> **Tip**
>
> The `plone_templates` directory is not the only place where templates are found. All of the objects in the `plone_portlets` directory are technically templates that control the various Plone slots. Other directories also might contain templates, placed there by add-ons to your Plone installation.

As you can see by the numerous templates in this listing, almost all aspects of Plone are compartmentalized into their own individual templates. For example, the search box found in the top right of the standard Plone template is controlled by the `global_searchbox` template. The contents of this template are detailed in Listing 7.1.

CHAPTER 7 Additional Content-Related Techniques

LISTING 7.1: Contents of the `global_searchbox` Template

```
 1: <html xmlns="http://www.w3.org/1999/xhtml" xml:lang="en" lang="en"
 2:       i18n:domain="plone">
 3: <body>
 4: <!-- THE SEARCHBOX DEFINITION -->
 5: <div id="portal-searchbox" metal:define-macro="quick_search">
 6:     <form name="searchform"
 7:         action="search"
 8:         tal:attributes="action string:${portal_url}/search" >
 9:         <label for="searchGadget" class="hiddenStructure"
10:             i18n:translate="text_search">Search</label>
11:         <input id="searchGadget"
12:             name="SearchableText"
13:             type="text"
14:             size="20"
15:             value=""
16:             alt="Search"
17:             title="Search"
18:             accesskey="accesskeys-search"
19:             i18n:attributes="alt accesskey title"
20:             tal:attributes="value request/SearchableText|nothing;
21:             tabindex tabindex/next" class="visibility:visible" />
22:         <input class="searchButton"
23:             type="submit"
24:             value="Search"
25:             accesskey="accesskeys-search"
26:             tal:attributes="tabindex tabindex/next"
27:             i18n:attributes="value accesskey" />
28:     </form>
29: </div>
30: </body>
31: </html>
```

Zope templates always look like valid HTML documents, in that they contain the <HTML></HTML> tag pair as well as the <body></body> tag pair. Usually, templates always contain this amount of whitespace, with tag attributes each on separate lines, to make it easy for programmers to find exactly what they're looking for. Zope templates are nothing if not tidy.

In this example, there might not be much that you'd ever want to change regarding the search box. You might want to change the length of the text field, from 20 to 30 or more (line 14). You might want to add text such as "Looking for something?" before the search field (at around line 6), or put the Submit button on a different line (put a few <br/> tags at the end of line 21). All of these things are done within this template, but in your own custom version.

> **Tip**
>
> If you've never seen the <br/> tag, don't be alarmed. It is simply an XHTML-compliant, strict version of the
 (line break) tag.

You can create a custom version by clicking on the Customize button while viewing the read-only version of the template within the ZMI. An editable version is created that you can modify and then save in the Custom folder. The version in the custom folder overrides the standard template when Plone renders any page, but the standard template entry still is available if you want to revert to it. Any time you create a custom template, you can test its appearance by selecting the Test tab within the ZMI. However, for changes to take effect in the live Plone site, you need to restart Zope.

Creating a New Plone Template

Within the ZMI, creating a new Plone template is no different than adding a new image object or DTML document, for example. After you have logged in to the ZMI, select your Plone instance from the navigation pane and select Page Template from the drop-down list of items available to add. Press the Add button. You will see a form with two fields: Id and File. The Id field is required; it provides a name for your new template object. The optional File field can be used to upload content from an existing file on your file system. After you enter a value in the Id field, press the Add and Edit button to create the object. When the form is submitted, the resulting screen will be the editing form, shown in Figure 7.2.

As you can see, a basic template framework was created for you during the addition process. This framework is shown in Listing 7.2.

LISTING 7.2: Template Framework

```
1: <html>
2: <head>
3:     <title tal:content="template/title">The title</title>
4: </head>
5: <body>
6:    <h2><span tal:replace="here/title_or_id">content title or id</span>
7:       <span tal:condition="template/title"
8:             tal:replace="template/title">optional template title</span></h2>
9:
```

CHAPTER 7 Additional Content-Related Techniques

LISTING 7.2: Continued

```
10:     This is Page Template <em tal:content="template/id">template id</em>.
11: </body>
12: </html>
```

FIGURE 7.2 Editing the `testing_template` template.

To get a feel for creating your own template, start by editing the title, the form field at the top of the page that is currently blank. Use something similar to My Template, and then press the Save Changes button. You should see a message that your changes have been saved, and the editable form will still be in front of you.

At lines 3, 6, 8, and 10, you can see TAL statements, which control which text actually is displayed when this template is rendered. In line 3, now that a title has been added, the text `The title` will be replaced with the content that you just entered in the form field called `Title`. In line 6, the text `content title or id` will be replaced with the Plone instance title or id, whichever is present. Note the difference between `template/title` in the TAL attribute in line 3 and the `here/title` value of the TAL attribute in line 6.

Line 7 shows an example of a TAL condition statement. This condition says that if there is a value for `template/title`—and there is because you added one earlier—then replace the text `optional template title` with the actual text (line 8). Line 10 says to replace the text `template id` with the value of `template/id`, which you created when you added the new template. As you can see, HTML markup surrounds the TAL statements; the content title and template title printed in lines 6 and 8 are surrounded by the `<H2></H2>` tag pair. The `template id` printed in line 10 is surrounded by the `<em></em>` tag. Both of these tags are defined in the Plone style sheet, using elements stored in the `base_properties` file.

Save your changes and then click on the Test tab. You will see the contents of your template with the appropriate text replaced by the referenced values. Figure 7.3 shows the new template, with the custom different values called out for easy identification.

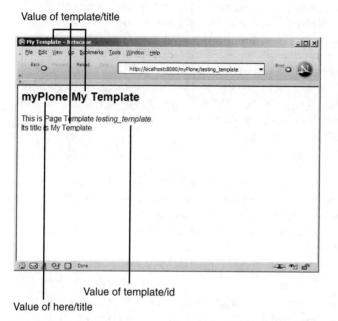

FIGURE 7.3 Viewing `testing_template`.

The goal of this brief example was simply to show how content in Plone is rendered via Plone templates and is not meant as a comprehensive example of all the things you can do with TAL. Two excellent tutorials for working with Zope page templates, written by Zope developer Evan Simpson, are an integral part of the Plone documentation set:

- "Zope Page Templates—Getting Started," at http://plone.org/documentation/zpt1
- "Zope Page Templates—Advanced Usage," at http://plone.org/documentation/zpt2

Depending on the type of website and the level of customization required, a Plone developer might never have to create new templates or even modify existing ones—you might be able to apply your corporate theme through the use of `base_properties` and the Plone style sheet. However, if you want to create your own dynamic slots or other content areas, or if you want to modify any of the existing Plone templates, spending time with the previously mentioned articles is highly recommended. The "Getting Started" article shows you how to use the basic attributes of TAL to display dynamic content. The "Advanced" article involves conditional programming and more advanced TAL syntax.

Implementing Content Syndication

If your Plone site will contain timely news articles or other press-release types of material, you might want to enable readers to syndicate this content. Content syndication typically takes place via RSS, which can be an acronym for "Really Simple Syndication" or "Rich Site Summary"—there's actually a debate, but it's not important to understanding what RSS actually does. In brief, RSS produces a list of title and summary content within a syndicated folder and allows for this information to be transferred through specialized RSS reader software to the end user. In other words, a user can read the syndicated portions of your content without ever viewing your well-designed Plone site. In the next few sections, you'll learn a bit about RSS and how to syndicate the content of your Plone site.

How RSS Works

RSS feeds—the streams of content read by users—are based on XML. Elements of the RSS feed are segmented into content-related definitions such as headlines, descriptions, and the URL leading to the full information. Providing an RSS feed of the content stored in your Plone site does not require you to learn XML—those tricky bits are taken care of via the syndication tools, which you'll learn about shortly. All you'll end up doing as the site administrator is remembering to turn on the correct switches via the ZMI so that users can subscribe to your content and read it at their leisure.

As an end user, one of the greatest advantages of subscribing to RSS feeds is that you can be immediately notified when a site has been updated with new content. You don't have to spend time clicking links and refreshing your browser, and you don't have to subscribe to multiple email lists that end up producing more spam than news. Instead, you simply subscribe to a feed through any of the RSS *aggregators* that are available.

> **Note**
>
> An RSS *aggregator* is a piece of software that reads the RSS feeds and displays their content. These are usually freely available and customizable to check for new content at specific timed intervals. For a list of stable aggregators used on multiple platforms, visit `http://www.mnot.net/rss/tutorial/#Aggregators`.

The benefits to the content owner vary depending on the type of content you offer and the frequency with which you offer it. At first glance, it might seem as if you are giving up site traffic—and any advertising revenue that goes along with it—just so the end user can have a nice, neat little package of news, off-site. In fact, providing a newsfeed will likely drive more traffic to your site because readers will know exactly when your content has been updated and will thus head on over to see any other changes that have occurred.

Say your Plone site represents the web presence for a software company. If the RSS feed serves up the company's press releases, and one of those releases concerns the public availability of a long-awaited piece of software, your site subscribers will be among the first to know. These readers will likely come to the site for additional technical specifications, whitepapers, case studies, and a credit card in hand for ordering your product. Without an RSS feed, you rely on the whims of users to randomly wander by and notice that your product has been released. Users appreciate that they don't have to sell their soul just to subscribe to your RSS feed and will likely be more loyal clients, up-to-date on what your company has to offer.

Syndicating a Plone Folder

Enabling content syndication within a Plone folder is a very simple process, yet it yields great results: the capability to provide an RSS feed for your readers. The first step in enabling any content syndication is to make a modification through the ZMI, enabling syndication for your entire Plone site. This does not mean that a feed will be created for your site; it simply tells Zope to prepare for the possibility.

In the ZMI, click on your Plone instance in the navigation pane and then select the `plone_syndication` object in the workspace pane. You should see a completed form, as in Figure 7.4.

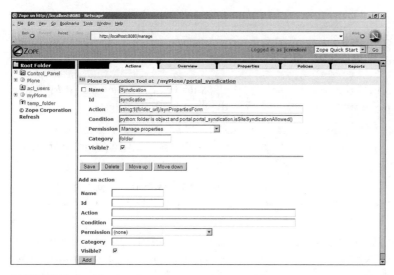

FIGURE 7.4 Viewing the `plone_syndication` object.

Ensure that the check box next to the label `Visible?` is checked, meaning that a Syndication tab will now be visible in the content view of your Plone site, if you are the content owner or have permission to perform actions on the content. If you have to check the check box in this form, press the Save button to save your changes. After these changes have been saved, or after you verify that the check box has been checked, click the Properties tab.

You will now see a large form submission button that reads Enable Syndication. Press this button to enable syndication and automatically move on to the syndication settings form, as shown in Figure 7.5.

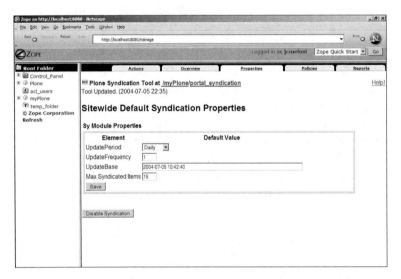

FIGURE 7.5 The site-wide syndication settings form within the ZMI.

Four fields in this form control the basic settings of the RSS feed that will be created for any syndicated area of content within your site. These are the modifiable settings:

- **UpdatePeriod**—This is the time frame over which the RSS feed is updated. You can set this to be hourly, daily, weekly, monthly, or yearly. If it is left blank, daily is assumed. Unless you are running a news-heavy site or a blog, daily updating is sufficient.

- **UpdateFrequency**—This setting controls the number of updates per update period. If `UpdatePeriod` is hourly and `UpdateFrequency` is 4, the feed will be updated four times per hour. The default value is 1.

- **UpdateBase**—This field contains the base date, used in conjunction with `UpdatePeriod` and `UpdateFrequency` to produce a new feed on the correct schedule. The format of this date string is `yyyy-mm-dd hh:mm`, as in `2004-07-05 10:42:40`.

- **Max Syndicated Items**—This field defines the number of items that are included in the feed. The default—and recommended maximum—is 15.

When you have made the appropriate changes, press the Save button to store your settings. Restart Zope to ensure that all your changes have taken effect throughout your Plone site.

Implementing Content Syndication

Making these changes is the last syndication-related modification made through the ZMI; all other modifications are made as a content administrator, within the confines of the Plone site itself. Log in to your Plone site and navigate to a folder in your member area, or any other area in which published content exists.

> **Tip**
>
> If you don't have a folder with content already created, take a moment to create and publish a folder that contains a few fake files, news items, events, or whatever content types you'd like to use for your test feed. Be sure to take the items through the publishing process so that they are published and visible to all users.

In the content view of this folder, you will see that a Syndication tab is now present along with the Contents, View, Sharing, and Properties tabs. Click on the Syndication tab within the folder that you want to syndicate, and you will see a form similar to the one in Figure 7.6.

FIGURE 7.6 The folder-specific syndication settings form within the Plone interface.

The contents of this form look remarkably like the site-wide syndication settings you saved from within the ZMI; the difference is that these settings are only for this particular folder. Feel free to choose the same values for the Update Period, Update Frequency, Update Base, and Maximum Items fields as you did for the site-wide settings, or you can customize this particular folder to update more or less frequently. When you have completed your modifications, press the Save button to deploy your changes.

After it is saved, your RSS feed is accessible via a URL, such as http://yourserver/ yourPlonesite/yourFolder/RSS. For example, I syndicated the books folder within the myPlone instance on the server running on localhost, so the URL to my RSS feed is http://localhost/myPlone/books/RSS. When this is live, you should put a link to your RSS feed in a prominent place—you might even create a custom slot that contains static links to different types of RSS feeds available for your site.

Figure 7.7 shows how the RSS feed is read through a particular RSS aggregator—in this case, the SharpReader software for Windows (see http://www.sharpreader.net).

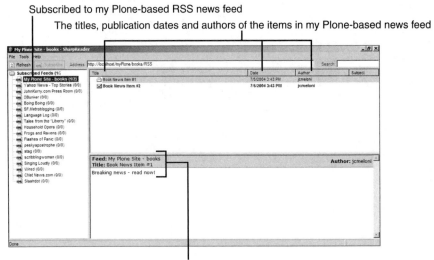

FIGURE 7.7 Viewing an RSS feed within an RSS aggregator.

Although each RSS aggregator looks and acts differently, especially on different platforms, the main idea and outcome are still the same: Readers connect to the RSS URL, which feeds standardized content to the software, which is then displayed to the user. Users can read the item synopses and then connect to the actual site to read the full article, resulting in targeted traffic to your website (that is, people who actually want to be there and who are looking for specific, useful information).

Creating and Using New Content Types

In the final content-related section of this chapter, you'll learn a few tricks to help you repurpose the structure and programmatic elements of existing content types into different types that you can use. For example, you might want to use the news item content type as a base to create a specifically formatted press release item. The subsequent sections outline this process.

> **Note**
>
> The instructions for repurposing an existing content type are expanded from those found in Chapter 8 of the online Plone documentation, at http://plone.org/documentation/book/8. Feel free to consult the official documentation for additional methods of adding new content types and extending Plone.

In this example, the goal is to create a functioning Press Release content type, based on the News Item content type. The only differences between the two will be the name of the content type, the identification icon, descriptive text about the type, and a certain amount of footer text that will be automatically applied to the bottom of each new press release. To get started, log in to the ZMI, select your Plone instance from the navigation pane, and select the `portal_types` object from the workspace pane. From the drop-down menu, select Factory-based Type Information, as shown in Figure 7.8.

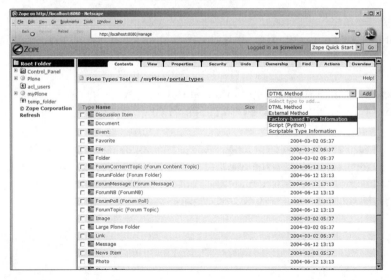

FIGURE 7.8 The list of existing `portal_types`; choosing to add a new type based on an existing one.

Press the Add button to continue; you will see a form containing two fields: Id and Use Default Type Information. Because you are creating a new type for press releases, enter Press Release in the Id field. Because the Press Release type will be based on the existing News Item type, select CMF Default: News Item from the drop-down of existing default types. Press the Add button to create this new type.

> **Tip**
> At this point, the Press Release type will be available in the Add New Item drop-down list within the Plone site itself, although it will act exactly like a news item because customization has not been completed within the ZMI.

The next step is to modify the fundamental information about the Press Release content type; currently, it's just a News Item with a different name. Navigate to the portal_types listing in the ZMI, and select the Press Release object in the workspace pane. You will see the underlying properties of this type within an editable form. In the next section, you'll make the customizations necessary for your new content type to act like a press release.

Customizing the New Content Type

Values are assigned to the fundamental properties of your new content type through the editable form in Figure 7.9. The default values are those for the News Item type because the Press Release type has been copied from it.

These are the properties for a Plone content type:

- **Title**—The optional title for your content type. It already has an Id of Press Release, so there's no need to give it a title of Press Release, but you can do so for the sake of completeness.

- **Description**—The description of the content housed in this content type. The description is shown as part of the addition form within Plone, when a user adds a new item with this content type.

- **Icon**—The object Id, not the filename, of the icon you want to associate with this content type. You can retain the value assignment of newsitem_icon.gif, although, in that case, there would be no way to differentiate the content type of documents within a listing because both News Item and Press Release types would use the same icon.

Creating and Using New Content Types

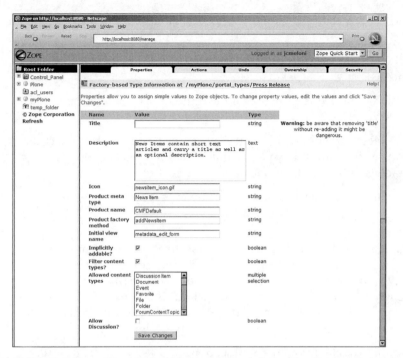

FIGURE 7.9 Editing the factory-based type information for a press release.

> **Tip**
> To use a custom icon such as `pressrelease_icon.gif`, first add an Image object via the ZMI and then associate a new image file with that object. After you have added it to your Plone assets, you can change the value of the `Icon` property for the Press Release content type to your new object.

- **Product Metatype**—The metatype of the content. Use Press Release for this new content type.

- **Product Name**—The Plone product to which the content type is associated. `CMFDefault` is appropriate.

- **Product Factory Method**—The method called by the product to create a piece of content with this new type. Continuing to utilize the `AddNewsItem` method is appropriate in this instance because the Press Release content type was intended to reuse available programming elements.

- **Initial View Name**—Deprecated and currently unused in Plone, but it remains in the form. Do not edit it.

- **Implicitly Addable?**—If checked, this content type can be added within a folder. The default value is checked.

- **Filter Content Types?**—Check this value only if the content type is a folder and, thus, can hold other objects.

- **Allowed Content Types?**—If the Filter Content Types check box is checked, select the allowable content types from this list. None is required for the Press Release type because it is not a folder and, thus, has no folder-related filtering.

- **Allow Discussion?**—If checked, readers can leave comments at the end of an item of this type.

After you have entered and selected the appropriate values for the Press Release properties, the next step in the process is to modify the templates used for this new content type. Because the News Item type has been the basis for the Press Release type since you started this process, you will simply reuse the News Item templates for this portion as well. However, before customizing versions of the News Item templates, you need to know how many different actions—and, thus, how many different templates—you'll be dealing with.

In the ZMI, select the portal_types tool from the workspace pane, select the Press Release object, and click on the Actions tab. The Actions tab provides you with a list of actions specific to the content type and enables you to add your own. Figure 7.10 shows the contents of the Action tab for the Press Release content type, which contains all the information for the News Item content type from which it was copied.

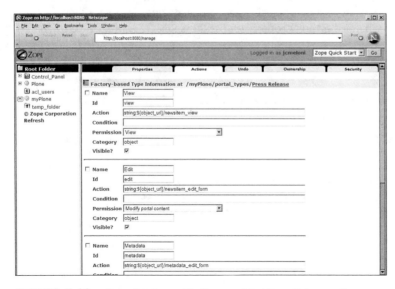

FIGURE 7.10 Preparing to modify the associated Press Release actions.

Creating and Using New Content Types

The first action in the list is the View action, which is the action that controls how the content is displayed when the user accesses a press release to read it. The View action, in this case, currently points to the News Item View action:

string:${object_url}/newsitem_view

Modify this line so that it points to an as-yet-to-be-created Press Release View action, as shown here:

string:${object_url}/pressrelease_view

You'll create this View action template soon enough; for now, continue to modify the entries within this form. The Edit action template controls the content that is displayed when a user wants to add or edit a document of the Press Release type. In this case, too, modify the News-specific action to something appropriate for the Press Release type, such as this:

string:${object_url}/pressrelease_edit_form

Save the changes on this form by pressing the Save button. Next, navigate back to the root of your Plone instance and select the `portal_skins` object from the workspace pane, followed by the `plone_content` object. The `newsitem_view` object referenced in the Actions form is a template within the `plone_content` object. To make a custom copy, click the `newsitem_view` object. You will see a read-only version as well as the Customize button. Press the Customize button to place an editable copy of this template in the `portal_skins/custom` directory. Repeat the process for the `newsitem_edit_form` object as well.

Navigate to the portal_skins/custom directory. You should see the two `newsitem_*` objects you just coped. Select the check boxes next to each of them, and press the Rename button; you want these two items to be named `pressrelease_view` and `pressrelease_edit_form`, respectively. With your objects now properly named, you can begin to edit the template language they contain. Select the `pressrelease_view` object. You should see an editable template containing the code shown in Listing 7.3.

LISTING 7.3: Original Contents of the `pressrelease_view` Template

```
1:  <html xmlns="http://www.w3.org/1999/xhtml" xml:lang="en"
2:     lang="en"
3:     metal:use-macro="here/main_template/macros/master"
4:     i18n:domain="plone">
5:  <body>
6:  <div metal:fill-slot="main">
7:    <tal:main-macro metal:define-macro="main"
8:         tal:define="len_text python:len(here.text)">
```

CHAPTER 7 Additional Content-Related Techniques

LISTING 7.3: Continued

```
9:         <h1 tal:content="here/title_or_id" class="documentFirstHeading">
10:            Title or id
11:        </h1>
12:        <div metal:use-macro="here/document_actions/macros/document_actions">
13:            Document actions (print, sendto etc)
14:        </div>
15:        <div class="documentDescription" tal:content="here/Description">
16:            News summary
17:        </div>
18:          <p tal:condition="python: not len_text and is_editable"
19:           i18n:translate="no_body_text"
20:           class="discreet">
21:            This item does not have any body text, click the edit tab to change it.
22:        </p>
23:          <div class="stx"
24:            tal:condition="len_text"
25:            tal:omit-tag="python:here.text_format != 'structured-text'">
26:          <div tal:replace="structure python:here.CookedBody(stx_level=2)" />
27:        </div>
28:        <div metal:use-macro="here/document_byline/macros/byline">
29:            Get the byline - contains details about author and modification date.
30:        </div>
31:     </tal:main-macro>
32: </div>
33: </body>
34: </html>
```

Lines 9–11 display the Title or Id of the document (whichever is available). Lines 12–14 are used to print the line and action icons (Edit, Send to Friend, Print, Add to Favorites) that appear beneath the title. Lines 18–22 display any body text that has been associated with the document, and lines 28–30 print the author and last-modified details for the document.

Unless you want to dramatically alter the way in which a Press Release type is displayed, relative to a News Item type—and unless you have become intimately familiar with the Zope Template Language—just make a few modifications that will set this template apart from the others. Namely, add a static footer that will display corporate disclaimer information at the end of each press release so that the site administrator does not have to type the content each time a new press release is added.

To add the custom static footer, place the following (or text much like it) after the current line 27 of the code listing:

```
<p><b>About MyCompany</b><br/>
It's very cool, all my trademarks are my own (unless they're not).
All statements may become moot at any time, without warning.</p>
```

Save this custom template by pressing the Save button. Go through the same process for the `pressrelease_edit_form` template, making any changes in descriptive text that you feel are necessary for the Press Release Add/Modify form. When you have completed all of your template-related changes, restart Zope to ensure that these changes take effect. From this point forward, any time you add, edit, or view a document of the Press Release type within your Plone site, these custom templates will drive that display.

Other Methods for Adding Content Types

The Plone developers have already created content types for the most common types of documents used in a website. Using third-party add-on products also tends to add specialized content types, such as photo albums, wikis, and blogs. All of these predefined content types provide a variety to choose from when you want to repurpose a type into a custom type, as you just did in the previous section.

However, if you have a firm grasp on the Python language as well as the overall Zope and Plone architecture, you can create a specialized content type entirely from scratch. This type of modification is now handled by Archetypes, which is an add-on Zope product that aids in the creation of new content types by providing a framework for development. More information on Archetypes, including the Developers Guide and downloadable product files, can be found at `http://plone.org/documentation/archetypes/`.

Troubleshooting

When creating new Zope page templates or modifying existing ones, the ZMI uses a built-in syntax checker that ensures that templates with errors are not published. When you press the button to save template additions or changes, the ZMI displays the error type and location (using line numbers) and does not save the file until those items are fixed. However, the nature of these error messages might require further explanation if you are not well versed in the Zope Template Language. Keep handy Appendixes A and C of *The Zope Book*: "DTML Reference" and "Zope Page Templates Reference," respectively. The URL to the current *Zope Book* is `http://www.zope.org/Documentation/Books/ZopeBook/2_6Edition/`. After your templates have been published, if you decide that you don't like your changes, the Undo tab is only one click away, as always.

Summary

This chapter introduced you to the structure of Zope templates and how they interact with the properties and styles you learned about in the previous chapter. Additionally, you learned the basics of content syndication and how to repurpose existing content types to extend the types available to you in Plone. The next chapter introduces you to some of the administrative basics that will enable you to keep your Plone site up and running. You'll also learn how to configure Plone so that it can be run on top of other web servers, and how to get the most bang for your buck when it comes to site optimization and content caching.

Technical Administration

IN THIS CHAPTER

- Basic Plone Administration
- Backing Up Your Plone Site
- Caching Elements in Plone
- Using Plone with Other Applications
- Troubleshooting

In this chapter, you'll learn some of the basics for keeping your Plone site running smoothly. Additionally, you'll see how to change some of the more technically oriented preferences within Plone, such as indicating on which ports you want Plone to run and how and when to access SMTP servers.

Beyond the very basic sections on technical settings and optimization methods such as content and object caching, this chapter also provides a crash course on running Plone with other web servers, such as Apache and Microsoft IIS. Having Apache or Microsoft serve as the front end for this "new" technology can go a long way toward implementing Plone within your existing corporate infrastructure, if you're being met with resistance.

Basic Plone Administration

When you are logged in to your Plone site as the manager, the Plone Setup screen offers you several basic administrative options related to the day-to-day administration of the site functions and users. A few more of these types of options are found in the Zope Management Interface (ZMI). In this section, you'll learn about some of these basic administrative details.

The Plone Setup Screen

Some items found on the Plone Setup screen were explained in previous chapters of this book. For example, in Chapter 4, "Additional Plone Elements," you followed the Add/Remove Products link on the Plone Setup screen to add some items from the CMF Collective to your Plone installation. Users who are assigned the Manager role will see the link to the Plone Setup screen as part of their standard navigation.

The next few sections describe some of the elements found within the Plone Setup screen and how they can be used to administer your Plone site.

Add/Remove Products

Following the Add/Remove Products link from the Plone Setup screen displays a list of the available Plone add-ons that can be installed or that are already installed. Depending on the information provided by the creator of each package, a link to the package description also might be present. If you unsuccessfully attempted to install an item, a link to the relevant error log entry is present. If an item was successfully installed, a link is present to its installation log.

> **Note**
>
> As you learned in Chapter 4, you can also add and remove products through the Zope Management Interface. Simply log in to your manager account at `http://yourhost:8080/manage` and navigate to your Plone site. When you're there, click on the `portal_quickinstaller` object in the navigation page. The workspace area is populated with the same sort of add/remove product form that you see on the Plone Setup screen. You can check one or more boxes next to items that you want to add or install, en masse.

Error Log

This is not your typical error log, in the sense of a long text file with ambiguous entries. The initial Plone error log screen shows you line items representing the time, the user who caused the exception, and a short description of the exception itself.

Clicking on the exception description provides a wealth of information about the problem:

- **Time**—The date and time that the error occurred.

- **User Name (User ID)**—The user who was logged in and who performed the action that caused the error.

- **Request URL**—The URL that caused the error.

- **Exception Type**—The type of error, such as `AttributeError`. Reporting the error type is crucial to a successful bug report.

- **Exception Value**—A potentially more detailed message regarding the error that occurred. An example would be `global name 'keep_entries' is not defined`. This is also very important for tracking down the potential problem.

- **Traceback**—This includes a link to display the traceback of the error as text. This is the most important entry in the error log because it provides a line-by-line notification of what the system was doing when the exception occurred.

- **Environment Variables**—These variables show the environment in use when the exception occurred, such as the browser type and request method.

- **Instructions for Reporting the Error**—These step-by-step instructions show where, when, and how to report your problem to the proper developers, either Plone developers or the responsible party for a package that has produced an error.

- **Version Information**—This includes the version information for Zope, Plone, CMF, and the browser used when the error occurred.

- **Installed Products**—These include currently installed add-on products.

Any time you view your error log and find exceptions, it's a good idea to review the exception thoroughly, to try to find potential long-term issues with your installation. For instance, if you find that an exception is being caused by a particular module, you might want to track down the offending lines of code and fix this (if you have the Python skills), or offer suggestions to the development team. Similarly, using the information found in the error log to report issues to the Plone development team helps not only you, but all the other Plone users out there.

If an error occurs within a Plone add-on product, the error summarization will instruct you to contact the owner of the add-on product or to report the issue within the bug tracker at the Collective. It's important to discern, by reading your error log carefully, whether the error is due to an add-on product or the internals of Plone. If you submit your bug to the wrong place, it will be rejected,

For example, in the error report, you will see a heading titled "How to Report This Issue." In step 1 under this heading, you must determine whether your error or issue is related to Plone internals, add-on products, or Archetypes. If it is specific to Plone internals, skip to step 2 of the process; otherwise, continue on to determine which link to follow. The link for reporting errors from elements obtained from the Plone Collective takes you to the bug-tracking system specifically for Collective items. These bugs, questions, and other issues can be reviewed and addressed by anyone with appropriate access to that area. Similarly, if your error is regarding Plone Archetypes (an add-on product maintained by the Plone team, but not a standard part of Plone), follow the named link to add your comments to the bug-tracking system for Archetypes-related issues.

In step 2 of the process for reporting Plone-specific issues, two links are generated for you that run a search query against issues that already might be in the bug collector. You should follow as many links as are generated, to ensure that you have performed an exhaustive search. If you receive hits on your query, be sure to thoroughly read any notes, tips, and hits provided for fixing your error. However, if no entries match your issue, move on to step 3 and add your issue.

Adding an issue to the Plone bug collector ensures that someone on the development team will review the problem. When adding an item, you must enter your name, version information, and step-by-step instructions for reproducing the error. Most important, however, is the traceback. This traceback is crucial for showing the reviewers exactly what was happening at the time of the error. The version information and traceback information already are part of your error log and can be easily be copied and pasted into the bug-collection form.

> **Note**
>
> You can also examine your error log through the Zope Management Interface. Simply log in to your manager account at `http://yourhost:8080/manage` and click on the `error_log` object in the root folder. The workspace area is populated with the same list of exceptions that you would see in the Error Log section of the Plone Setup screen.

Mail Settings

You might have set some Plone actions to send email to users, such as when they invoke the password-reminder mechanism, when they want to be notified when forum posts are made, and so forth. In the Mail Settings tool, reached through the Plone Setup screen, you can indicate the name and port for the SMTP server that Plone should use. The default server name is localhost, and the default port is 25, but you can modify these as needed. For example, if you use an external mail server called mail.yourcompany.com, enter that in the `SMTP Server` field of this screen.

> **Note**
>
> You can also modify the value of the SMTP server through the Zope Management Interface. Simply log in to your manager account at `http://yourhost:8080/manage` and navigate to your Plone site. When you are there, click on the `MailHost` object in the navigation page. The workspace area displays the form necessary for entering the SMTP server name and port number.

If your SMTP server requires username and password authentication, you will need to install the ESMTPMailHost add-on, available at `http://zope.org/Members/bowerymarc/ESMTPMailHost`. After downloading, expand the contents of the archive into your Products folder and restart Zope. After Zope restarts, log in to the Zope Management Interface and click on your Plone instance from the navigation frame. Select the `MailHost` object, and you will see the standard

Basic Plone Administration

MailHost properties form, with two additional fields at the end. This form is shown in Figure 8.1.

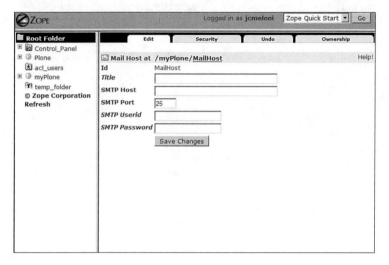

FIGURE 8.1 The MailHost properties form, after installing ESMTPMailHost.

You can now enter the username and password required for SMTP authentication on your server. When the changes have been made, press the Save Changes button.

Portal Settings

The Portal Settings tool, within the Plone Setup screen, enables you to set basic portal-wide settings for your Plone site. These settings range from very simple, such as the name of the site (myPlone), to action-related settings such as how a user's initial password is created. An example of the Portal Settings form is shown in Figure 8.2.

The form elements are fairly straightforward:

- **Portal Title**—A required field whose content is displayed as the title on the main page of the Plone portal, as well as other places.

- **Portal Description**—Optional, but used in syndicated content and other areas, so a brief description of your portal is warranted.

- **Portal From Name**—The name in the From field of all emails generated from your Plone site.

- **Portal From Address, Required**—The email address used in all emails generated from your Plone site.

- **Default Language**—The default language setting for all localized items within the Plone site.

- **Password Policy**—The setting that enables users to choose their own passwords when their accounts are created or if they are automatically generated.

- **Enable External Editor Feature**—Enables users to use an external editor to modify content, if one has been installed.

FIGURE 8.2 The Portal Settings form.

Skins

The creation of new skins and the modification of existing skins were covered in Chapter 6, "Creating and Implementing a Custom Skin." In the Skins area of the Plone Setup screen, the administrator can select the skin used by the Plone site and can also set two other skin-related options. One option gives users the ability to select any skin they want via their Preferences screen within their member folder. The second option has to do with cookie

Basic Plone Administration

persistence regarding skins and whether this should be set to never expire. By default, cookies persist for the length of the user session, but if users chooses to change the length, they may, based on their own personal tastes.

Users and Groups Administration
Following the Users and Groups Administration link from the Plone Setup screen places you in the User Administration area. As an administrator, you can modify the record of any other member in the system. When you first select the Users and Groups Administration link, you will see an alphabetical list of the usernames in the system, along with a search interface for quickly finding a user record. From this screen, you can check the boxes to reset a user's password or remove a user from the system entirely. The initial Users screen is shown in Figure 8.3.

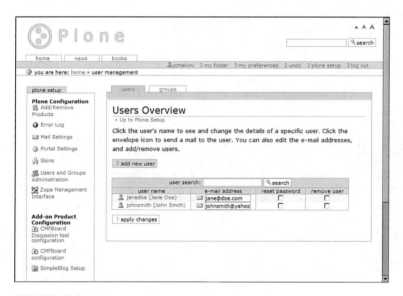

FIGURE 8.3 The User Administration menu.

You also can click on the username link to display the member profile form and make several different changes to the record, including these:

- **Full Name**—Optional. This is the full name of the user, such as Jane Doe.
- **E-Mail**—Required. This is the email address of the user.
- **Content Editor**—This is a drop-down list of available editors for the user. Use it to select the default.
- **Listed in Searches**—Select this box if you want the user to appear as a result in relevant member searches.

CHAPTER 8 Technical Administration

- **Allow Editing of Short Names**—Check this box if members can change the automatic short names that are generated when a new item is added in their member folder.
- **Portrait**—This is an image of the user, displayed in the member record and other areas such as in forum postings. A check box is also available for portrait deletion.

If you select the Groups tab, you will see the management interface for groups, as shown in Figure 8.4.

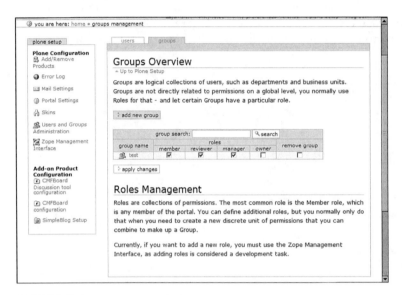

FIGURE 8.4 The Groups Administration menu.

Groups are collections of users; users can belong to one or more groups, or no special group. When you land on this page, you will see a list of current groups (if any exist) along with a button to add a group.

If you add a group, you are asked for a short name, description, and email address. Only the short name is required. After the group is created, you will see the member listing along with member search box. Use this listing to select the members that you want to place in your new group. When you modify the role of the group, all members in that group receive the same role permissions.

Zope Management Interface

Following the link to the Zope Management Interface drops you into the workspace for your Plone site. Many of the items listed previously, such as mail settings, skin settings, list of installed products, and so on, can be seen in this view as well, only in a different format.

Additionally, you can view and modify many other Plone actions, such as the Control Panel tool; you can modify the elements present in the Control Panel tool by checking the appropriate check box and pressing the Delete button.

The Zope Management Interface is explained in more detail in Appendix B, "Introduction to Zope and the ZMI." In the next section, you'll read about how to back up your Plone site before moving on to optimizing your Plone and Zope installations.

> **Note**
>
> Depending on the third party add-ons you have installed and the options they contain, your Plone Setup screen might also show an area beneath the ZMI entry called Add-On Configuration. Any add-ons that have configurable options have links present in this area. These links are explained in part in Chapter 4.

Backing Up Your Plone Site

When dealing with any amount of data, obviously you should back it up regularly. But "regularly" is relative. If your site is going through very little content changes, there's no reason to back it up every night—you could get away with backing it up weekly or even every two weeks. But for any site on which content changes frequently, it's typical to do a backup every night. Midnight is always a good time, unless your site is devoted to night owls and receives the majority of visitors at that time.

In addition to deciding when to back up your site, you need to decide what exactly needs to be backed up. Following are some options:

- **The Zope Object Database (ZODB)**—When performing a backup, this should be the absolute required item in the list. All of your Plone data is stored in the ZODB, in a file called `Data.fs` within the `Data/Var` directory in your Plone installation directory. `Data.fs` is the only file you need to back up; any other files, such as `Data.fs.tmp` or `Data.fs.index`, are variations of the file in different states and will be rebuilt (in the case of the index) or are temporary/swap (in the case of the `.tmp` file).

- **Log files**—Backing up the error logs and access logs is a good idea if you often analyze these logs for reporting purposes, or if you use these logs to monitor the goings-on in your server.

- **Plone files**—If you have made any custom modifications to the source code that runs Plone, be sure to back up these files as well. Otherwise, although you can reinstall Plone and use the backed-up `Data.fs` file, your customizations will be lost.

- **CMF and add-on product files**—Similarly to backing up Plone files, if you made any changes to the internals of the CMF or any of your Plone add-on products, be sure to back these up.

Before backing up the ZODB, you might want to pack it. Depending on your settings, packing the ZODB removes old objects and ensures that you're backing up only what you really need.

To perform packing, log into the Zope Management Interface and select the Control Panel link from the leftmost navigation frame. You should see a list of system administration information (such as uptime) and management functions—links to items such as Database Management and so forth. Clicking the Database Management link produces links to all the databases available, usually main and temporary. Click the main link to display information and available actions for this database, as seen in Figure 8.5.

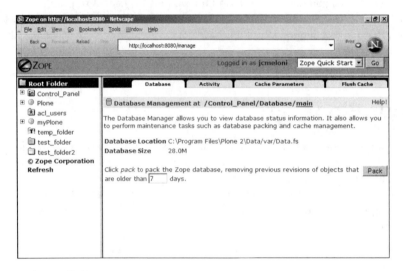

FIGURE 8.5 Database Management control panel.

A 28.0MB Data.fs file was packed to 5.8MB—much more compact than its original size. You can customize the database packing by specifying a minimum age before objects are removed. If you specify that you want only items older than seven days old to be packed, that is what will occur. You still can undo any actions on objects modified within the last seven days, while freeing up whatever space you can.

In the next section, you'll learn about some of the different types of caching that can be done with Plone, to provide faster application response times.

Caching Elements in Plone

You can be proactive in your Plone site administration by monitoring and caching several different elements that make up the site. For example, you can control the number of objects cached in the Zope Object Database, and you can cache the content of pages and slots—items that usually contain dynamic content. The next few sections provide some basic insight into how to cache Plone elements so that your users experience even faster response times than usual.

ZODB Caching

Earlier in this chapter, you used the Zope Management Interface to access the Database Management control panel. You can use this area to monitor the elements within the ZODB and modify any cache settings, as needed. Click on the Activity tab to display a real-time graph of the number of objects stored and loaded in the ZODB. An example is shown in Figure 8.6.

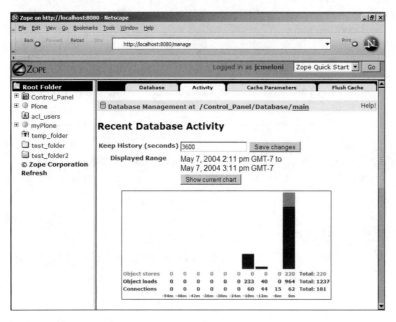

FIGURE 8.6 Zope Object Database activity snapshot.

The statistics in this chart will help you to determine whether changes are needed in your cache parameters. According to Plone developers, you should be concerned if you see 800–1,200 object loads continually over the activity period, and you should then think about modifying your cache parameters to reduce these numbers. Your mileage might vary, of course, because a machine with large amounts of RAM and processing speed can handle more transactions than a server with the minimum recommended configuration.

Cache parameters are managed under the aptly named Cache Parameters tab. Under this tab, you will see a list of current statistics:

- **Total Number of Objects in the Database**—This includes objects stored in memory and on the file system.
- **Total Number of Objects in Memory from All Caches**—This helps you determine the amount of memory currently used by Zope.
- **Target Number of Objects in Memory Per Cache**—This isn't a ceiling; it's a target. When processing a request, the ZODB allows the number of objects to surpass this number, if required, but it immediately reduces the number of objects to the target or below when the request is complete.
- **Total Number of Objects in Each Cache**—This is a heading for a table that displays each current object cache, the number of objects in the memory of that cache, and the number of ghost objects in that cache.

> **Note**
> A ghost object is a very small object that you don't need to worry about because it has a very small footprint.

Next, you'll learn a bit about the HTTP Accelerated Cache Manager and the RAM Cache Manager, both of which are installed in the Root folder of your Zope instance during the Plone 2.0 setup.

Additional Cache Managers

When Plone is installed, two cache managers are installed along with it, in the Root folder of your Zope instance.

> **Tip**
> If you do not see these managers already installed, you can add both via the drop-down menu in the ZMI workspace frame.

These are the default Zope cache managers:

- **HTTP Accelerated Cache Manager**—Adds cache-related headers to objects
- **RAM Cache Manager**—Caches objects in RAM to hasten their retrieval

The HTTP Accelerated Cache Manager

The HTTP Accelerated Cache Manager enables the administrator to modify the cache headers of outbound activity. For example, unless you plan to constantly change the icons used to represent different content types—files, URLs, images, and so forth—you can attach headers to these items so that they will stay cached for a very long time. Similarly, if you have some documents that change but not all that often, you can cache them for a day or even a week. By setting these cache-related headers, you reduce the number of incoming requests to the web server and, in turn, the request of objects from the Zope server.

To use the HTTP Accelerated Cache Manager, follow the HTTP Accelerated Cache Manager link in the Plone instance of the Zope Management Interface. To set the overall HTTP Accelerated Cache Manager settings, go to the Properties tab for this object. You will see the following form fields:

- **Title**—Optional. This is the name of your instance.
- **Interval (Seconds)**—This is the number of seconds for the object to be cached. It defaults to 3600 seconds (1 hour).
- **Cache Anonymous Connections Only**—If this is checked, it caches only requests made anonymously, or by users who are not logged in.
- **Notify URLs (via PURGE)**—You can specify the URLs of caches that should receive PURGE directives, thus clearing their caches at the appropriate times.

The RAM Cache Manager

Unlike the HTTP Accelerated Cache Manager, the RAM Cache Manager performs no tasks related to network traffic. Instead, the RAM Cache Manager stores the results of DTML methods, Python scripts, and SQL queries in memory, for faster retrieval when repeatedly requested.

To use the RAM Cache Manager, follow the RAM Accelerated Cache Manager link in the Root folder of the Zope Management Interface. To set the overall RAM Accelerated Cache Manager settings, go to the Properties tab for this object. You will see the following form fields:

- **Title**—Optional. This is the name of your instance.
- **REQUEST Variables**—These are used as the cache key(s).
- **Threshold Entries**—This defaults to 1000 and represents the maximum number of entries stored in the cache. If the cache is taking up too much memory, reduce this number.
- **Maximum Age of a Cache Entry (Seconds)**—This defaults to 3600 seconds (1 hour).
- **Cleanup Interval (Seconds)**—This defaults to 300 seconds. Reduce this number if the RAM cache causes too much fluctuation in memory usage.

Caching Items in Plone

When you have decided to cache an object, you must decide which cache manager to use. If you are caching a document, an image, or another similar content type, the HTTP Accelerated Cache Manager is for you. Through the Zope Management Interface, navigate to the object that you want to cache and select it. The object should have a Cache tab. Under this tab, use the drop-down menu to select the appropriate response to Cache This Object Using and press the Save Changes button. The item then is cached.

To see a list of items that are regularly requested but are not cached, follow the HTTP Accelerated Cache Manager link in the PloneInstance folder in the ZMI, and then select the Statistic tab. You will see a list of documents, such as /PloneInstance/zope_icon.gif, a static image file. Click on the linked name of this item, select the cache manager to use, and press the Save Changes button. The object then is cached.

Using Plone with Other Applications

Although Zope is a full-featured application server, you might be able to use Plone in an enterprise environment only if it utilizes your company's standard set of applications, such as Microsoft IIS or Apache as a web server, or a different relational database server. In the next sections, you'll learn some methods for integrating these technologies.

Zope Virtual Hosts

If you want Apache or Microsoft IIS to serve your Plone pages, the first thing you need to do is create a virtual host object inside the folder that you want to serve via the alternate web server. Zope virtual hosts are added and controlled through a Virtual Host Monster, which is added through the Zope Management Interface. Despite its name, the Virtual Host Monster (VHM) is not a big scary thing; it simply changes the URLs generated by your Zope/Plone objects.

To install a VHM, log in as the manager to the Zope Management Interface at http://yourdomain:8080/manage and click on the Root Folder link so that the contents of the root folder are in the workspace frame. From the pull-down menu, select Virtual Host Monster and press the Add button.

Enter the ID for the VHM. In this case, I used myPloneVHM. Then press the Add button. The VHM is added to your Zope application server; the remaining configuration occurs within the alternate web server, which you'll learn about in a moment. When the VHM is added in the root folder of your Zope server, you do not need to add other VHMs. If you refresh the contents of the root folder and click on the VHM object you just added, you will see a page full of information regarding the inner workings of the VHM, with the primary point being "one is enough." Next, move on to making the appropriate modifications to either Apache or Microsoft IIS.

Using Plone with Other Applications

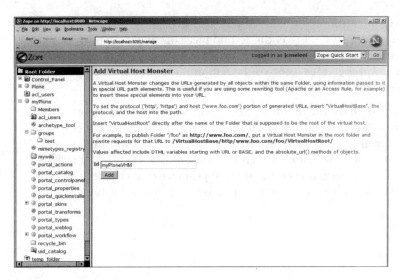

FIGURE 8.7 Adding a Virtual Host Monster.

Running Plone with Apache

This section discusses how to run Plone with Apache as the core web server. This section assumes that you already have a working version of Apache (either version 1.3.x or 2.0.x) configured and happily running on your system; the instructions detail the changes that must occur to Apache, Zope, and Plone.

> **Note**
>
> If you haven't already done so, visit http://httpd.apache.org/ to download Apache. Then follow the instructions included with the Apache distribution to successfully install Apache on your system. Configuration instructions are provided next for both Apache versions 1.3.x and 2.0.x.

If Apache is already your primary web server, it is likely already listening on port 80. However, if you're just getting into the game and are installing Apache after Zope and Plone have been running, you'll need to modify the port on which Plone is running to some unused port such as 81. Zope can still run on port 8080; in fact, you want to keep your Zope configuration just so.

The goal is to have Apache act as a proxy for your Plone site so that you can access http://*yourdomain*/ and have that be your Plone site—none of this http://*yourdomain*/myPlone sort of URL. To achieve this goal, Apache must act as a proxy for Plone, which occurs through the activation of the mod_proxy Apache module, and the Zope application server needs to know that a virtual host is in the mix.

Apache Configuration Modifications

With your Zope Virtual Host Monster in place, the second piece of the puzzle is to configure Apache. Configuring Apache to act as a proxy or to rewrite requests requires the addition of a virtual host directive to the Apache `httpd.conf` configuration file. First, however, you might want to think about one security-related element.

If you are creating a proxy, you have the option of limiting access to it at the server level; this is a good idea if you want to limit access to your Plone site to people within your corporate network, for example. Although your site will retain all of its user account-related security, if you don't want anonymous visitors who are truly anonymous—those who are not even part of your company—you'll want to restrict even the sheer appearance of your site from the outside world. To do so, add the following directive in `httpd.conf`, replacing `191.111.0` with your own netblock:

```
<Proxy *>
Order Deny,Allow
Deny from all
Allow from 191.111.0
</Proxy>
```

> **Note**
> If you are not the system administrator for the Plone server, or if you are unaware of your netblock, ask your system administrator or hosting provider before continuing.

After modifying the `httpd.conf` file, the next step is to create the virtual host directive; the instructions are slightly different, depending on whether you are using Apache version 1.3.*x* or 2.0.*x*.

> **Note**
> If you are using Apache 1.3.*x* and did not install mod_proxy when you originally installed Apache by specifying the `--enable-module=proxy` and `--enable-module=proxy_http` configuration flag on Linux/Unix or uncommenting the appropriate modules in the `httpd.conf` configuration file on Windows, do so before continuing. Similarly, Apache 2.0.*x* users need to have mod_rewrite activated.

In the instructions that follow, substitute the following with your own values:

- **yourdomain**—Use your own domain name, such as company.com or mysite.net.
- **yourPlone**—Use the name of the Plone folder on your Zope server.

Using Plone with Other Applications

For Apache 2.0.x users, the following virtual host directive is appropriate:

```
<VirtualHost *:80>
ServerName     yourdomain
ServerAlias    yourdomain
ServerSignature On

 <IfModule mod_rewrite.c>
   RewriteEngine On
   RewriteRule ^/(.*) \
   http://localhost:8080/VirtualHostBase/http/yourdomain:80/yourPlone/VirtualHostRoot/$1
➥[L,P]
 </IfModule>
</VirtualHost>
```

Apache 1.3.x users should use the following virtual host directive:

```
<VirtualHost *:80>
ServerName     yourdomain
ServerAlias    yourdomain
ServerSignature On

ProxyPass / \
     http://localhost:8080/VirtualHostBase/http/yourdomain:80/yourPlone/VirtualHostRoot/
ProxyPassReverse / \
     http://localhost:8080/VirtualHostBase/http/yourdomain:80/yourPlone/VirtualHostRoot/
</VirtualHost>
```

Although they are written differently and use different modules, both virtual host entries achieve the same goal: to take a request from your domain (port 80) and find the appropriate matching elements on your domain, port 8080—the Zope instance. To see this in action, simply make the configuration changes and restart Apache. When you type the URL to access your Plone site, you no longer have to type http://yourdomain/yourPloneSite; you type only http://yourdomain/.

Running Plone with Microsoft IIS

This section discusses how to run Plone through Microsoft IIS instead of the Zope web server. This section assumes that you already have a working version of Microsoft IIS on your system. The common method for implementing Plone with Microsoft IIS comes in the form of an ASP script found at http://www.zope.org/Members/hiperlogica/ASP404. According to the authors, when it is implemented, this script forwards requests to the Zope server and relies on the Zope Virtual Host Monster to send back the correct URLs.

To get started, download the `ASP404` script from the URL referenced previously, and open the file in a text editor so that you can set some configuration variables. Only a few are necessary, but the authors have written a plethora of instructions in their code so that you have the information necessary to make additional modifications, if you want.

You must enter these primary configuration variables:

- **zopeAddress**—The location of your Zope server, such as `http://yourdomain:8080`. Do not use a trailing slash, and do not use folder names.

- **zopePath**—The folder that you want to serve via Microsoft IIS, such as `/yourPlone`. Again, do not use a trailing slash.

Next, place your modified file in your IIS folder, such as `C:\Inetpub\wwwroot`, and open the Internet Services Manager. From the Internet Services Manager, right-click on the folder that you want to serve from, such as Default Web Site, and then choose the Properties tab. Access the Custom Errors tab and look for the entry for 404. You will modify the properties of how 404 errors are handled, so click Edit Properties and select URL from the Message Type drop-down list. In the URL field, enter **/default.asp**, the name and location of the script you just configured. Repeat the process to assign `/default.asp` to the 405 error, and then restart IIS.

> **Note**
>
> Depending on the configuration of IIS, you might have to modify the order of your default documents if `default.asp` is not the primary default document. To change the precedence, open the Internet Services Manager and click on the folder for the Default Web Site (or a specific site). Then click Properties, followed by the Documents tab. Use the Move Up or Move Down buttons to change the order of existing documents, or use the Add button to create a new default document. Be sure to restart IIS after making changes.

Now when you access `http://yourdomain/`, you should see your Plone site instead of the default main page of the vanilla web server.

Troubleshooting

Most of the items described in this chapter are tool based, such as working with the Database Management tools within the Zope Management Interface. As such, any errors will result in the typical error messages—complete with debugging information—that you've seen throughout the examples in this book.

With regard to modifications to Apache or Microsoft IIS, any errors might be more difficult to track down, depending upon your familiarity with these pieces of software. Both applications have error logs of their own, however, which are useful if you think you have configured a virtual host properly but are not seeing the expected page. If you instead see an error, you can look in the Apache or IIS error logs for extended information. If you are completely stuck, visit the Plone site (`http://www.plone.org`) or Zope site (`http://www.zope.org`) for additional documentation related to integrating other server technologies.

Summary

This chapter provided an overview of the basics of Plone administration and also covered how to integrate Plone with other web server software. As you've seen, some administrable elements are found within the Plone Setup screen and are available to administrators, while others are found strictly in the Zope Management Interface. Many of the tips and tricks for Plone administration are the same as those for running any other sort of server: Keep an eye on system usage and back up your data on a regular basis.

PART

Appendixes

A Using Python for Greater Customization

B Introduction to Zope and the ZMI

Using Python for Greater Customization

IN THIS APPENDIX

▶ Getting Started with Python

▶ More Information

The underlying programming language of the Plone application is Python. Although it is not a language on the tip of the tongues of many programmers, and certainly not the mainstream media, Python is a viable object-oriented programming language. Having been on the scene for almost 15 years now, Python is comparable to Perl, Tcl, and Java in its structure and features.

> **Note**
>
> A common question is "How did Python get its name?" because it's not an acronym such as PHP. Python was named by its creator, Guido van Rosson, in reference to *Monty Python's Flying Circus*.

Because Python is a long-standing and stable language, many companies use it, including Red Hat, Google, and Yahoo!, among many others. As with most object-oriented programming languages—especially those in the open-source family—Python is a popular choice because it is so flexible and can be used to solve many different types of problems. The Plone application sits on top of the Zope application server, and Zope itself is written in Python, so it was only natural to use Python to write Plone and all its accompanying extras.

You, too, can use Python to extend your Plone installation by creating additional products that will plug into the overall framework. Or, because the majority of popular add-ons to Plone are open source, you can use your Python skills to modify core functionality of such elements.

Of course, such tasks are far beyond the scope of this book. This appendix serves only as a basic introduction to working with Python; if you want to learn more, a visit to the Python website (http://www.python.org/) is recommended, as is a good book such as *Python Essential Reference* (Pearson Education, 2001), by David M. Beazley and Guido Van Rossum, or *Python Developer's Handbook* (Pearson Education, 2000), by Andre S. Lessa.

Getting Started with Python

Python scripts are interpreted, meaning that no compilation is necessary. You simply create your script and run it through the interpreter. This interpreter can be used interactively, meaning that you can test snippets of code on the fly before integrating them into your overall script. When writing Python scripts, you can utilize modules—either your own or those written by others—to perform specific tasks such as system calls and socket usage. This is similar to Perl and the Perl module library that programmers cannot live without.

One main feature of Python is its compact and readable scripts. Even though Python is a similarly powerful object-oriented language to C and C++, its scripts tend to be much shorter. The structure of the language enables you to express complex functionality in a single statement rather than multiple statements over numerous lines of code. Also, unlike in C and C++, variable declarations are not necessary. This point alone removes numerous lines of code from the mix.

In the next few sections, you'll learn about the very basics of Python, such as how scripts are structured and how to use the Python interpreter. If you have a proclivity for programming, these sections should whet your appetite enough to study further on your own; eventually you'll be tying it all together and using your Python skills to extend your Plone application.

Working with the Interpreter

The Python interpreter is just called `python` and is usually found in the `/usr/local/bin/` directory on Linux/Unix machines, or in the default installation directory on Windows machines (usually `C:/Python/`), where it is called `python.exe`. Other installation locations are possible, however, depending on your Linux/Unix distribution and your own preferences regarding file placement.

> **Note**
>
> The process of downloading and installing Python is not covered here because Python will have already been installed with your Plone installation. However, if you want to try Python on a different machine, you can find downloading options and installers at http://www.python.org/download/.

Getting Started with Python

To begin the interactive interpreter on Linux/Unix, you simply type the following at the shell prompt:

`# python`

You also can use one of the various tools that are part of the Windows installation, such as IDLE, the Python GUI. This enables you to write and execute snippets of code.

You can also write scripts as separate files, such as `helloworld.py`, and invoke the interpreter using this command on Linux/Unix machines:

`# python helloworld.py`

This interprets the file called `helloworld.py`.

Finally, on Linux/Unix machines your scripts can be made executable just like shell scripts, by beginning the file with the following and granting executable permissions to the file:

`#!/path/to/python`

At that point, you can simply type the name of the file at the shell prompt, and the script will be interpreted.

> **Note**
> The previous concepts described for Linux/Unix systems are applicable to Windows systems as well—substitute the Windows path to `python.exe`.

When working directly within the Python interpreter, two different prompts are used:

- `>>>` is the primary prompt.
- `...` is the secondary prompt.

> **Note**
> The secondary prompt is used to indicate a continuation of a line in your script.

Lines output from the interpreter are not preceded by a prompt.

The last item that you need to know about when working within the interpreter is how comments are used. Comments are preceded by the # character:

APPENDIX A Using Python for Greater Customization

```
>>> # this is a comment
>>> TEST = 1  # this is also a comment
```

The Python interpreter ignores comments, whether they are part of interactive coding or part of a standalone script.

A quick way to get accustomed to using the Python interpreter is to try some mathematical expressions. The mathematical operators in Python are not unlike those of other languages: The + operator performs addition, - performs subtraction, * is used for multiplication, and / is used for division.

For example, type the following at the primary prompt:

```
>>> (142*4-12)/7
```

You will see this result:

79

> **Note**
>
> In integer division, the result is always rounded toward minus infinity.

You can use the = operator to assign values to variables and then use them—for example:

```
>>> x = 15
>>> y = 12
>>> x * y
180
```

Working with Strings

Python can also work with strings such as the following, which assigns a value to a variable called message:

```
>>> message = "I like Python"
```

Strings can be enclosed in single or double quotes, with the applicable escaping of these quotes, if you need to use them within your string:

```
>>> message = 'He\'s a smart guy'
```

or

```
>>> message = "Did you say \"Hi\"?"
```

Typing this:

```
>>> print message
```

results in this:

```
Did you say "Hi"?
```

> **Note**
> There is no functional difference whether you enclose your strings in single or double quotes. When the interpreter prints a result string, it encloses it in double quotes if it contains a single quote, and it encloses it in single quotes if it contains double quotes, so no character escaping is shown in a result. You can also enclose your strings in triple quotes (""")—and if you do that, you get around having to escape single or double quotes that you use within your string.

If you need to enter line breaks in your strings, use the newline character (\n):

```
>>> message = "This is a long line. \nBlah Blah"
>>> print message
This is a long line.
Blah Blah
```

Similarly, use the tab character (\t) to display tabs:

```
>>> sampletext = "test\ttest\ttest"
>>> print sampletext
test    test    test
```

In Python, the concatenation operator (+) is used to put strings together:

```
>>> smushed = "Test" + "String"
>>> print smushed
TestString
```

Strings can also be indexed, meaning that each character in a string has an assigned number, beginning with 0 for the first character. Continuing with the TestString example, the first letter is accessible via this code:

```
>>> smushed[0]
'T'
```

APPENDIX A   Using Python for Greater Customization

You can slice the word into parts, such as starting at the first position and selecting the next three characters:

```
>>> smushed[0:3]
'Tes'
```

You can even start at the end and select the last five characters:

```
>>> smushed[-5:]
'tring'
```

As with the numerical and mathematical examples, these are very brief examples of how Python works with strings, but hopefully you're starting to get the picture. Conceptually, Python is not unlike other programming languages you've likely encountered.

Working with Lists

In Python, a list is akin to something you might have encountered in other languages, called an array. A list is a compound data type used to group values. The syntax of a list is shown here:

```
>>> myList = ['apple', 'orange', 'banana', 'python']
```

As with indexed words, lists are indexed and start at position 0. Thus, this input:

```
>>> print myList[3]
```

will print the following:

```
python
```

The same type of slicing that you saw with strings is also possible with lists. One difference, however, is that you can change an individual element of a list, whereas you cannot change an individual element in a string.

For example, the following does not produce the new string bolt:

```
>>> myString = 'boot'
>>> myString[2] = 'l'
```

In fact, you would get an error:

```
TypeError: object doesn't support item assignment
```

However, you could use this to replace orange with peach in the original list example:

```
>>> myList[1] = 'peach'
```

Getting Started with Python

The new list would be this:

```
>>> print myList
['apple', 'peach', 'banana', 'python']
```

You can do plenty of other things with lists. In fact Python has some handy built-in methods for dealing with them:

- **append**—Adds an item to the end of a list:

    ```
    >>> myList = ['apple', 'orange', 'banana', 'python']
    >>> myList.append('grapes')
    >>> print myList
    ['apple', 'peach', 'banana', 'python', 'grapes']
    ```

- **extend**—Extends the list by appending the items in another given list:

    ```
    >>> myList = ['apple', 'orange', 'banana', 'python']
    >>> myOtherList = ['red', 'blue', 'black']
    >>> myList.extend(myOtherList)
    >>> print myList
    ['apple', 'peach', 'banana', 'python', 'grapes', 'red', 'blue', 'black']
    ```

- **insert(i,x)**—Inserts an item into a list at a given position, where i is the index before which the new item should be inserted and x is the item itself:

    ```
    >>> myOtherList = ['red', 'blue', 'black']
    >>> myOtherList.insert(2,'yellow')
    >>> print myOtherList
    ['red', 'blue', 'yellow', 'black']
    ```

- **remove(x)**—Removes the first instance of x from the list:

    ```
    >>> myOtherList = ['red', 'blue', 'black']
    >>> myOtherList.remove('yellow')
    >>> print myOtherList
    ['red', 'blue', 'black']
    ```

- **pop(i)**—Removes the item at index i from the list:

    ```
    >>> myOtherList = ['red', 'blue', 'black']
    >>> myOtherList.pop(2)
    'black'
    >>> print myOtherList
    ['red', 'blue']
    ```

APPENDIX A Using Python for Greater Customization

- **index(x)**—Provides the index of value x in the list:

    ```
    >>> myOtherList = ['red', 'blue', 'black']
    >>> myOtherList.index('blue')
    1
    ```

- **count(x)**—Provides the number of times that value x appears in a list:

    ```
    >>> myOtherList = ['red', 'blue', 'black']
    >>> myOtherList.count('blue')
    1
    ```

- **sort()**—Sorts the items in a list:

    ```
    >>> myOtherList = ['red', 'blue', 'black']
    >>> myOtherList.sort()
    >>> print myOtherList
    ['blue', 'red']
    ```

    The sort() method sorts in ascending order, by default. However, you can define a custom sort order. The following creates a reverse sort by defining reverse_numeric and then using it within the call to the sort() method:

    ```
    >>> myNumList = [1, 5, 2, 6, 9]
    >>> def reverse_numeric (x,y):
    >>> return y-x
    >>> myNumList.sort(reverse_numeric)
    >>> print myNumList
    [9, 6, 5, 2, 1]
    ```

    Or, you could just use the reverse() function, which sorts items in reverse alphabetical order, as you'll see next.

> **Note**
>
> The reverse_numeric example is one of many sorting examples that appear in the sorting HOWTO at http://www.amk.ca/python/howto/sorting/.

- **reverse()**—Reverses the elements of the list:

    ```
    >>> myOtherList = ['red', 'blue', 'black']
    >>> myOtherList.reverse()
    >>> print myOtherList
    ['black', 'blue', 'red']
    ```

In other programming languages, you might have come across what are known as associative arrays, which are key/value pairs instead of index/value pairs. In Python, these are called dictionaries. In this example, a dictionary called products is created, containing keys that are product names, and values that are product prices:

```
>>> products = {'book': 19.99, 'CD': 12.99, 'water': 1.00}
```

Different methods of accessing dictionary elements include:

```
>>> products.keys() # shows all keys
['water', 'book', 'CD']
>>> products.values() # shows all values
[1.00, 19.99, 12.99]
>>> products['CD'] # will print the value of this key
12.99
```

Wasn't that exciting? Now that you've seen some simple one-liners, the next section provides you with an overview of flow control in Python scripts.

Operator Overview

Before moving on to flow control, this section provides a very brief refresher on standard operators. Operators tell the Python interpreter to "do something" with a variable: assign a value, change a value, compare two more values, and so on. Operators can be categorized as follows:

- **Assignment**—Used to assign values to variables
- **Arithmetic**—Used to perform arithmetic operations on variables
- **Comparison**—Used to compare two values and return either true or false
- **Logical**—Used to determine the status of conditions

You've already used an assignment operator if you've been following along in this appendix: The equals sign (=) is the basic assignment operator. Remember, = does *not* mean "equal to." Instead, == (two equals signs) means "equal to," and the single = means "is assigned to." Additionally, the + operator can be used for concatenation (and assignment) purposes. For example:

```
>>> a = 'hi'
>>> b = ' there'
>>> c = a + b
>>> print c
hi there
```

APPENDIX A   Using Python for Greater Customization

You've also seen some arithmetic operators in the previous examples; these simply perform basic mathematical tasks, as shown in Table A.1

TABLE A.1
Arithmetic Operators

OPERATOR	NAME	EXAMPLE
+	Addition	10+3
-	Subtraction	10-3
/	Division	10/3
*	Multiplication	10*3
%	Modulus	10%3

Next come the comparison operators, which compare two or more values. Table A.2 shows the comparison operators. The result of a comparison is either true or false.

TABLE A.2
Comparison Operators

OPERATOR	NAME	RETURNS TRUE IF...
==	Equivalence	Left is equivalent to right
!=	Non-equivalence	Left is not equivalent to right
>	Greater than	Left is greater than right
>=	Greater than or equal to	Left is greater than or equal to right
<	Less than	Left is less than right
<=	Less than or equal to	Left is less than or equal to right

Finally, the logical operators are used in conditions. These operators—or, not, and and—are often found in flow-control structures, which you'll learn about in the next section.

Basic Flow Control in Python

Again, if you've used other programming languages, you'll recognize the basic flow-control constructs:

- if ... elif ... else statements
- for statements
- while statements

The if ... elif ... else statement begins with just the simple if construct—if something is true, do something else:

Getting Started with Python

```
>>> num = 10
>>> if num == 10:
        print "you got it!"
```

This results in:

you got it!

Suppose that the value of num was 5; the output would be nothing because although the if statement is not true, there is nothing else for the script to do. This is where elif or else comes in:

```
>>> num = 5
>>> if x > 5:
...         print 'too large!'
... elif x < 5:
...         print 'too small!'
... else:
...         print 'just right!'
just right!
```

Next, the for statement iterates over a list of items and performs a specific task. For example, given a list containing four numbers, this for statement prints the number and then the square root of all the numbers:

```
>>> import math
>>> numList = [2, 34, 5354, 1034939]
>>> for x in numList:
        print x, math.sqrt(x)
2 1.41421356237
34 5.83095189485
5354 73.1710325197
1034939 1017.31951716
```

The while loop is also likely familiar to you. This construct continues to loop for as long as the given condition is true. For example, for as long as the value of i is less than 5, the while loop will print the value of i:

```
>>> i = 0
>>> while i < 5:
        print i
>>> i = i + 1

0
1
```

APPENDIX A   Using Python for Greater Customization

2
3
4

When using `for` and `while` loops, additional constructs can control the iteration of these loops: `break` and `continue`. When encountered, the `break` statement breaks out of the current loop. Similarly, the `continue` statement continues with the iteration of the current loop.

Nesting of loops is perfectly fine—just don't get all crazy with them (that's true with any language, not just Python). For example, this example of nested loops displays a few multiplication tables:

```
>>> for multiplier in range(2,6):
    for t in range(1,6):
        print "%d times %d equals %d" % (t, multiplier, t*multiplier)
    print "\n";
```

In English, this script says that, given a multiplier (2,3,4,5) and a base number (1,2,3,4,5), multiply the two together and display the base number (t), the multiplier, and then the result (t*multiplier), followed by a new line.

The result is this:1 times 2 equals 2
2 times 2 equals 4
3 times 2 equals 6
4 times 2 equals 8
5 times 2 equals 10

1 times 3 equals 3
2 times 3 equals 6
3 times 3 equals 9
4 times 3 equals 12
5 times 3 equals 15

1 times 4 equals 4
2 times 4 equals 8
3 times 4 equals 12
4 times 4 equals 16
5 times 4 equals 20

1 times 5 equals 5
2 times 5 equals 10
3 times 5 equals 15
4 times 5 equals 20
5 times 5 equals 25

You can nest any looping condition, but remember to break out of your loop where necessary, or you'll have programmed an infinite loop that does nothing more than suck away all your resources.

File Access with Python

One common programming task—with any language, not just Python—is accessing (creating, reading, writing to) files on your system. In Python, the open() function is used to open a file, and this must be done before any other actions, such as reading and writing, are performed. The function takes two arguments: the full file pathname and the mode. The common modes are listed here:

- **w**—Opens the file for writing. An existing file of the same name is overwritten.
- **a**—Opens the file for appending, starting at the end of the current file.
- **r**—Opens the file for reading.
- **r+**—Opens the file for both reading and writing.

So, if you wanted to open the file myFile in the /home/me/ directory for reading only, the command would be this:

```
>>> f = open('/home/me/myFile', r)
```

Similarly, to open a new file for writing, you would use this:

```
>>> f = open('/home/me/newFile', w)
```

The f used in the previous examples is called the file object. After this is created, you can use one or more of the numerous built-in file-related methods to read data, append data, and do countless other things. For example, if the contents of the file in question are Python is cool, the following outputs this information:

```
>>>   f = open('/home/me/myFile', r+)
>>> f.read()
'Python is cool.'
```

Other file-related methods are listed here:

- **readline()**—Returns a list of all the lines in the file.
- **write(string)**—Writes the content of string to the file.
- **tell()**—Displays the current position within the file object, in bytes. It can be changed using the seek(offset,reference_point) method

▶ **close()**—Used to close the file when you are finished using it, to free up system resources.

These are not the only file-related actions that you can perform; you'll learn more by reading the Python Language Reference at http://www.python.org/doc/.

Defining Your Own Functions and Modules in Python

When you have familiarized yourself with coding in Python, you can begin to create reusable elements such as functions and modules. In Python, a basic function begins with the definition:

```
>>> def myFunction(n):
```

This is followed by the code in the function:

```
>>> i = 0
>>> while i < n:
    print i
i = i + 1
```

Then you call the function:

```
>>> myFunction(7)
```

Finally, you watch the output:

```
0
1
2
3
4
5
6
```

The `return` statement is used within functions to break out of a function and return a value from it. For example:

```
>>> def mult(x,y):
    return x*y
>>> print mult(6,7)
```

Getting Started with Python

These are very simple examples and do not delve into the intricacies of writing functions; it just shows you the structure. At the end of this appendix, you will find links to far more documentation than you ever thought imaginable for a programming language, and you can learn all about the inner workings of user-created functions.

Modules are different from functions. They contain definitions and statements external to the code that you are typing or the script that you are calling, and you import them when you need them. You can write your own modules or use open-source modules written by others. For example, suppose that the myFunction function lives in a module called mine. Before using the myFunction function, you would have to import the mine module:

```
>>> import mine
>>> myFunction(3)
0
1
2
```

You can learn much more about creating functions and modules, in the Python documentation. In the next section, you'll learn a bit about the standard library that comes along with Python; it contains many useful elements that will help you avoid reinventing the wheel, so to speak.

What's in the Standard Library?

The Python standard library contains several modules, each containing numerous functions that enable you to quickly write scripts without duplicating your efforts. With all of the modules listed next, you can use the dir() command to show a list of the functions in the module, and you can use the help() command to show the manual page for that module. For example, the os module provides numerous functions related to the operating system. First, you import the module:

```
>>> import os
```

Next, you can show a list of the module functions, using dir():

```
>>> dir(os)
['F_OK', 'O_APPEND', 'O_BINARY', 'O_CREAT', 'O_EXCL', 'O_NOINHERIT',
 'O_RANDOM', 'O_RDONLY', 'O_RDWR', 'O_SEQUENTIAL', 'O_SHORT_LIVED',
 'O_TEMPORARY', 'O_TEXT', 'O_TRUNC', 'O_WRONLY', 'P_DETACH', 'P_NOWAIT',
 'P_NOWAITO', 'P_OVERLAY', 'P_WAIT', 'R_OK', 'TMP_MAX', 'UserDict', 'W_OK',
 'X_OK', '_Environ', '__all__', '__builtins__', '__doc__', '__file__', '__name__',
 '_copy_reg', '_execvpe', '_exists', '_exit', '_get_exports_list',
 '_make_stat_result', '_make_statvfs_result', '_pickle_stat_result',
```

APPENDIX A Using Python for Greater Customization

- '_pickle_statvfs_result', 'abort', 'access', 'altsep', 'chdir', 'chmod',
- 'close', 'curdir', 'defpath', 'dup', 'dup2', 'environ', 'error', 'execl',
- 'execle', 'execlp', 'execlpe', 'execv', 'execve', 'execvp', 'execvpe',
- 'extsep', 'fdopen', 'fstat', 'fsync', 'getcwd', 'getcwdu', 'getenv',
- 'getpid', 'isatty', 'linesep', 'listdir', 'lseek', 'lstat', 'makedirs',
- 'mkdir', 'name', 'open', 'pardir', 'path', 'pathsep', 'pipe', 'popen',
- 'popen2', 'popen3', 'popen4', 'putenv', 'read', 'remove', 'removedirs',
- 'rename', 'renames', 'rmdir', 'sep', 'spawnl', 'spawnle', 'spawnv',
- 'spawnve', 'startfile', 'stat', 'stat_float_times', 'stat_result',
- 'statvfs_result', 'strerror', 'sys', 'system', 'tempnam', 'times',
- 'tmpfile', 'tmpnam', 'umask', 'unlink', 'unsetenv', 'utime',
- 'waitpid', 'walk', 'write']

For information about the module itself and documentation for all of the functions listed, use help():

```
>>> help(os)
```

The resulting output is quite long, but here is an example of something you will see in the manual page for the os module:

```
getcwd(...)
    getcwd() -> path
    Return a string representing the current working directory.
```

You can test this (results will vary):

```
>>> import os
>>> os.getcwd()
'C:\\Python'
```

Other modules in the standard library include these:

- **datetime**, which contains functions used to manipulate dates and times.
- **glob**, which contains a function for making file lists from directory searches.
- **math**, which contains all mathematics-related functions defined by the C standard.
- **random**, which provides access to a plethora of random variable–generation functions.
- **re**, which provides access to regular expression tools.
- **shutil**, which contains functions for use with file and directory management.
- **smtplib**, which contains functions used to interface with SMTP.

- **sys**, which contains numerous functions used to interact with the interpreter, including stdin, stdout, and stderr for program input and output.

- **urllib2**, which contains functions used to open and read from URLs using multiple protocols.

- **zlib, gzip, bz2, zipifile**, and **tarfile**, each containing functions used for their respective compression format. For example, the gzip module contains functions used to gzip files, while tarfile contains functions used to tar/untar archives.

These are just a few of the modules included in the standard library, but they are the most commonly used. If you have aspirations of modifying the code used to create elements of Plone or Plone-related add-on packages, as you've seen in this book, you'll need to refer to much more of the Python documentation than what is found here. But this appendix should have given you enough of an introduction for you to determine whether it's something you want to try. In the next section, you'll find a partial listing of all the freely available reference information and outlets for help within the world of Python.

More Information

The home of all things Python is the Python website, at http://www.python.org/. One click from the main page is the Documentation area (http://www.python.org/doc/), which contains comprehensive and well-written documents for the new programmer, the advanced user, and just about everyone in between. Some highlights include these:

- The "Beginner's Guide to Python" isn't simply a tutorial document; it's an annotated collection of documents for how to proceed if you are new to the language.

- The "Python Tutorial" is a tutorial; it contains many sections, covering some of the same core material found in this appendix, but to the nth degree.

- "Python for the Nonprogrammer" is another annotated collection of information, such as links to articles on how to think like a programmer, Python 101, and so forth.

- The "Python Library Reference" is a reference work that documents the core components of the Python library. The Python library contains those built-in functions and modules that you saw to some extent with file system functions, for example, but again to the nth degree. What you saw in this appendix is about 5% of what you can do with Python.

- The "Python Reference Manual" is yet another large reference work that differs from the Library Reference, in that this manual discusses the inner workings of the language itself. As it warns, it is not a tutorial.

APPENDIX A Using Python for Greater Customization

▶ You'll also find a collection of HOWTO guides, book reviews, essays by the creator of Python, and so forth.

As with most open-source languages, there's never a lack of documentation available.

If the documentation doesn't answer your burning Python questions, there's always the Community section of the website (http://www.python.org/community/), which contains links to the Python-related mailing lists, IRC channels, user groups, and more.

Introduction to Zope and the ZMI

IN THIS APPENDIX

- Fun with Application Servers
- The Zope Framework
- Zope and Objects
- The Zope Management Interface (ZMI)
- Where to Find More Information

In Chapter 1, "Introduction to Plone and Content Management," you learned that the underlying architecture of Plone is the Zope Application Server. Throughout the rest of the chapters, you saw examples of using the Zope Management Interface (ZMI) to install Plone add-ons, manage security, and perform other administrative tasks. Although Zope itself has been the topic of many books and is a very broad subject to write about, it only seems fair that this appendix cover some of the basics of Zope, its management and optimization, and how to use the ZMI to further enhance your Plone installation.

This appendix sets out to do just that, but in no way should you consider this to be comprehensive or the only resource you should read about these topics. Instead, think of it as an advertisement, or something to whet your appetite for all the comprehensive books, articles, and websites devoted to Zope.

Fun with Application Servers

Ask someone for the 5-second definition of Zope, and you'll get "It's an application server." This is a true statement, but not a very helpful one if you're a manager charged with evaluating products that will become the framework of your company's web presence. If your web presence is small and fairly static, a web application server is likely not what you need—you just need a plain ol' web server such as Apache.

The plain ol' web server performs one task, albeit a very important one: to serve web pages when requested by an end user. The pages are static HTML files, each of which must be manually modified when a content change is required. Think of the classic situation in which you have a few hundred static pages, all of which need their footer changed to reflect a new copyright date or link to a privacy policy. Each of those pages must be modified manually, and that's not a small task. It's more tedious than difficult, but it's still not among my list of favorite things in the world to do.

Suppose that you decide to get fancy and use an interpreted language such as PHP, JSP, or even ASP to dynamically add a footer to each of your HTML files. Now you have a dynamic page and a very basic sort of web application. The only real difference between a website and a web application is that the web application has this sense of dynamism to it. It might be only one line of footer information, or it might be a change in the entire navigation set or color scheme of the template, but dynamic is dynamic. When you have created this sort of dynamic site, the web server that answers requests for pages has now become a web application server. It might be only a simple web server with, for example, the PHP parser built into it, or it might be something like Zope, which provides a developer with an entire application framework, not just a web server with a few add-ons.

The Zope Framework

The core of the Zope application server contains all the bare necessities that are crucial for operations. But in the Zope framework, developers can add utilities to this core set of elements to extend their applications even further. Consider the topic of this book: Plone is a software application that is an add-on to the Zope Application Server, which results in a dynamic, content-oriented environment for the end user.

Using the underlying Zope framework, a developer can do the following:

- Easily manage dynamic content
- Create and maintain sophisticated rules for content creation
- Manage users and their roles
- Integrate existing systems
- Scale, scale, and scale some more

The ultimate goal of using an application server such as Zope, which is both flexible and scalable, is to increase productivity while decreasing costs (and thus increasing profit). To wit:

- Zope is free and distributed under the open source license. It does not cost the tens or hundreds of thousands of dollars that other application servers and frameworks will eat from your budget.

- ▶ The Zope Application Server contains all the components you need to get up and running, such as the web server and the relational database server. If you don't want to use the Zope-brand servers, you can plug your own (Apache, MySQL, and so forth) into the framework. The next section has a list of the core components of Zope.

- ▶ The Zope framework runs on just about any platform: all flavors of Linux, Windows NT/2000/XP, Solaris, the BSD family, and Mac OS X.

- ▶ The Zope community shares its creations. If you want to integrate a blog into your Zope-based site, you can quickly find an add-on that will seamlessly plug into the Zope framework.

- ▶ Zope is built for collaboration. Whether your teams are sitting in cubicles on the same floor or in 10 different countries, Zope can authenticate users against numerous authentication systems. After being authenticated, users can work together without duplicating or overwriting the work of others, using Zope's built-in version-control mechanisms.

The Components of the Zope Framework

Earlier you learned that the Zope Application Server contains all the components to get you up and running. This list shows you just what comes in the package:

- ▶ **Zope Core**—This is the engine behind the whole product.

- ▶ **Zserver**—This underlying web server also serves content via FTP, WebDAV, and XML-RPC. Or, you can use your own, such as Apache or Microsoft IIS.

- ▶ **Object Database**—This stores all the objects you'll use when working with Zope.

- ▶ **ZClasses**—These enable you to create new types of objects for use with Zope.

- ▶ **Products**—These are used to add new types of objects to Zope.

- ▶ **Relational Database**—This is used for the storage of content. You can also use your own, such as MySQL or Oracle.

- ▶ **File System**—The file system of your server is accessible to Zope.

Zope and Objects

In Zope, a web application is built out of objects. These objects perform myriad tasks but are usually one of the following types:

- ▶ Content objects, which hold types of data such as documents, images, and other retrievable files

- Presentation objects, often called templates
- Logic objects, which enable you to perform tasks with your object using a language such as Python

The concept of object orientation is often a difficult one to grasp for the uninitiated, but it's an important concept to understand to fully appreciate the powers of Zope. Everything in Zope is an object: folders, forms that you create, an instance of a file, and so on. Next you'll read perhaps the world's shortest primer on objects.

The Basics About Objects

In a non-object-oriented environment, there are two elements to deal with: data and code. These are two separate entities. Data is any stored content, and code is the procedural bits of programming that allow the data to get to its intended audience. But with Zope, you're dealing with objects and object orientation. As such, you have only one element, an object. The object comes to the table as a bundle of code and data, all nicely packaged together and ready for use.

The following object-related vocabulary will be helpful to you as you learn more about Zope; this is not intended to be a tutorial on object orientation.

- Objects store data and code together, along with logic that makes them perform a task.
- Classes contain the basic instructions for each type of object. For example, all folder objects come from the same class; their attributes make them different from one another. Objects created from a class are called *instances* of a class. For example, the `fancy_folder` object is an instance of the `folder` class, the `graven_image` object is an instance of the `image` class, and the `secret_document` object is an instance of the document class.
- The data stored in an object is defined by its attributes (also known as *properties*). For example, when you create a folder object, the folder has a `name` attribute and a `description` attribute. All of the attributes of an object, taken together, make up its state. When one or more of these attributes is changed, the state of the object is said to have changed.
- The tasks performed by objects are called its methods. For example, if you want to print the name of a folder, you might use a method called `getFolderName`. If you want to change the state of a folder object by changing its name, you might use a method called `setFolderName`. Objects from the same class share the same set of methods.
- Objects talk to one another using messages. Using the example of a folder object again, think of how you would display a list of folders in a directory tree. You might create an object called `FolderList`, whose only purpose is to communicate to all the disparate

folder objects and ask their names—for example, by calling the `getFolderName` method of each of these scattered folder objects.

▶ Objects can inherit behavior from each other. They can also override defined methods of their parent class.

Clear as mud? Thousand-page books have been written solely on object-oriented programming, and whole-semester classes have been taught at universities on this topic. So these simple bullet points are enough to provide you with the basic terminology you need to survive and read more about the subject. Although a full understanding of objects and object-oriented programming is not required to successfully use Zope, it will open your eyes to the ease with which you can extend and scale your Zope application server.

Publishing and Managing Objects

If your web application consists of objects that coexist and talk to one another, it's the responsibility of Zope to publish these objects so that your users can access them. Through simplistic yet powerful design, the hierarchical nature of the Zope object structure provides a template of its own for producing URLs that it can then successfully interpret. A URL such as `http://www.yourserver.com/myPlone/members/jane/` is a request for the folder object called `jane` inside the folder object called `members`, inside the Plone instance known as `myPlone`.

In the world of static web servers, the mapping of elements from a URL also occurs, but only to files on a file system. For example, `http://www.mycompany.com/index.html` asks for the static file `index.html`. The URL `http://www.yourserver.com/myPlone/members/jane/index.html` might look and act the same way to the end user, but `index.html` on the Zope server is actually a document object called `index.html`, not a static file of the same name.

When working in your Plone site, each time you add a new image, document, file, or other content type to your member folder, you add an object into the mix. Outside of Plone, you can add and manage objects through the Zope Management Interface, a truly wonderful web-based tool. In the next section, you'll learn a great deal about the ZMI and how you can use it to completely manage your content outside of the framework of the Plone application.

The Zope Management Interface (ZMI)

When you installed the Plone package, you also created a manager account, used not only for the management of Plone, but also for authenticating yourself as the manager of the Zope application server itself. The Zope Management Interface (ZMI) is the web-based environment that presents itself to you when you access `http://zopeserver:8080/manage`, as shown in Figure B.1.

APPENDIX B Introduction to Zope and the ZMI

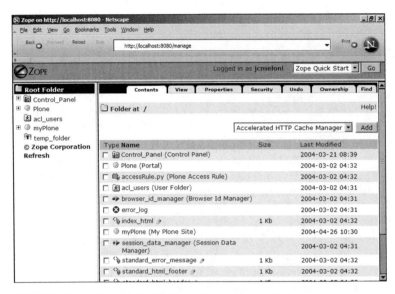

FIGURE B.1 The Root folder Zope Management Interface.

> **Note**
>
> The view in Figure B.1 is of the Root folder of Zope. This is the starting point of the application, so to speak. You will see this view upon logging in or when you click on the Root Folder link in the navigation pane.

What might look to you like a web-based document tree is actually a representation of the Zope object hierarchy. Objects in Zope are stored in the Zope Object Database (ZODB), also known as the really important file called Data.fs that you want to make sure you never delete from your filesystem. The ZMI is a window into the ZODB; folder objects are shown, as are document objects within the folders, objects that are snippets of text or Python scripting, and so forth.

In Zope, everything is an object, and in the ZMI, every object is a manageable element. Selecting a check box next to a folder icon and clicking the Rename button takes you to a form that modifies the attribute of that folder object. It might seem to you that you're simply changing the name of something, and although that's true, you can get fancy and refer to it as modifying an attribute of an object whose state has now changed.

The Zope Management Interface is frame based, which is not the greatest usability feature in a website, but it actually works quite well in this sort of administrative environment. These are the three frames:

- **Navigator frame**, the leftmost frame. It is used to expand and contract the overall object hierarchy.
- **Workspace frame**, the rightmost frame. It is used to display the different views of the object you have selected from the Navigator frame. Any actions that you perform occur in this Workspace frame; this includes adding, removing, and renaming products; performing security tasks; administering the databases and other products; and so forth.
- **Status frame**, the top frame. It simply displays the name of the logged-in user and provides a few quick links, such as Set Preferences or Logout, specific to the user and the ZMI.

The following subsections provide a more detailed look at each frame in the ZMI and show you some basic tasks that greatly improve the quality of life for web application managers who use Zope.

The ZMI Navigator Frame

The leftmost frame in the ZMI is the Navigator frame. This frame shows the object hierarchy of your Zope installation, and all elements are clickable. Figure B.2 shows an example of the elements in a navigation frame.

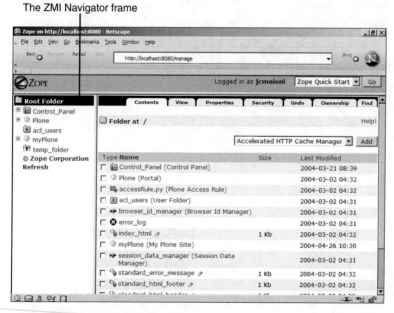

FIGURE B.2 Example of the ZMI Navigator frame.

The Root folder is where all things begin; it's the topmost container element in the Zope object hierarchy and holds all other elements. Clicking the Root folder populates the Workspace frame with the folders and files that live inside it, many of which are part of the Navigator frame already because they are high-level folders. Control Panel, Plone, and myPlone are examples of folders in this figure.

Any time you see a plus mark next to a folder, you can click on it to expand its contents within the Navigator frame. Similarly, a minus mark indicates that the folder is expanded; clicking on that mark contracts it back to its closed state. Expanding a folder does not show its contents in the Workspace frame. Only clicking on an item in the Navigation frame populates the Workspace frame with something meaningful.

The ZMI Workspace Frame

The rightmost frame in the ZMI is the Workspace frame, and all the fun happens in this frame. The Workspace frame shows you all the information about the element you have clicked in the Navigation frame, and it enables you to perform requested actions initiated in either the Navigation frame or the Workspace frame. Figure B.3 shows an example of the elements in the Workspace frame after clicking on the Root folder in the Navigation frame.

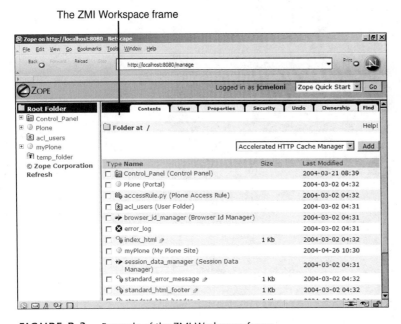

FIGURE B.3 Example of the ZMI Workspace frame.

The Zope Management Interface (ZMI)

In the body of the Workspace frame, you can see the individual objects that are present within the Root folder object. For example, the error_log object is part of the Root folder. Clicking on the error_log object populates the Workspace frame with the configuration options for this object, such as how many exceptions to keep in the log.

Across the top of the Workspace frame are several tabs. Each of these tabs performs a specific task on the object you are viewing. For example, if you clicked on the Root folder in the Navigation frame, the tabs in the Workspace Frame are relevant to the Root folder object. Similarly, after you select the error_log object from the Workspace Frame, the actions following those tabs are relevant to that object.

The Status Frame

The Status frame is quite simple, as shown in Figure B.4.

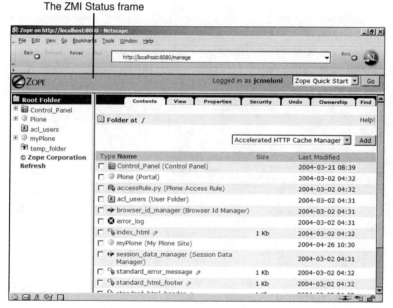

FIGURE B.4 Example of the ZMI Status frame.

Besides displaying the name of the logged-in user, the drop-down menu provides a few useful quick links:

- **Zope Quick Start**—Displays the appropriately named Quick Start page. The Quick Start page has numerous links to the main Zope site, Zope documentation, and much more.

APPENDIX B   Introduction to Zope and the ZMI

- **Set Preferences**—Enables you to modify the frames and some of the other template elements used in the ZMI.
- **Logout**—Logs you out of Zope and the ZMI.

With the third of the three frames out of the way, the next section provides some insight to working with the objects displayed in the ZMI.

Working with Objects in the ZMI

Adding objects to your Zope instance is so easy that it's almost an absolute joy to do. With the ZMI open and the Workspace frame in front of you, look for the drop-down list with the Add button next to it. This is called the Add List, and it's your quick tool for adding almost anything you can think of to your Zope instance. Want to add a folder object, an image object, a Plone object, a blog, or a wiki? You can do it all from this drop-down list.

To test the process of adding an object via the ZMI, click on the Root folder in the Navigation pane; then select Folder from the drop-down list and, in the Workspace pane, press the Add button. This adds a folder within the Root folder. The Workspace pane now contains a form so that you can add information about your new folder object, as shown in Figure B.5.

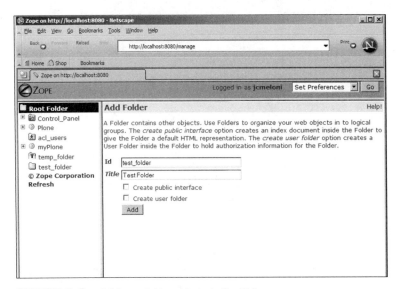

FIGURE B.5   Adding a folder object via the ZMI.

This form shows two attributes that need to be populated with values: Id and Title. In this example, the folder object has an Id attribute value of test_folder and a Title attribute value of Test Folder. After you press the Add button, this object is created and placed in the object hierarchy. You now can navigate to it via the Navigation frame.

Clicking the test_folder object in the Navigation frame populates the Workspace frame with its contents, of which there are none. However, if you select DTML Document from the Add list and press the Add button, the Workspace frame is populated with the form used to add a DTML Document object.

> **Tip**
>
> A DTML Document is an object that can hold HTML, XML, plain text or structured text, and DTML scripting tags. For more information on DTML, read Appendix A, "DTML Reference," of *The Zope Book*: http://zope.org/Documentation/Books/ZopeBook/2_6Edition/AppendixA.stx.

The possible attributes for a DTML object are Id and Title. The File field is present for ease of use, if you want to import data from an existing file. Enter an Id for your DTML object, such as testdoc.html, and a Title, such as Test Title. This is the second form in two examples that required an Id attribute, and for good reason: The Id becomes part of the URL to the item. In this example, I've created a sample DTML Document object inside a folder object, as shown in Figure B.6. The URL to this object is http://zopeserver/test_folder/testdoc.html. Notice the use of the Id attributes for each object.

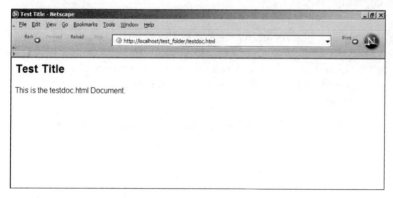

FIGURE B.6 Successfully adding a DTML Document object.

You will notice that although I didn't perform an action in the ZMI related to entering text into this DTML Document object, there is indeed a title and a string of text present in the object. This is part of the standard template for the object. To actually edit the object, expand the test_folder object in the Navigation frame and then click on the testdoc.html object in the Workspace frame. You will see a form with a text area in which you can type the content for this object, in any of the markup types discussed previously.

The process of modifying objects is as easy as the process of adding them. In fact, the format is quite similar, in that you have a form field labeled with the attribute name prepopulated with the existing information. So, if you click on the `test_folder` object in the Navigation frame and then select the Properties tab within the Workspace frame, you see a field called `Title` populated with the string `Test Folder`. The `Id` is not modifiable in this view; you change the `Id` through the Rename action.

The Rename action is available to you in the Workspace frame, such as when you click the `test_folder` object in the Navigation frame and see the list of objects within the Workspace frame. Selecting the check box next to the `testdoc.html` DTML object and then pressing the Rename button displays a form that enables you to change the `Id` attribute of that object.

When viewing objects in a list such as the one described earlier, other important actions are available to you:

- **Cut** places the selected object on the Clipboard for pasting later. The object is not removed from its existing location until it is pasted somewhere else.
- **Copy** places the selected object on the Clipboard for pasting later.
- **Paste** places cut or copied objects into their new locations. The name `copy_of_object-name` is used if you paste an element in the same location as the original item. You can't have two objects with the same `Id` attribute in the same location—in Zope or in any directory structure.
- **Delete** removes objects completely.

You can cut, copy, delete, and rename objects anywhere except the Control Panel, the `browser_id_manager` object, and the `temp_folder` object. Other items in the Root folder can be cut, copied, removed, or renamed, but it's not recommended unless you know what you're doing and have a good reason to make the changes. If you want to play around with Zope, make a bunch of folders and have at it.

The next section covers a very important aspect of content management, the value of the Undo feature.

Undoing Actions

How many times have you yelled "Undo! Undo!" after inadvertently deleting something, as if yelling the command would magically fix the error? With the ZMI, you can Undo any action (even an Undo action) without the yelling, and with success. In Figure B.7, I have accessed the Undo tab within the Workspace frame after selecting the Root folder from the Navigation frame. As such, all of the Undo-able actions listed are Zope-wide.

Tip

Had I selected the Undo tab after selecting just `temp_folder` from the Navigation frame, I would have seen only the actions that were performed on the `temp_folder` object.

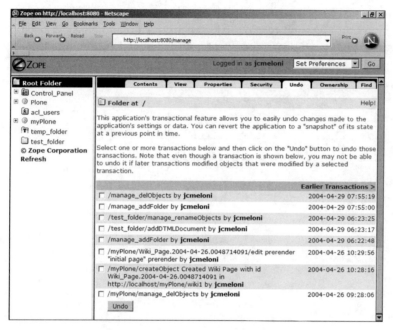

FIGURE B.7 The list of actions that can be undone.

If you select the fourth item in the list:

`/test_folder/addDTMLDocument by jcmeloni`

and press the Undo button, the action is undone. Because this action was to add the DTML Document object called `testdoc.html`, undoing the action removes the document. If you decide that wasn't what you wanted to do, you can also undo the Undo action.

When you perform an Undo action, it is logged just like any other action. As such, it is an entry that is available for selection under the Undo tab. If you select it and press the Undo button, it reverts the object to the state before the Undo occurred. In other words, the DTML Document object called `testdoc.html` reappears.

The Undo action has its limitations: You cannot undo an action when a subsequent action depends on it, and you can go only one step backward at a time when the actions were performed in the same object. In addition, you can select the entire series of actions and press the Undo button, to achieve the same result.

The Undo feature is useful when multiple people are modifying the same content, and perhaps someone has placed content into an object that shouldn't be there. Not only can you undo the action, but you also can use the History feature to see who added the bad content and when.

Object History

The history of an object shows the time and type of actions performed on an object, as well as who performed the actions. Figure B.8 shows the history of the DTML Document object called testdoc.html.

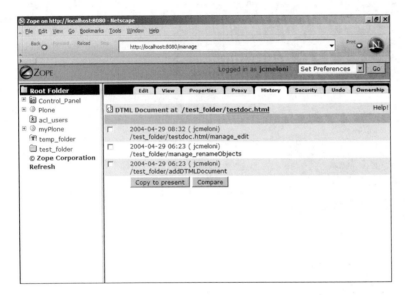

FIGURE B.8   The history of an object.

This history shows that the object was first created, then renamed, and then edited. At this point, you could select any one of the actions and press the Copy to Present button, which essentially reverts the state of the object to the state it was in before the selected action was completed.

If you're not entirely sure of the changes that have been made, or if you simply want to compare two different versions of the object, you can select two revisions and press the Compare button. This action shows a *diff* between the versions (see Figure B.9). You then can decide whether the state should be reverted or whether you simply want to make a few edits to the current version.

> **Note**
>
> A diff shows the difference between two items. New lines are preceded by a plus sign (+), while lines that have been removed are preceded by a minus sign ([nd]). Any changes within a line are noted with an exclamation point (!).

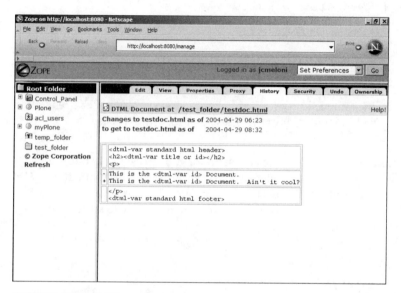

FIGURE B.9 Diff between revisions.

Here ends the quick trip through the Zope Management Interface. The ZMI is by far one of the best management interfaces out there in terms of ease of use and number of tasks performed—not to mention the price (or lack thereof). The final section of this appendix points you in the right direction to find more information about Zope.

Where to Find More Information

The starting point for all things Zope is http://www.zope.org/. This site is not the home of the Zope Corporation (http://www.zope.com/); it's "The Web Site for the Zope Community," so says its tagline. Arguably the most important section of the Zope site is the Documentation section, which is as comprehensive and well written as the application server itself. You can start to see the community aspect come into play: Users can leave comments within the documentation to improve and clarify elements.

These are other very good community-based sites:

- Zope Documentation Project, at `http://zdp.zope.org/`
- ZopeZen, at `http://www.zopezen.org/`
- ZopeLabs, at `http://www.zopelabs.com/`
- ZopeNewbies, at `http://www.zopenewbies.net/`
- ZopeWiki, at `http://zopewiki.org/ZopeWiki`

Invariably, all of these sites have links to their own preferred informational sites, so a little exploring will garner a ton of additional information.

There's also the Zope Magazine, at `http://www.zopemag.com/`, as well as more Zope-related mailing lists than you can shake a stick at, at `http://www.zope.org/Resources/MailingLists`.

If you like your information in book form, there are plenty of good Zope books out there, such as *The Zope Book*, by Amos Latteier and Michael Pellatier (Pearson Education, 2001); *The Zope Bible*, by Michael Bernstein (John Wiley & Sons, 2002); and *The Book of Zope*, by Casey Duncan (ed.) (No Starch Press, 2001). As you can tell by their names, they're rather comprehensive and, no doubt, extremely thick.

Index

Symbols

!= (nonequivalence) operator, 200
% (modulus) operator, 200
* (multiplication) operator, 200
> (greater than) operator, 200
+ (addition) operator, 200
- (subtraction) operator, 200
/ (division) operator, 200
== (equivalence) operator, 200

A

About slot, 16
actions, undoing (ZMI), 220-222
Add/Remove Products link (Setup screen), 170
adding
    objects (ZMI), 218-219
    Web sites via Zope Application Server, 35-37
addition operator (+), 200
administrative options (sites), 169
    backup mechanisms
        add-on product files, 177
        log files, 177
        source code files, 177
        ZMI packing feature, 178
        Zope Object Database (ZODB), 177

caching mechanisms
  HTTP Accelerated Cache Manager, 180-181
  RAM Accelerated Cache Manager, 181
  ZODB, 179-180
Plone Setup screen, 169
  Add/Remove Products link, 170
  error log, 170-172
  group record settings, 175-176
  mail settings, 172-173
  portal settings, 173-174
  skin settings, 174
  user record settings, 175-176
aggregators (RSS), 156
  feeds, reading, 160
Apache
  downloading, 183
  proxy server configuration, 184-185
  running Plone under, 183-185
append method for lists (Python language), 197
applications, CMS integration, 15
Archetypes tool, 167
architecture
  Web sites, design process 142-143
  Zope Application Server
    Content Management Framework (CMF), 6
    Python language, 6
    Zope.org Web site resources, 6
arithmetic operators (Python), 199-200
assignment operators (Python), 199
associative arrays for lists (Python language), 199
asterisk (*) as multiplication operator, 200
attributes of objects (ZMI), 218-219

B

backgroundColor property (skins) 133
backup options (sites), 177
  add-on product files, 177
  log files, 177
  packing feature, 178
  source code files, 177
  Zope Object Database (ZODB), 177
base properties (skins)
  backgroundColor, 133
  borderStyle, 133
  borderStyleAnnotations, 133
  borderWidth, 133
  columnOneWidth, 137
  columnTwoWidth, 137
  contentViewBackgroundColor, 135
  contentViewBorderColor, 135
  contentViewFontColor, 135
  discreetColor, 136
  evenRowBackgroundColor, 135
  fontBaseSize, 132, 140
  fontBaseSize, 140
  fontColor, 132
  fontFamily, 132
  fontSmallSize, 132
  globalBackgroundColor, 134
  globalBorderColor, 134
  globalFontColor, 134
  headingFontBaseSize, 134
  headingFontFamily, 134
  helpBackgroundColor, 136
  inputFontColor, 135
  linkActiveColor, 133
  linkColor, 133
  linkVisitedColor, 133

logoName, 132
notifyBackgroundColor, 136
notifyBorderColor, 136
oddRowBackgroundColor, 135
plone skin, 132
portalMinWidth, 137
textTransform, 135
title, 132

blogs
   CMFWeblog
      entry additions, 94
      entry publishing, 94-95
      folder additions, 93-94
      installing, 91-92
   SimpleBlog, 90-91

The Book of Zope, 224
borderStyle property (skins) 133
borderStyleAnnotations property (skins) 133
borderWidth property (skins) 133
bugs, error log, viewing, 171-172
bulleted lists, structured text, 57
bz2 module, Python standard library, 207

C

C2.com Web site, wiki resources, 99
Cache tab (ZMI), 182
caching options (sites)
   HTTP Accelerated Cache Manager, 180-181
   RAM Accelerated Cache Manager, 181
   ZMI, 182
   ZODB activity snapshots, 179-180
Calendar slot, 17
character sets, international, 124-125

close() function, Python language, 204
CMFBoard
   forum folders
      creating, 77-78
      forumNBs, 78-82
   installing, 75-77
   member preferences, 82
   message boards, creating, 74

CMFCollective, 73-74
CMFForum, 25
CMFMessage
   installing, 83
   instant messaging functions, 82
   messages
      sending, 84-86
      viewing, 84-86
   slots, viewing, 83

CMFPhotoAlbum
   installing, 87
   photo albums
      creating, 87-88
      photo additions, 88-89
      viewing, 89-90

CMFQuick Installer, 25
CMFUserTrackTool
   installing, 83
   logged-in member listings, 82
   slots, viewing, 83

CMFWeblog
   blog entries
      adding, 94
      publishing, 94-95
   blog folders, adding, 93-94
   installing, 91-92

CMFWiki, 25

CMS (content-management system), 5
   applications, integration with, 15
   content and design separation, 13-16
   design versus content areas, 13
   error rollback features, 14
   features overview, 13-16
   HTML markup, 14
   images, customizing, 119-120
   international settings, 120-121
      character sets, 124-125
   localized settings, 120-124
   logos, customizing, 119-120
   metadata, 14
   page templates, 14
   perceived disadvantages, 8
   Plone add-on tools
      CMFBoard, 74-82
      CMFCollective, 73-74
      CMFMessage, 82-86
      CMFPhoto, 87
      CMFPhotoAlbum, 87-90
      CMFUserTrackTool, 82-83
      PlacelessTranslationService, 120-121
      PloneLanguageTool, 121-124
      SimpleBlog, 90-95
      troubleshooting resources, 102
      Zwiki, 96-102
   reasons to use, 13
   site content areas, 48
      advanced searching, 70-72
      discussion feature, 69-70
      documents, 49-54
      events, 49, 61-63
      files, 49, 63-64
      folders, 49
      images, 49, 64-66
      links, 49
      news items, 49, 61-63
      publishing, 66-68
   site examples
      NASA/Jet Propulsion Labs Mars Rover, 8-10
      Southern Utah Online, 11-12
   sites
      searching, 70
      joining, 39-40
      logging in, 41-43
      Member folder (member home pages), 44-46
      member home pages, 43-44
      undo feature, 48
      user preferences, 47
   slots
      About, 16
      Calendar, 17
      custom creation, 112-114
      Events, 17
      Favorites, 17
      location, changing, 103-106
      Login, 17
      Navigation, 19
      News, 19
      Related, 19
      Reviews, 19
      visibility, members only, 109-112
      visibility, modifying, 107-109
   style sheets, 14
   tabs
      adding, 116
      changing, 115-119
      order of, 117-119
      removing, 116

troubleshooting, 20
user access roles, 14
columnOneWidth property (skins), 137
columnTwoWidth property (skins), 137
commercial licensing versus GNU General Public License, 6
comparison operators (Python), 199-200
components (Zope Application Server)
    file system, 211
    object database, 211
    products, 211
    relational database, 211
    Z classes, 211
    Zope Core, 211
    Zserver, 211
content areas (sites)
    add-on development tools
        CMF Collective, 73-74
        CMFBoard, 74-82
        CMFMessage, 82-86
        CMFPhoto, 87
        CMFPhotoAlbum, 87-90
        CMFUserTrackTool, 82-83
        PlacelessTranslationService, 120-121
        PloneLanguageTool, 121-124
        SimpleBlog, 90-95
        troubleshooting resources, 102
        Zwiki, 96-102
    advanced searching, 70-72
    discussion feature, 69-70
    documents, 49
        creating, 49-54
        modifying, 49-54
    events, 49
        adding, 61-63

    files, 49
        adding, 63-64
        editing, 63-64
    folders, 49
    forum folders
        creating, 77-78
        forumNBs, 78-82
    images
        adding, 64-66
        customizing, 119-120
        editing, 64-66
    international settings, 120-121
        character sets, 124-125
    links, 49
    localized settings, 120-124
    logos, customizing, 119-120
    message boards, 75-77
    news items, 49
        adding, 61-63
    publishing, 66-68
    searching, 70
    slots
        custom creation, 112-114
        relocating, 103-106
        visibility of, 107-109
        visibility to members only, 109-112
    tabs
        adding, 116
        changing, 115-119
        order of, 117-119
        removing, 116
Content Management Framework (CMF), 6
content objects (Zope Application Server), 211
content syndication (RSS), 156
    feeds, 156-157
    folders, 157-160

Max Syndicated Items setting, 158
UpdateBase setting, 158
UpdateFrequency setting, 158
UpdatePeriod setting, 158

content teams, separation from design teams, 15-16

content types
adding, 167
Allow Content Types? property, 164
Allow Discussion? property, 164
Archetypes tool, 167
customizing, 162-167
Description property, 162
Filter Content Types? property, 164
Icon property, 162
Implicitly Addable? property, 164
Initial View Name property, 164
Original Contents of the pressrelease_view Template (Listing 7.3), 165-167
Press Release, customizing, 162-167
Product Factory Method property, 163
Product Metatype property, 163
Product Name property, 163
repurposing, 161-162
Title property, 162

content-management system. *See* **CMS**

contentViewBackgroundColor property (skins), 135

contentViewBorderColor property (skins), 135

contentViewFontColor property (skins), 135

count method for lists (Python language), 198

custom skins
creating, 129-131
Governor of Texas Web site example, 145-148
use preparations, 129-131

custom slots, creating, 112-114

customizing new content types, 162-167

D

datetime module, Python standard library, 206
definition lists, structured text, 57
Description property (content types), 162
design teams, separation from content teams, 15-16
designing
sites
architecture, 142-143
display elements, 144
goals of, 142
navigational elements, 144
style sheet customizations, 145
skins, 141-142

development tools
CMFBoard
forum folders, 77-82
installing, 75-77
message board development, 74
CMFCollective, 73-74
CMFMessage
installing, 83
instant messaging functions, 82
messages, viewing, 84-86
slots, viewing, 83
CMFPhoto, installing, 87
CMFPhotoAlbum
album creation, 87-88
album photo additions, 88-89
installing, 87
viewing albums, 89-90
CMFUserTrackTool
installing, 83
logged-in member listings, 82
slots, viewing, 83
PlacelessTranslationService, 120-121

PloneLanguageTool, 121-124
SimpleBlog
    entries, adding, 94
    entries, publishing, 94-95
    features, 90-91
    folders, adding, 93-94
    installing, 91-92
    readme.txt file, 95
    troubleshooting resources, 102
Zwiki, 96-97
    installing, 97-99
    wiki modifications, 99-102
discreetColor property (skins) 136
discussion feature, content areas, enabling, 69-70
division operator (/), 200
documents
    content areas
        advanced searching, 70-72
        creating, 49-54
        discussion feature, 69-70
        event additions, 61-63
        file additions, 63-64
        image additions, 64-66
        modifying, 49-54
        news additions, 61-63
        publishing, 66-68
        searching, 70
    text types
        HTML, 50
        plain, 50
        structured, 50-61
downloading
    Apache, 183
    Plone, 24-25

E

em unit, 137
email, property settings (Setup screen), 172-173
entries in blogs
    adding (CMFWeblog), 94
    publishing (CMFWeblog), 94-95
equivalence operator (==), 200
error log (Setup screen)
    information settings, 170-172
    site backup option, 177
    viewing, 171-172
error rollback features, 14
evenRowBackgroundColor property (skins) 135
events in content area, 49
    adding, 61-63
Events slot, 17
exceptions in error log, viewing, 171-172
extend method for lists (Python language), 197
External Editor 0.6, 25

F

Favorites slot, 17
feeds (RSS)
    content syndication, 156-157
    reading via aggregators, 160
file system component (Zope Application Server), 211
files
    accessing
        close() function (Python), 204
        open() function (Python), 203
        readline() function (Python), 203
        tell() function (Python), 203
        write() function (Python), 203

content area, 49
  adding, 63-64
  editing, 63-64
Filter Content Types? property, 164
flow-control constructs (Python)
  for statement, 200-203
  if, elif, else statement, 200-203
  while statement, 200-203
folders
  blogs, adding (CMFWeblog), 93-94
  content area, 49
  content syndication, 157-160
fontBaseSize property (skins), 132, 140
fontColor property (skins), 132
fontFamily property (skins), 132
fonts, em unit, 137
fontSmallSize property (skins), 132
footnote references, structured text, 60
for statement (Python), 200-203
formatting structured text, 58-59
forum folders
  creating (CMFBoard), 77-78
  forumNBs, 78
    member preferences (CMFBoard), 82
    topic/post additions (CMFBoard), 78-81
forumNBs
  member preferences, 82
  member test forums, 78
  public test forums, 78
  states, 78
  topics/posts, adding, 78-81
forward slash (/), use as division operator, 200
frames (ZMI)
  Navigator, 214-216
  Status, 214-218
  Workspace, 214-217
functions in Python language, 204-205

G

generic users in Plone sites, creating, 39-40
glob module, Python standard library, 206
global roles, 21
globalBackgroundColor property (skins), 134
globalBorderColor property (skins), 134
globalFontColor property (skins), 134
global_searchbox template (Listing 7.1), 151-153
GNU General Public License versus commercial licensing, 6
Governor of Texas Web site, Plone customization example, 145-148
greater than operator (>), 200
groups, record settings (Setup screen), 175-176
gzip module, Python standard library, 207

H

hardware, installation requirements, 23
headingFontBaseSize property (skins), 134
headingFontFamily property (skins), 134
headings, structured text, 56
helpBackgroundColor property (skins), 136
history of objects (ZMI), 222-223
hosting options (sites), Virtual Host Monster (VHM), 182
HTML (Hypertext Markup Language)
  markup knowledge, 14
  specifications, W3C Web site 139
  tags, use in style sheets 139
  text, document types, 50
HTTP Accelerated Cache Manager, site caching options, 180-181
hyphen (-), use as subtraction operator, 200

I - J - K

Icon property, content types, 162
Id attribute for folder objects (ZMI), 218-219
if, elif, else statement (Python), 200-203
images
- changing, 119-120
- content area, 49
  - adding, 64-66
  - editing, 64-66
- skins, 128-129

index method for lists (Python language), 198
inputFontColor property (skins), 135
inserts method for lists (Python language), 197
installing
- CMFBoard, 75-77
- CMFMessage, 83
- CMFUserTrackTool, 83
- CMFWeblog, 91-92
- Linux/Unix platforms, 30-33
- Mac OS X platforms, 28-30
- Plone
  - bundled installers and components, 24-25
  - troubleshooting areas, 37-38
- Plone upgrades, 33-34
- Windows platforms, 25, 28
  - component options, 26-27
  - manager accounts, 27
  - Plone Controller, 27-28

instant messaging (CMFMessage), 83
- sending, 84-86
- viewing, 84-86

integration in enterprise applications, 15

interface
- accessibility standards, 6
- usability of, 6

international character sets, 124-125
international settings for sites, modifying, 120-121, 124-125
Internet Information Server (IIS), running Plone under, 185-186
interpreters, Python language, 192-194
intranets
- educational, 7
- enterprises, 7

joining Plone sites
- generic user creation, 39-40
- user registration forms, 40

L

less than operator (<), 200
licensing, 6
linkActiveColor property (skins), 133
linkColor property (skins), 133
links in content areas, 49
linkVisitedColor property (skins), 133
Linux
- Plone downloads, 25
- Plone installations, 30-33

listings
- Contents of the global_searchbox Template (7.1), 151-153
- Original Contents of the pressrelease_view Template (7.3), 165-167
- The portlet_announce Code (5.1), 112-114
- Template Framework (7.2), 153-155

lists
    bulleted, 57
    definition, 57
    numbered, 57
    Python language
        append method, 197
        associative arrays, 199
        count method, 198
        extend method, 197
        index method, 198
        inserts method, 197
        pop method, 197
        remove method, 197
        reverse method, 198
        slicing, 196
        sort method, 198
        syntax, 196
local roles, 21
localized settings for sites, modifying, 120-124
Localizer, 25
log files, site backup option, 177
logging in Plone sites, 41-43
    Forgot/Lost Password links, 41
    member home pages, 43-44
logic objects (Zope Application Server), 212
logical operators (Python), 199
Login slot, 17
logoName property (skins) 132
logos (CMS), changing, 119-120
look and feel of Web sites, design process, 144

M

Mac OS X, Plone installations, 28-30
mail settings (Setup screen), 172-173

mailto links, 59
managers
    accounts on Windows platforms, creating, 27
    administrative options (Plone Setup screen), 169-176
    roles, 21-22
    site backup options
        add-on product files, 177
        log files, 177
        packing feature, 178
        source code files, 177
        Zope Object Database (ZODB), 177
    site caching options
        HTTP Accelerated Cache Manager, 180-181
        RAM Accelerated Cache Manager, 181
        ZMI, 182
        ZODB activity snapshots, 179-180
    site hosting options, Virtual Host Monster (VHM), 182
math module, Python standard library, 206
math operators, 200
Max Syndicated Items setting, content syndication (RSS), 158
Member folder (member home pages)
    Contents tab, 45
    item management, 44-46
    Properties tab, 46
    Sharing tab, 46
    View tab, 46
member home pages
    Member folder, item management, 44-46
    Plone sites, logging in, 43-44
    undo feature, 48
    user preferences
        content editor, 47
        name, 47

passwords, 46
portraits, 47
member roles, 22
message boards, installing (CMFBoard), 74-77
messages (CMFMessage)
  sending, 84-86
  viewing, 84-86
metadata, 14
Microsoft IIS (Internet Information Server)
  proxy server configuration, 185-186
  running Plone under, 185-186
migrating Plone upgrade versions, 33-34
minus sign (-), subtraction operator, 200
MNOT.net Web site, RSS aggregators, 156
modules (Python)
  functions, standard library, 205-207
  defining, 205
modulus operator (%), 200
multiplication operator (*), 200

N

naming skins, 129
NASA/Jet Propulsion Labs Mars Rover Web site, 8
  account creation, 10
  discussion forums, 10
  login status, 10
  main sections, 8
  navigation sets, 9-10
navigation in Web sites, design process 144
Navigation slot, 19
Navigator frame (ZMI), 214-216
news items in content areas, 49
  adding, 61-63

News slot, 19
nonequivalence operator (!=), 200
notifyBackgroundColor property (skins), 136
notifyBorderColor property (skins), 136
numbered lists, 57

O

object database component (Zope Application Server), 211
objects
  adding (ZMI), 218-219
  folder attributes (ZMI), 218-219
  history (ZMI), 222-223
  modifying (ZMI), 220
  viewing (ZMI), 220
  Zope Application Server
    basic functions of, 212-213
    content type, 211
    hierarchy, 214
    logic type, 212
    managing, 213
    presentation type, 212
    publishing, 213
oddRowBackgroundColor property (skins), 135
open source software versus commercial software, 6
open() function, Python language, 203
operators
  arithmetic operators, 200
  Python
    arithmetic, 199-200
    assignment, 199
    comparison, 199-200
    logical, 199

How can we make this index more useful? Email us at indexes@samspublishing.com

P

packing backup files, 178
page templates, 14
passwords
    forgotten/lost, site logins, 41
    user preferences, setting, 46
percent sign (%), use in modulus operator, 200
photo albums (CMFPhotoAlbum)
    creating, 87-88
    photo additions, 88-89
    viewing, 89-90
Placeless Translation Service, 25
    international/localized site settings, 120-121
plain text document types, 50
platforms, Plone upgrades, migrating, 33-34
Plone
    access requirements, 23-24
    bundled installers and components, 24-25
    downloading, 24-25
    installation
        Linux/Unix platform, 30-33
        Mac OS X platform, 28-30
        Windows platform, 25-28
    installations
        requirements, 23-24
        troubleshooting, 37-38
        wizards, 26
    intranet uses, 7
    template customization, 8
    upgrade versions, installing, 33-34
    version numbers, 25
    Web browser support, 23-24
Plone Controller, use with Windows installations, 27-28

plone skin property (skins), 132
Plone.org Web site
    custom template examples 148
    download site, 24-25
    installation help areas, 38
    online documentation, 161
    slot resources, 16
PloneLanguageTool, localized site settings, 121-124
plus sign (+), use in addition operator, 200
pop method in lists (Python language), 197
portal settings (Setup screen), 173-174
portalMinWidth property (skins), 137
presentation objects (Zope Application Server), 212
Press Release content type
    customizing, 162-167
    Original Contents of the pressrelease_view Template (Listing 7.3), 165-167
products component (Zope Application Server), 211
properties, style sheets, 139-141
proxy servers
    Apache, configuring, 184-185
    Microsoft IIS, configuring, 185-186
publishing
    blog entries (CMFWeblog), 94-95
    content areas, 66-68
    objects (Zope Application Server), 213
***Python Developer's Handbook*, 192**
***Python Essential Reference*, 192**
Python Imaging Library (PIL), 24
Python language, 6, 191
    corporate use, 191-192
    features overview, 191-192

file access
    close() function, 204
    open() function, 203
    readline() function, 203
    tell() function, 203
    write() function, 203
flow control constructs, 200-203
functions, defining, 204-205
lists
    append method, 197
    associative arrays, 199
    count method, 198
    extend method, 197
    index method, 198
    inserts method, 197
    pop method, 197
    remove method, 197
    reverse method, 198
    slicing, 196
    sort method, 198
    syntax, 196
modules, defining, 205
name origins, 191
operators
    arithmetic, 199-200
    assignment, 199
    comparison, 199-200
    logical, 199
reference resources, 192
scripts
    compactness, 192
    interpreters, 192-194
    readability of, 192
standard library, module functions, 205-207
strings
    concatenation operator, 195
    indexing, 195-196
    line breaks, 195
    quotes syntax, 194-195
    tab display, 195
    value assignments, 194
    Zope.org Web site resources, 7
Python.org Web site
    documentation resources, 207-208
    installation help areas, 38

R

RAM (random access memory), Plone requirements, 23
RAM Accelerated Cache Manager, site caching options, 181
random module, Python standard library, 206
readline() function, Python language, 203
Related slot, 19
relational database component (Zope Application Server), 211
relocating slots via ZMI, 103-106
remove method in lists (Python language), 197
ReportLab 1.15, 25
repurposing content types, 161-162
reverse method in lists (Python language), 198
Reviews slot, 19
roles (users)
    global, 21
    local, 21
    manager, 21-22
    member, 22
    workflow, 22-23
        private status, 22
        reject status, 23
        retract status, 23
rollback features, use with errors, 14

root folder (ZMI), 213
RSS (Rich Site Summary/Really Simple Syndication), 156
    content syndication, 156
        feeds, 156-157
        folders, 157-160
        Max Syndicated Items setting, 158
        UpdateBase setting, 158
        UpdateFrequency setting, 158
        UpdatePeriod setting, 158
    feeds, reading via aggregator, 160

S

scripts in Python language
    compactness, 192
    interpreters, 192-194
    readability of, 192
searching content areas, 70
    advanced types, 70-72
selectors in style sheets, 138
Setup screen, 169
    Add/Remove Products link, 170
    error log, information settings, 170-172
    group record settings, 175-176
    mail settings, 172-173
    portal settings, 173-174
    skin settings, 174
    user record settings, 175-176
SharpReader.net Web site, RSS aggregator software, 160
shutil module, Python standard library, 206
SimpleBlog
    entries
        adding, 94
        publishing, 94-95
    features, 90-91
    folders, adding, 93-94
    installing, 91-92
    readme.txt file, 95
sites
    add-on development tools
        CMFBoard, 74-82
        CMFCollective, 73-74
        CMFMessage, 82-86
        CMFPhoto, 87
        CMFPhotoAlbum, 87-90
        CMFUserTrackTool, 82-83
        PlacelessTranslationService, 120-121
        PloneLanguageTool, 121-124
        SimpleBlog, 90-95
        troubleshooting resources, 102
        Zwiki, 96-102
    administration options, Plone Setup screen, 169-176
    backup options
        add-on product files, 177
        log files, 177
        packing feature, 178
        source code files, 177
        Zope Object Database (ZODB), 177
    caching options
        HTTP Accelerated Cache Manager, 180-181
        RAM Accelerated Cache Manager, 181
        ZMI, 182
        ZODB activity snapshots, 179-180
    CMS examples
        NASA/Jet Propulsion Labs Mars Rover, 8-10
        Southern Utah Online, 11-12
    content areas, 48
        advanced searching, 70-72
        custom slot creation, 112-114

discussion feature, 69-70
documents, 49-54
events, 49, 61-63
files, 49, 63-64
folders, 49
forum folders, 77-82
images, 49, 64-66, 119-120
international settings, 120-121, 124-125
links, 49
localized settings, 120-124
logos, customizing, 119-120
message boards, 75-77
news items, 49, 61-63
publishing, 66-68
searching, 70
slot relocation, 103-106
slot visibility, 107-112
tabs, 115-119

hosting options, Virtual Host Monster (VHM), 182

logging in, 41-43
    Forgot/Lost Password link, 41
    member home pages, 43-44

member home pages, 44-46

undo feature, 48

user preferences
    content editor, 47
    name, 47
    passwords, 46
    portraits, 47

skins
base properties, 128-131
    backgroundColor, 133
    borderStyle, 133
    borderStyleAnnotations, 133
    borderWidth, 133
    columnOneWidth, 137
    columnTwoWidth, 137
    contentViewBackgroundColor, 135
    contentViewBorderColor, 135
    contentViewFontColor, 135
    discreetColor, 136
    evenRowBackgroundColor, 135
    fontBaseSize, 132
    fontBaseSize, 140
    fontColor, 132
    fontFamily, 132
    fontSmallSize, 132
    globalBackgroundColor, 134
    globalBorderColor, 134
    globalFontColor, 134
    headingFontBaseSize, 134
    headingFontFamily, 134
    helpBackgroundColor, 136
    inputFontColor, 135
    linkActiveColor, 133
    linkColor, 133
    linkVisitedColor, 133
    logoName, 132
    notifyBackgroundColor, 136
    notifyBorderColor, 136
    oddRowBackgroundColor, 135
    portalMinWidth, 137
    textTransform, 135
    title, 132
creating, 128-129
custom
    creating, 129-131
    Governor of Texas Web site example, 145-148
    use preparations, 129-131
elements, 127-128

images, 128-129
naming, 129
selecting, 127-128
settings (Setup screen), 174
style sheets
    design elements, 138
    element properties, 139-141
    entry structure, 138
    selectors, 138
    syntax, 139-141
    tag values, 139
style sheets, 128-131, 138
Web sites, design process 141-142

slash (/) use in division operator, 200

slots (CMS)
    About, 16
    Calendar, 17
    CMFMessage, viewing, 83
    CMFUserTrackTool, viewing, 83
    custom, creating, 112-114
    Events, 17
    Favorites, 17
    location, changing, 103-106
    Login, 17
    Navigation, 19
    News, 19
    Plone.org Web site resources, 16
    The portlet_announce Code (Listing 5.1), 112-114
    Related, 19
    Reviews, 19
    visibility
        changing, 107-109
        members only, 109-112

smtplib module, Python standard library, 206

software
    open source versus commercial, 6
    skins, 127-128

sort method in lists (Python language), 198

source code files, site backup options, 177

SourceForge.net Web site, CMF Collective, 73

Southern Utah Online Web site
    current events, 11
    home page, 11
    links page, 12
    shopping page, 11-12

standard library (Python), module functions, 205-207

Status frame (ZMI), 214-218

strings in Python language
    concatenation operator, 195
    indexing, 195-196
    line breaks, 195
    quotes syntax, 194-195
    tab display, 195
    value assignments, 194

structured text
    document types, 50-61
    footnote references, 60
    formatting, 58-59
    headings, 55-56
    lists
        bulleted, 57
        definition, 57
        numbered, 57
    mailto links, 59
    paragraph indentations, 55-56
    text levels, 55-56

style sheets, 14
    skins
        design elements, 138
        element properties, 139-141

entry structure, 138
selectors, 138
syntax, 139-141
tag values, 139
skins, 128-131
skins, 138
specifications, W3C Web site, 139
Web sites, design and customization, 145
subtraction operator (-), 200
sys module, Python standard library, 207

T

tabs (CMS)
adding, 116
changing, 115-119
order of, 117-119
removing, 116
tal-attributes statement (TAL), 150
tal-condition statement (TAL), 150
tal-content statement (TAL), 150
tal-define statement (TAL), 150
tal-repeat statement (TAL), 150
tarballs, Linux/Unix installations, unpacking, 31-33
tarfile module, Python standard library, 207
teams (site design), 141
architectural development, 142-143
display elements, 144
goals of, 142
navigational elements, 144
style sheet customizations, 145
tell() function, Python language, 203

Template Attribute Language (TAL)
tal-attributes statement, 150
tal-condition statement, 150
tal-content statement, 150
tal-define statement, 150
tal-repeat statement, 150
Zope.org Web site resources, 150
templates, 149
Contents of the global_searchbox Template (Listing 7.1), 151-153
creating, 153-155
customization of, 8
plone_templates directory, viewing, 151-153
syntax checker (ZMI), 167
Template Attribute Language (TAL)
tal-attributes statement, 150
tal-condition statement, 150
tal-content statement, 150
tal-define statement, 150
tal-repeat statement, 150
Zope.org Web site, 150
textTransform property (skins), 135
Title attribute, folder objects (ZMI), 218-219
title property (skins), 132
topics/posts, adding (forumNBs), 78-81
troubleshooting
add-on development tools, 102
CMS, 20
Plone installations, 37-38
templates, syntax checker (ZMI), 167
via Undo action 148

U - V

undo feature, 48
undoing actions (ZMI), 220-222
   troubleshooting, 148
Unix
   Plone downloads, 25
   Plone installations, 30-33
unpacking tarballs for Linux/Unix installations, 31-33
UpdateBase setting, content syndication (RSS), 158
UpdateFrequency setting, content syndication (RSS), 158
UpdatePeriod setting, content syndication (RSS), 158
upgrading Plone, 33-34
urllib2 module, Python standard library, 207
user registration forms on Plone sites, 40
user roles
   global, 21
   local, 21
   manager, 21-22
   member, 22
   workflow, 22-23
      private status, 22
      reject status, 23
      retract status, 23
users
   access roles, 14
   Plone sites, logging in, 41-43
   record settings (Setup screen), 175-176

viewing
   objects (ZMI), 220
   site templates in plone_templates directory, 151-153
Virtual Host Monster (VHM), installing, 182

visibility of slots
   changing, 107-109
   members only, 109-112

W

W3C (World Wide Web Consortium) Web site
   HTML specifications 139
   style sheet specifications 139
web browsers, Plone support, 23-24
web servers
   Apache, running Plone under, 183-185
   Microsoft IIS, running Plone under, 185-186
web sites
   adding to Zope Application Server, 35-37
   C2.com, 99
   CMS (content-management system)
      About slot, 16
      application integration, 15
      Calendar slot, 17
      content and design separation, 15-16
      design versus content areas, 13
      error rollback features, 14
      Events slot, 17
      Favorites slot, 17
      features overview, 13-16
      HTML markup, 14
      images, customizing, 119-120
      international settings, 120-121, 124-125
      localized settings, 120-124
      Login slot, 17
      logos, customizing, 119-120
      metadata, 14
      Navigation slot, 19
      News slot, 19

page templates, 14
reasons to use, 13
Related slot, 19
Reviews slot, 19
slots, changing location of, 103, 105-106
slots, custom creation, 112-114
slots, visibility of, 107-112
style sheets, 14
tabs, adding, 116
tabs, changing, 115-119
tabs, removing, 116
troubleshooting, 20
user access roles, 14

content syndication (RSS), 156
feeds, 156-157
folders, 157-160
Max Syndicated Items setting, 158
UpdateBase setting, 158
UpdateFrequency setting, 158
UpdatePeriod setting, 158

content types
adding, 167
customizing, 162-167
repurposing, 161-162

design teams
architecture development, 142-143
display elements, 144
goals, defining, 142
navigational elements, 144
style sheet customizations, 145

Governor of Texas, Plone customization example, 145-148

Plone.org
custom template examples, 148
download site, 24-25
online documentation, 161
slot resources, 16

Python.org, documentation resources, 207-208
SharpReader.net, RSS aggregator software, 160
skins
creating, 128-129
design process, 141-142
selecting, 127-128
SourceForge.net, CMF Collective, 73
templates, 149
creating, 153-155
plone_templates directory, 151-153
Template Attribute Language (TAL), 150
Template Framework (Listing 7.2), 153-155
W3C
HTML specifications, 139
style sheet specifications, 139
Zope Documentation Project, 224
Zope Magazine, 224
Zope.com, 223
Zope.org, 223
architectural concepts, 6
Python concepts, 7
troubleshooting resources, 20
Zope Template Language resources, 167
ZopeLabs, 224
ZopeNewbies, 224
ZopeWiki, 224
ZopeZen, 224
Zwiki.org, 102

while statement (Python), 200-203
wikis
C2.com Web site, 99
editing (Zwiki), 99-102
function of, 96-97
structure of, 99
Zwiki, installing, 97-99

Windows 2000, Plone installations, 25-28
Windows NT, Plone installations, 25-28
Windows XP, Plone installations, 25-28
workflow roles, 22-23
    private status, 22
    reject status, 23
    retract status, 23
Workspace frame (ZMI), 214-217
write() function, Python language, 203

Z

Z classes component (Zope Application Server), 211
zipifile module, Python standard library, 207
zlib module, Python standard library, 207
ZMI (Zope Management Interface), 103
    accessing, 213
    actions, undoing, 220-222
    administrative options, Setup screen, 169-176
    backup options, packing feature, 178
    Cache tab, 182
    custom skins, creating, 129-131
    frame
        Navigator, 214-216
        Status, 214-218
        Workspace, 214-217
    objects
        adding, 218-219
        folder attributes, 218-219
        history, 222-223
        modifying, 220
        viewing, 220
    root folder, 213

slots
    custom creation, 112-114
    relocating, 103-106
    visibility, members only, 109-112
    visibility, modifying, 107-109
templates, syntax checker, 167
Zope
    resource sites
        Zope Documentation Project, 224
        Zope.com, 223
        Zope.org, 223
        ZopeLabs, 224
        ZopeNewbies, 224
        ZopeWiki, 224
        ZopeZen, 224
    templates, Template Attribute Language (TAL), 150
Zope Application Server, 209-210
    access requirements, 23
    components
        file system, 211
        object database, 211
        products, 211
        relational database, 211
        Z classes, 211
        Zope Core, 211
        Zserver, 211
    Content Management Framework (CMF), 6
    content objects, 211
    features, 210-211
    framework features, 210
    goals of, 210-211
    installation requirements, 23
    logic objects, 212

objects

    basic functions of, 212-213

    managing, 213

    publishing, 213

presentation objects, 212

Python language, 6

sites, adding to, 35-37

Zope Object Database (ZODB), 7

The Zope Bible, **224**

The Zope Book, **7, 224**

Zope Core component (Zope Application Server), 211

Zope Documentation Project web site, 224

Zope Magazine **web site, 224**

Zope Management Interface. *See* **ZMI**

Zope Object Database (ZODB), 7

    object hierarchy, 214

    site backup option, 177

    site caching options, 179-180

Zope.com web site, 223

Zope.org web site, 223

    architectural concepts, 6

    installation help areas, 38

    Python concepts, 7

    Template Attribute Language (TAL) resources, 150

    troubleshooting resources, 20

    Zope Template Language resources, 167

ZopeLabs web site, 224

ZopeNewbies web site, 224

ZopeWiki web site, 224

ZopeZen web site, 224

Zserver component (Zope Application Server), 211

Zwiki

    installing, 97-99

    wikis, 96-97

        editing, 99-102

        structure of, 99

Zwiki.org Web site, 102